FINAL JOURNEYS

FINAL JOURNEYS

A Practical Guide
for Bringing Care and Comfort
at the End of Life

Maggie Callanan

BANTAM BOOKS

FINAL JOURNEYS
A Bantam Book / April 2008

Published by
Bantam Dell
A Division of Random House, Inc.
New York, New York

Book design by Robert Bull

Bantam Books is a registered trademark of Random House, Inc., and
the colophon is a trademark of Random House, Inc.

Library of Congress Cataloging-in-Publication Data
Callanan, Maggie.
Final journeys : a practical guide for bringing care and comfort at the
end of life / Maggie Callanan
p.   cm.
Includes index.
ISBN 978-0-553-80367-9 (hardcover)
1. Palliative treatment.   2. Terminal care.   3. Terminally ill—Family
relationships.   I. Title.
R726.8.C345 2008
616'.029—dc22   2007042077

Printed in the United States of America
Published simultaneously in Canada

www.bantamdell.com

10 9 8 7 6 5 4 3 2 1
BVG

Dedicated with love
to
Ellie, Tallie, Lily, Bear, and Will

The brightest stars in my universe
who light up my life with immeasurable joy

And
with gratitude
to all the dedicated home health aides and
certified nursing assistants
who are the backbone of hospice care
and critically important to our medical system,
but often are not given the respect and recognition
they so richly deserve.
Thank you for being there for my patients and for me.
I could not do what I do without you.

The stories in *Final Journeys* are true. Names and other identifying details of patients and their families have been changed to protect the privacy of those involved. If any incidents described in this book seem familiar to the reader, it is because such experiences occur frequently in the care of the dying.

CONTENTS

FINAL
JOURNEYS

INTRODUCTION:

"I Don't Know How to Do This"

My father was second-generation Irish American, a proud, meticulous man.

He was a career diplomat for the State Department, and honor and dignity were his core values. He was introspective by nature, a man of few words, but the things he did say to me in our private talks became anchors in my life. His introspection intensified in 1981 as he became sicker and more debilitated from the emphysema and heart disease that would eventually take his life.

I lived in a neighboring state, a forty-five-minute drive from my parents' home. I had two young children at this point and worked full time, but I visited my parents as often as I could to help them as they dealt with my father's illness. They had hired a private nurse's aide, Sela, who lovingly tended to his personal care. My mother spent her time cooking, running up and down the stairs to meet my father's many fastidious requests, and worrying—after being married for forty-five years—about how she would cope with the rest of her life alone.

I just wanted to be there and do whatever I could to make my father know how important he was to me, and to share with my mother in our common grief. I cleaned, shopped, cooked, and rubbed my father's back—when he let me. Often I just sat on the bed near him and held his hand, grateful for each moment we were together. But it never felt like enough. I wasn't ready to let him go, even as his inner focus intensified and he seemed to be getting further and further away from us.

Holding his hand, I thought of what I had learned from him throughout my life. So much was by example rather than by words. I never ceased to be moved by the image of this brilliant and successful man kneeling humbly in prayer like a child by the side of his bed every night. It was never discussed, and we were never told we had to do the same. But my father's nightly ritual of prayer was important to him, and he never missed it—until the awful night when he was too weak to get up and my mother had to call for a neighbor's help to lift him into bed. That was when we knew that his life had really started to unravel. He never knelt again, but he seemed to be lost in thought, or possibly prayer, much more often as the days and weeks went by. I recall wondering what could be important enough to rob us of his attention. And yet I had a strong sense that I should not intrude: he was clearly busy, mentally and emotionally, on something very important. I had the feeling that when he finally shared it with me it would change my life.

So it was with excitement and anticipation that I ascended the stairs to his bedroom near the end of his illness when my mother said he wanted to talk to me. He patted the chair next to his bed, inviting me to sit near him. He seemed to have a particularly purposeful gaze that afternoon. He put his hand over mine. *This is it!* I thought, and I felt my heart race.

He spoke with a determination that was my father's to the end. "Listen to me," he said. "This is important. I've figured it out." He paused.

"What, Dad? Tell me," I finally said hesitantly.

"The odds are against us," he said. "One out of one dies." I felt an almost comical disbelief. *That's it?* I thought. *That's what he's been working on all this time?*

Then he continued: "There are classes in parenting, financial planning, maintaining your house, building a deck. Why aren't there how-to classes in dying? Why don't we talk about death? I don't know how to do this." He looked deep into my eyes. "I want to do it right. How can I be a good example to all of you in my dying? I have tried to live my life right, and now I want to die right!" He gripped my hand with surprising strength. "What does it feel like to die?" he asked with an urgency that I had never before heard in his voice.

I was unnerved by his profound questions, but the good nurse in me fumbled for an answer. I explained what I'd learned in school about vital signs, electrolytes, and other bodily processes. But my father just shook his head and asked again, "But what does it *feel* like to die—not the physical part, the *feeling* part? If no one gets out of this world alive, why don't we know these things? Why do we go in fear?" At that moment my personal and professional journey changed.

The fibers that weave the cloth of who I have become were formed in large part by my hospice experiences. Hospice has never been just work for me; rather, it has become a philosophy—not of dying but of living. Much of what you read here will refer to hospice because that is how I understand the world. But I am also aware that even today, only about 30 percent of people in the United States die under the care of hospice, and no matter what circumstances have brought you to these pages, I believe that what I have learned can be of comfort and use to you. I am writing this book for anybody and everybody who faces the profound journey called dying. I am writing this book for all of us.

When my father reached the final stage of his illness, I had already been a nurse for eighteen years, but I had been with hospice for only a year and a half. Hospice, which is now a huge worldwide movement, began in the Middle Ages when Irish convents on pilgrimage routes opened their doors as places of shelter where the tired, sick, or dying could rest and receive food and care. Centuries later, *hospice* still refers to a safe place of shelter that provides care and comfort for travelers on a journey.

In 1967, Dame Cicely Saunders, a British physician, opened the first modern-day hospice, St. Christopher's, outside London. She and her staff implemented a sophisticated approach to the care of the terminally ill using a new concept called palliative care. The treatments they provided sought not to cure the patient but rather to control the symptoms of discomfort, especially pain. St. Christopher's continues to be the prototype for the thousands of hospices today.

I loved the challenge of working in this field of specialized care for the dying. I was amazed at what could be done to keep people free of physical pain and suffering in the last stages of their life, while they were in familiar and comforting surroundings, often at home, and being cared for by their friends and families. I found that the hospice philosophy blended the best of modern medicine with true compassion and creativity.

But my training did not address the questions that my father had so urgently asked. His concerns haunted me, and I set out to find the answers. I recognized that the true experts were my dying patients and their families, and I began quietly to learn from them. In this book, I pass along the lessons that they have taught me. They have taught me that dying is hard work. It is, perhaps, our most challenging and difficult experience. But they have also taught me that facing death can be affirming and enriching, a creative time of closeness, growth, and memory making, despite all its difficulty and grief.

Final Journeys distills all the "tricks of the trade" that I've learned since 1981 as a hospice nurse who has been privileged to care for more than two thousand dying people and their families. I hope it will be your companion and your advocate, a source of understanding and support throughout the time ahead. I have tried to touch on all the challenges you may face— medical, emotional, spiritual, practical, legal, ethical, and creative. However, not every chapter fits every journey, so please feel free to choose the topics and issues that match your situation and skip the rest. Some of my chapters are addressed primarily to the dying person, others primarily to caregivers, family, and friends; most of us will play more than one of these roles. Above all, I have tried to make *Final Journeys* the "how-to guide" that my father wished for.

As you will discover in the stories of my patients, the dying person *can* be in charge. You *can* make choices that will help you control your comfort, your alertness, and other important aspects of this journey. You *can* teach your family and friends how to do this with dignity. As uniquely as you have lived your life, you can write this last chapter of your life's story in a manner that is uniquely yours, and that will be treasured by those who care about you. *Final Journeys* will help guide you.

Ultimately, I hope this book will make the journey of dying less frightening for all of us. When we're afraid, we tend to shut down, becoming quiet and withdrawn. Some of us freeze and hunker down like small animals in the dark, trying to make ourselves invisible. Perhaps we think that if we do, death will pass us by. Others turn to anger and rage, or quiet desperation and depression.

It does not have to be that way. After all, as my father asked, "If no one gets out of this world alive, why do we go in fear?" This book offers other possibilities.

PART I

REFRAMING THE JOURNEY

"TOOLS, NOT TISSUES"

How beautiful these leaves were just last week, I thought. *How ironic that they're the most vibrant right before they fall and die. Now all we're left with is big piles of wet drabness and this bone-chilling weather.*

This is how so many patients feel, I thought. One moment your life is going along beautifully, and the next your doctor walks in with your tests in his or her hand and says, "I have bad news."

Once you or someone you love receives that diagnosis, your lives will never be the same. A good friend, diagnosed with cancer, told me, "The disease took away life's innocence. I always feel like there's a stranger lurking in the shadows now, ready to jump out and do me harm again. The shadow person—that negative presence—is always there."

I thought of my friend and the end of innocence as I steered my car past the leaf piles toward the only stretch of visible curb in a neighborhood of wide lawns and large colonial-style homes. Then I quietly reviewed the intake information sheet on the new patient I was about to meet.

JAKE

Jake was barely sixty years old, diagnosed with pancreatic cancer just three months before, and already terminally ill. He and his wife of many years had two married children, both living nearby, both with babies of their own. How sad, I thought: just as life was getting easier—kids launched, retirement around the corner, time to travel and enjoy the benefits of all those years of hard work, grandbabies to spoil—this happened. How unfair!

I suspected that this family, like so many others I meet, had held off calling hospice for as long as possible, and now they were near crisis. As I climbed the steps to the front door, I noticed a woman glancing through the bay window of the living room. Was this Jake's wife, Julie? I rang the bell and sensed her presence behind the front door, but it was a long minute before she opened it, her face puffy from crying.

Even after so many years as a hospice nurse, I'm still in awe of the raw courage it takes to open the door and let someone like me in for the first time. Most of the patients and families that I work with have clung to the hope of a miracle, a medical breakthrough, or even a misdiagnosis until the eleventh hour. My presence means that the end is unavoidable. Those who *have* acknowledged the truth often feel that the limited time they have left together is private and fear that my visits will be an intrusion. I know that everything I represent is frightening. Nobody *ever* wants to have to deal with me. Yet I knock on front doors again and again because in my heart I know I can make these last weeks or months better and more meaningful.

Julie introduced herself and escorted me into a sun-filled kitchen decorated with blue Delft tiles.

"Tell me about your husband," I said to Julie as we sat down at the kitchen table.

It always interests me what people do with that question. It's like asking someone you meet, "What's going on in your life?" instead of "How are you?" The first question allows for real information to be shared; the second almost always elicits a perfunctory response. My first goal when I visit a new patient and his or her family is to connect in a genuine way. I need to know their focus, concerns, and fears. Julie's answer would tell me these things.

Julie gave me a list of her husband's symptoms and problems, and details of the treatments he had undergone. They had been in and out of hospitals for tests. They had traveled out of state to major cancer centers for second, third, and fourth opinions. The treatments they had chosen quickly overwhelmed Jake and had to be discontinued. Julie described a regimen that sounded truly hellish. And now they were finally back at home and having to deal with me. They were out of hope and running out of time. I took a deep breath, now knowing what direction to take. Julie was totally focused on the physical part of Jake's illness, so that's where we would start.

"I can see how much you and your husband have gone through in the past months. You must be physically and emotionally exhausted. I'm sure I'll have some very specific suggestions for better relief of his physical problems, but what else can I do today to help *you*?"

Julie's face quivered as she attempted to keep her composure. I wanted to reach across the table and put my hand on her arm to comfort her. My concern must have showed, because she suddenly drew herself up and almost fiercely said, "Please don't be nice to me! I feel like I'm made of bits of paper that are barely held together. The slightest kindness and I will fall apart and blow away. I *must* be strong for him. He's depending on me. I don't know how to do this! I need strength, not sympathy. I need tools, not tissues. I'm terrified! *Help me!*"

"That is exactly why I am here," I said. "Of course you don't know how to do it. No wonder you're terrified. Your husband's illness is being carried in his body, but its devastation is rippling through his life, your life, and the lives of your children and grandchildren, his colleagues, and your neighbors and friends. Everyone feels the turmoil. Hearts start breaking the moment the word *incurable* is uttered. What's vitally important is to focus on what you can do, rather than on what has been done and failed or how little time is left."

"It's just so overwhelming," Julie said. "I don't know *what* I need anymore."

I've heard these words so many times—the first words on the journey of dying. I reassured Julie. "I can tell you've done a great job of staying involved and informed at every stage," I said. "I am here to ensure that you have the very best possible care from the experts you need for each problem your husband might have or develop. I'm also here to help everyone else in the family deal with this life-changing event in as positive a way as possible. I will coordinate the people who will be taking care of all of you. This is a team that will include your doctor, a social worker, a chaplain, a nursing assistant, volunteers, a grief counselor, a nutritionist, a physical therapist, and me, your nurse. So not for one moment do I want you to think that you are in this alone, because you're not."

"But the doctors say there's nothing more we can do. He's going to die," Julie sobbed.

"How frightening and heartbreaking it must have been to hear that news," I replied. "But there's a *great deal* we can do. We have highly effective and easy ways of keeping your husband as comfortable and alert as possible. We can help him—and you— live as fully as possible every day he has left. This can be a very creative, intimate, and loving time for both of you—a time for making and celebrating memories that will last forever in your hearts. I am here to help you both be less frightened and more in charge. We can do this together!"

"I just want things to be the way they were," said Julie. "This is no way to live."

"This *has* changed your life," I replied, "but it need not destroy it. I suspect that each chapter of your husband's life story has been an important and rich one. I want to help you write the last chapter in a way that is a fitting tribute to him and the life you have created together. This is our chance to show him that it has mattered that he has been on this earth. I know you want to show him how important he has been to you."

Julie's eyes widened. I could see her focus shift, at least for a moment, away from the fear and the sense of burden that had been so much a part of Jake's physical journey. When I meet new patients and their families, as early as possible I try to re-frame the situation, to help people understand the loving and nurturing emotional journey that dying also includes. For a moment Julie seemed to be lighter, to grasp this possibility, but then her shoulders slumped again.

"But he's been so withdrawn, uncommunicative, almost sullen," she said. "And before that he was angry, snapping and snarling. Who could blame him? I think he just couldn't accept what was happening. That's why it took us so long to call for help," Julie said sadly.

"Anger and denial are two normal responses to terrible news," I said. "You may have heard of the psychologist Dr. Elisabeth Kübler-Ross, who changed the way we all look at the last stage of life with her book *On Death and Dying*. In it she describes five stages that dying people often go through: from denial, anger, and bargaining to depression and finally acceptance. These stages aren't necessarily a linear process; sometimes you can hear a seriously ill person touch on several during a single conversation. Not everyone experiences all of them, but I've learned that most people seem to experience some. This is true for the family as well as the patient.

"Denial is my personal favorite," I went on. "I try to use it in my own life as much as I can!" I was pleased to see a half smile on Julie's face as she relaxed a bit. "Denial is a wonderfully strong crutch that supports a person who is not yet emotionally ready to face what's happening all at once. If denial isn't causing any harm, let it be, unless you have something stronger to put in its place.

"You've already described anger. That's an easy stage to see and understand," I continued. "Bargaining is often very private. A man may promise that he'll work with the handicapped if he is cured, or a woman might resolve to go to church regularly if she can see her children grow up. We are usually not aware of someone else's bargaining. And then there are the stages of depression and, finally, acceptance."

"Well, I would say that Jake *has* been depressed recently."

"Let me go meet him. I'll check him and see if there's something we can do about that."

I went to Jake, whose den had become his sickroom so that he wouldn't have to go up and down the stairs. It was warm and inviting, lined with books. A hospital bed was set up in front of the fireplace. Jake was very foggy, in that drifty, dreamy state that pancreatic cancer often induces when it has spread to the liver.

"I've met your lovely wife," I said, biding my time, trying to help him lift himself out of the fog. "This is a beautiful house."

His eyes gradually became more focused and alert. I began to gently question him about how he was feeling and what concerned him. His voice was weak and wavering and his responses seemed dull and flat—not unusual for someone with depression. I asked what worried him most.

"I think this is too much for Julie," he said despondently. "I don't know how she'll manage to take care of me. It's too much. It'll kill her! Maybe it would be better for me to go to a nursing home."

Jake's fear was not so much about his own illness and death as it was about his wife's welfare. It moved me that he was willing to sacrifice staying in his own home to help her.

"I'm not just here for you," I told him. "I'll be making suggestions and keeping an eye on Julie to make sure she's okay. My focus will be on your entire family." His face relaxed and he sighed as his eyes filled with tears.

"Would it be okay if Julie joins us," I asked, "so you can tell her your concerns?"

Jake hesitated.

"Trust me," I reassured him. "It *will* be okay."

Julie came in, and with some gentle prodding, Jake shared what he had told me.

"You would leave home for *me*?" she asked. "How could you ever consider going someplace else?" Her tears came. "This is our life, our home. This was my wedding vow—for better or worse. I *want* to take care of you. We will do this together!"

He reached for her hand and began to sob. I tried to make myself invisible, giving them some privacy as they shared this powerful moment.

"Openness and honesty with each other are some of your strongest tools," I finally said. "If you can continue to use them, you've won half the battle.

"May I come back?" I asked, as I always do. Each patient and each family has the right to say no. "I think we can all work together as a team and make this better for both of you."

"Yes. Please, " Jake quietly said. Then he took my hand and shook it firmly for a long time.

After saying my goodbyes, I started for the front door. I stopped when Julie quietly called, "Wait, wait!" She wrapped her arms around me, and we hugged silently for a long moment before I left.

Changing the Journey

Jake's terminal diagnosis felt like a door slamming and locking behind them. It imprisoned Jake and Julie in a scary, inescapable place. Much of the emotional work I do with the dying and their families revolves around opening a new door that lets light, air, and *hope* into the room.

I do this by first acknowledging the grief a terminal diagnosis always brings. So many well-meaning people respond to terrible news by trying to smooth it over. Yet any statement that starts with "Well, at least . . ." diminishes the distress and comes across as a lack of caring—or even as a kind of one-upmanship. When I first meet people who are adjusting to a terminal diagnosis, I never try to diminish their emotions. "Yes, this is terrible news and it's very, very sad," I say. "You don't need to make excuses for the way you feel. You have a right to feel this way." These words identify and recognize the struggle the dying person and family are going through. Validation is one of the first and most important tools for opening a different door.

Only then do I try to help them focus on what's still possible, not on what's been lost. The idea of living until you die is extremely important. "There are things we *can* do," I assure my patients. "We can keep you comfortable, help you fulfill some of your dreams, make more good memories, and give you time for closeness and connection with the people you love."

For those still clinging to the hope of a miracle, I might say, "Yes, sometimes miracles do happen. Try whatever medical paths or alternatives you want—anything you think might help reverse your illness and improve your prognosis. But at the same time, let's also work together to fulfill your more personal goals. Then no time is lost. You will feel you have accomplished a great deal, and you will have as few regrets as possible."

When someone you care about receives a terminal diagnosis, you should offer your ear to listen, your shoulder to cry on, and your hand to hold. Along with your words of support, those small gestures can provide immense comfort. They were among the most valuable tools that Julie needed to help her and her husband share their difficult journey together.

THE BOTTOM LINE

A terminal diagnosis is not the end of the story. As one door closes, another can be opened.

2

"DON'T TELL MOM SHE'S DYING.
IT'LL KILL HER!"

"If I don't say it, it doesn't exist and I don't have to deal with it." People often feel that the realities of dying don't exist unless they're discussed. Both patients and family members want to know what to expect, but they're afraid to ask for or share information. Their hearts are breaking, but they fear that sharing their feelings will make everyone around them miserable, or that being open and vulnerable will mean "falling apart." So in the name of control, they keep everything inside.

Burying our thoughts and feelings can seem like protection, but it actually leads to isolation, for both caregivers and patients. Silence begets more silence, loneliness, and depression. The sick person thinks: *This is too hard for the people around me. I'd better take care of their fears and discomforts instead of my own.* So the sick person takes over the role of caregiver, avoids talking about anything that will upset the family, and in so doing further isolates him- or herself. Meanwhile, the caregiver thinks: *If I acknowledge what's happening, it will be too overwhelming to handle.*

I call this the "pink-hippopotamus-in-the-tutu syndrome." The pink hippo—the reality of dying—sits right in the middle of the room. Everyone sees it and walks around it, but no one mentions it, pretending it's not there. The atmosphere around the dying person becomes artificial and silent.

When families avoid being honest about what's happening, they inadvertently distance themselves emotionally from each other, which adds to their pain. Silence severs the possibility for human connection, the essential support we all need during this difficult time.

THE JACKSONS

On my first visit to the Jacksons', I was met by twelve very worried family members and friends. The gathering on the front porch had spilled over into the front yard. It was clear that before I would be allowed into the house to meet Mrs. Jackson, I would need to address the concerns of the group. I knew from long experience that these concerns would revolve around what I should and should not say to her.

"Granny doesn't know how sick she is," said one of her children. "She doesn't know that she's terminally ill," said another. "If you tell her she's dying, it will *kill* her!" said a third.

I was not to utter the words *cancer, terminal, dying,* or *hospice,* they told me. And I was to remove my hospice name tag. "Couldn't you just tell Granny that you're from the garden club?"

"If you saw what I did to plants, you would never ask me to say that!" I replied. The laughter that followed eased the tension somewhat, and I explained that I could not ethically remove my name tag. All patients have a right to know who is entering their home to provide care. Besides, if Mrs. Jackson was in denial, she wouldn't process what my name tag meant, anyway.

"Some of us use denial when we're under stress," I went on. "It's a strong shield that protects us from more than we can handle. I have great respect for denial and would never try to break through that shield unless I had something more protective to put in its place." The group mulled this over. "I also know that the shield disappears gradually by itself if and when we're ready to handle the truth," I continued. "In rare cases, it never disappears. But my feeling is that as long as no one is causing harm to themselves or to anybody else, denial is best left alone."

The people blocking the door now stepped aside reluctantly, allowing me to enter. I smiled to myself as various members of the Jackson clan followed me from room to room. Like temple guard dogs, they sat on either side of Mrs. Jackson's bed as I asked her questions about her health and what the doctors had told her about her illness.

"Mrs. Jackson, I'm Maggie Callanan. I'm a nurse, and your doctor asked me to stop by and see how you're doing," I said. "Tell me what the doctor has told you about what's going on with you."

She was a small woman with a shock of white hair, and she *did* seem vague and uninformed about her condition.

"I haven't been feeling well," she told me. "I need my rest. My kids fuss over me too much."

"Mrs. Jackson, would you mind if I asked your family to give us some privacy so I can check your blood pressure and listen to your lungs and abdomen?"

"Sure. That's fine. And please call me Granny. Everybody else does."

It took a few minutes for them all to file from the room. After they left, I could sense several anxious ears pressed to the other side of the door.

The second we were alone, Granny grabbed my hand and urgently whispered, "I know what's wrong with me. I know I'm going to die soon. But please don't tell my family yet; they're not ready to deal with it. If you told them now, it would *kill* them!"

It was comical in a way, but I didn't laugh. I knew both she and her family were very serious and showed great caring for each other.

After I examined Granny, I sat and held her hand. "Tell me," I said, "isn't it hard to keep this big secret from the people who love you so much?"

Her eyes filled with tears. "Oh, I guess it's hard, but I've been taking care of my babies all my life. And I'm not going to stop now—even though some of them are in their sixties, they're still my babies! Not talking about it is lonely. But I would hate to see them upset."

"I bet you didn't just take care of them all these years," I said. "I bet you taught them a lot along the way, didn't you?"

"Oh, Lordy, yes, I did!" she replied with a big smile.

"Well, who do you think is better suited to teach them about dying than you are? Each of them is going to have to die one day, and you seem to understand a lot about what's going on. You seem very comfortable, and you don't seem to be afraid of much. Don't you think that those are important things for them to learn about dying before they have to do it themselves? Wouldn't you be the most excellent and appropriate teacher for them?"

"I need to think about this a bit," Granny said warily.

"Fair enough," I replied. "I'll keep your promise not to tell them how sick you are, but I do need to spend a little time with your family now, to see how they're managing. I'll be back in a few minutes, okay?"

Granny nodded her assent.

I sat with the family at the kitchen table and reviewed how my hospice team and I could help with their problems. Their first concern was that Granny wasn't eating well and they were afraid she was going to "wither away." They also said that she was starting to spend more time in bed, and they wanted to know how to protect her skin against bedsores. Then, finally, the questions tumbled out: "What happens next?" "How often will you visit?" "What should we expect?" "How long do you think she has?" "What should we say if she asks us what's going on?"

I told them that Granny was blessed to have such a loving and concerned family around her, and that I would always let them know what was going on, what changes I thought were coming up, and what we should do about them.

"I have no doubt that together we'll be able to handle any-thing that lies ahead," I said. "But I *am* concerned about the amount of energy everyone is using in trying not to spill the beans. That energy could be better used to *be* with Granny, to recognize what's happening and to spend loving time together. This is a time for making memories and acknowledging your love for one another."

They were all quiet. "We need to think about this a bit," one of her daughters finally said.

I returned to Mrs. Jackson's room to ask her if I could con-tinue visiting her and her family in the future. "Oh, yes, baby girl!" she said, stroking my hand. "You ease my heart." I asked if there was anything else I could do for her just then, and she said with a big smile, "Tell my babies to come on in here. I've got some teaching to do! And could you stay a little longer to help me out a bit if I hit a rough patch?"

"You bet, Granny. I'm proud of you, and I know you'll be great!" I replied, squeezing her hand.

I stood in the back of the bedroom as Granny gathered her family around her, and I watched the glory of who she had been and who she still was. "Oh, my babies," she said, "I love you all so much, and I hate to leave you, but I know you'll be fine. The good Lord's waiting for me, and I'm getting ready to go home to Him. So we got some crying and laughing and praying to do here, but we'll do it together. I'm not afraid, and I don't want you to be, either, because whether I'm here or not, I'll *always* be watching over you."

The family crowded around to hug her and love her,

and the tears of relief flowed freely. I dried my own eyes and quietly left, knowing that they could now take this journey together.

THE BOTTOM LINE

Silence does not spare or protect; it isolates and causes loneliness.

3

BREAKING THE SILENCE

What do you do when you sense that the patient *wants* to talk about dying but is protecting you? How can you be sure your suspicion is true? What is the best way to open this kind of dialogue?

Please understand that it is normal to feel anxious and reluctant about doing this. Many doctors and nurses are also uncomfortable, and sometimes ineffective, in their attempts to talk openly with their dying patients. Some people are uncomfortable with almost any intense conversation, and death is not an easy topic for most people to discuss. But there are steps you can take to make breaking the silence easier for both of you.

How to Begin a Discussion

Consider Your Own Feelings About Death. Take a few private minutes, perhaps during a walk outside or while taking a hot bath. Consider whether some of your discomfort may be caused by your own fears. Does this situation make you worry about your own mortality? About how your family would manage without *you*? Do you feel powerless to do anything to really help? Are you afraid of breaking down in front of the dying person and adding more upset to an already emotionally charged situation? Are you afraid to watch how the process of dying unfolds?

All of these concerns are shared by the vast majority of

people. Understand, however, that the patient's concerns may be very different from yours. Try to focus on his needs rather than on your fears or discomforts. It will make communicating easier for both of you.

Consider the Patient's Style of Coping with Stress. If the dying person has always been a man of few words, prepare for a brief conversation. Perhaps you will need to have several talks before all is discussed. Is the patient an introvert, normally quiet and reflective? If so, he or she may become more so and seem withdrawn. Someone who is usually outgoing and inquisitive might need more interaction with you and others and may even seem demanding. Respect these personal differences and let them guide you as you try to help verbally.

Consider the Best Time to Talk. Two in the afternoon might be when you have a break from your caregiving tasks, but that doesn't necessarily make it a good time for the patient. He may be too tired from his morning care routine. However, it does give you an opportunity to open the door to future conversations. Here are some suggestions:

> *Describe what you see:* "You look so sad and lonely today. If talking about it would help, I'm here."
>
> *Clarify your concern:* "I'd like to better understand what's happening to you, and not just physically. If you ever want to talk about it, let me know, okay?"
>
> *Acknowledge the dying person's struggle:* "I bet you get real tired of being sick like this. It seems like really hard work; is it?"
>
> *Or simply:* "I'm here and I care about you."

A Caring Touch Can Often Be More Eloquent than Words. Such a simple expression of caring and concern may be enough to encourage the patient to open up.

If the Dying Person Doesn't Seem to Want to Talk. Even if a conversation doesn't immediately result from these suggestions, you've opened the door for communication by showing your willingness and concern. Now you must wait for the patient to decide if and when he's ready to walk through that open door. Know that some patients are *never* ready, and that's fine. And know that you did a good job by showing your care and concern, regardless.

A Note to Clinicians

One of the questions that consistently unnerved me in the early years of providing hospice care was "What does it feel like to die?" Quite aside from my own discomfort, I would feel sad that we had so little information to offer. Such a direct and honest question deserves a direct and honest answer. Today, I tend to say, "I have never died, so I can't tell you from my own experience. But I can tell you what I see when other patients die, and what they've told me dying is like for them."

I often recommend Dr. Raymond Moody's book *Life After Life*. It contains first-person accounts of near-death experiences, telling what dying felt like to people who, because of a car accident, drowning, heart attack, or other cause, were clinically dead for a brief time but were resuscitated. They often speak of joyful reunions, freedom from suffering, and a wonderful sense of peacefulness. Many of my patients and families have found this information very comforting. Dr. Moody's book can also be used as a way of opening a dialogue between patient and caregiver so that wishes, needs, and fears on both sides can be better understood.

Dying people don't expect us to have all the answers. There are many questions about dying, death, and what may come after that are unanswerable by anyone. In asking such questions, the dying person is really asking for our honest concern and support, and above all for our willingness to share his or her journey as much as we can. The following story illustrates this well.

EULA

I had been asked to do a presentation to a general hospital staff in Michigan on the topic "How to Be Present for the Dying." My host had told me that each staff department wore a different color of smock, and when I noticed a sea of burgundy in the audience, I asked him which department that was. To my surprise, his answer was "Housekeeping."

Part of my presentation was about how uncomfortable it can be to talk to someone about dying. At that point, Eula, whose burgundy smock carried a name tag reading "Supervisor," jumped to her feet and waved her arm. I nodded for her to speak.

One day, she told us, she had been mopping the floor in a patient's bathroom when she heard his physician come in and inform him that all the curative treatments had failed. There were no more options; sad to say, he was now terminal. The doctor sat with him for a few minutes, trying to soothe him as he cried, and then quietly left.

By now, Eula went on, the bathroom was *very* clean. She couldn't stay there, but she was unsure what to do. "So I put my head down and looked at the floor I was mopping, working fast to get out of the room without disturbing this poor man. Then he said right to me, 'How could God let this happen to me? I have always tried to live a good life. My wife and children need me. Now I'm going to die!' He was sobbing. 'How could God forsake me like this?' "

There was an awkward silence in the audience.

I asked Eula what she had done next. "Well," she said, "I leaned on my mop for a minute or so, and then I said, 'If I had the answer to those questions, do you think I'd be mopping floors?'" The audience gasped—and then started to giggle and laugh.

"How did he respond?" I asked.

"Well, he was still laughing when I left the room, but I did stop at the nurses' station to report this, so they could call the chaplain for him, or whatever."

After the presentation one of Eula's co-workers came up to me. "What Eula *didn't* tell you," she said, "is that she assigned herself to clean his room every day until he was discharged home. And every day she'd bring him a big caring smile and spend extra time making sure his room was spotless and that he was doing okay."

Eula gave him the very best she had to give, and he appreciated this simple gesture. Dying people do not ask us to analyze, diagnose, or solve their problems. They ask us to understand their anguish and be willing to listen and share their journey, good and bad, as far as we can.

A Word About Denial

I will make this point several times in this book because it is so important: denial is a powerful crutch that should not be yanked away unless you have something more powerful and supportive to put in its place. Let it be unless it causes behavior that is dangerous to the patient or to someone else. Denial will be given up if and when the patient (or family member) is able to deal with the truth. On rare occasions it is never given up. If that happens, so be it.

How do you talk honestly to someone in denial? You start by listening very carefully, for your quiet attention offers the person positive support. For example, Uncle Johnny, who's dying very soon, might say, "I'll be so glad when I get better and can go camping again with the guys in the spring." It would be cruel to say, "You're not going to get better, so forget camping!" Instead, consider the good times he's recalling: being in control of his world, freedom from day-to-day worries, enjoying nature, being relaxed and comfortable, doing something he loves while laughing and bonding with his friends.

These memories make him feel better and happier than dealing with his pain and losses every minute. So validate that positive mind-set by saying something like "Isn't it fun to think of those good times? Those guys are such nuts! I'll bet you did some outrageous things together. I'd love to hear about them." Can you see how you've reinforced and even expanded the positive moment and shared this happier mind-set for a while? It's like taking a mini emotional vacation with Uncle Johnny. It's refreshing and renewing.

On the other hand, never promise that the dream will come true. Saying "Absolutely, you'll be going!" is not the honest and compassionate way to respond. You could become the target of his rage later if he *does* let go of denial and sees that you have deceived him or attempted to keep him in denial. How can he believe anything you say—now and in the future? Even if he understands your motives, it will erode his trust in you.

Some people, particularly those who are confused, can be very insistent in their denial. They may demand immediate action. Distraction or deferring often helps in a situation such as this. For example, if Uncle Johnny says, "We're going camping *right now,* so bring the car around and get my gear," you might defuse this problem by saying, "Now *there's* a plan, but the car's not going *anywhere* until we get the tires replaced and that broken fan belt fixed. You've always taken very good care of that car and been so responsible about avoiding serious problems. It would be dangerous to go right now, but I'll take it to the shop tomorrow when it opens." This response doesn't reject or ridicule the denial but doesn't reinforce it, either.

By handling and responding to denial in this way, you can offer great emotional support while that crutch is still needed.

THE BOTTOM LINE

The journey is better shared if the silence can be broken and the denial understood.

4

"WE'RE NOT GIVING UP!
WE HAVE HOPE!"

It's normal to feel overwhelmed and grief-stricken when someone we love has been given a terminal diagnosis. It's also natural to fight against the prognosis. Affirming "We're not giving up! We have hope!" has helped many patients and their families. But if survival were a simple matter of just having hope, no one would ever die. We wouldn't need medical care. Hope and persistence would be enough.

A few years ago, I was sent to admit a new patient, an eighty-four-year-old woman with end-stage congestive heart failure who was living with her son and his family.

There are peaks and valleys in any chronic illness, and so it's often hard to judge when the end is near. But my prospective patient had experienced more frequent hospitalizations, with less improvement after each admission. She was now unable to walk across the room, and shortness of breath had made her increasingly dependent on a portable oxygen tank. Her son had asked for hospice's help, and her doctor had concurred.

I had been told that the woman's daughter was coming in from Ohio and might be there during our first meeting. I rang the doorbell and heard high heels clicking briskly on the floor inside. *Good!* I thought. *The daughter is here.*

The door opened, but only wide enough for the woman's body to block my entrance. "I'm sorry you wasted your time driving here," she said curtly. "My brother should have asked me before calling your organization. We don't need your services because we're not giving up. We have hope!"

Over the daughter's shoulder, I could see my potential patient, slumped in a wheelchair at the kitchen table. She briefly looked up and haltingly gestured with one hand for me to come to her. "Rose, please," she said. The daughter unwillingly stepped aside.

I went to the old woman's side. In the late stages of congestive heart failure, fluid collects in pockets in the body, including the lungs. She had the wide-eyed look of someone laboring to breathe. Her lips were bluish from her lungs inadequately absorbing the oxygen, and the swollen flesh of her ankles was hanging over her lace-up shoes.

"You look so uncomfortable," I said, stroking her hand. "I'm sorry this is happening to you. I know I could help make you feel better." For example, the right doses of diuretic medications would eliminate much of the excess fluid in her lungs so they could better absorb oxygen.

She rolled her eyes toward her daughter and weakly shrugged. "She says no." At that point, the daughter took me by the elbow and briskly escorted me through the door, which was then firmly closed behind me.

The daughter's intensity was probably in direct proportion to how upset she was that her mother was dying. It was an expression of love, a protectiveness that was fierce and touching in its way. But what does hope mean if maintaining it means that someone suffers unnecessarily from lack of appropriate care?

There are other problems with the mind-set of "We're not giving up—we have hope." If a person *is* dying, is he to blame for giving up? The sense of failure or despair that the dying feel in disappointing *us* is often a heavy burden on them. Many people who are terminally ill gradually become aware that they probably cannot win the battle. They *know*, more or less consciously, that they are dying. Family or caregivers who insist on not giving up may add to the sense of guilt they already feel about losing the fight against their illness. It's bad enough to know that soon you will leave the people you love, but also to fail them by your leaving is unbearable.

The death of the body is a physical process, not a mental one. Yes, a person's mind-set can certainly play a role in the progression of his or her illness, and sometimes it affects how quickly or slowly death approaches. But mind-set is *not* responsible for physical death. The illness is.

It is never necessary to continue suffering physical discomfort because you are "going for" or "waiting for" the cure. Relentless pain, nausea, vomiting, or constipation can take a devastating toll on a sick body, rendering it incapable of tolerating further treatments even if they become available. These and other unpleasant symptoms can be controlled so that the patient can take advantage of treatments to slow or even reverse the disease.

The first focus of hospice care is making sure the patient is as pain-free and as functional as possible, because if people are hampered by physical suffering, they are not mentally, emotionally, or spiritually free to deal with anything *but* their suffering. The following story shows how "giving up" allowed one family to achieve the kind of meaningful and loving finish to life that we all wish for.

FRANK

Frank was a retired letter carrier, a man who had always been proud of his day-in, day-out ability to perform his strenuous job. But now his cancer had spread to his bones, causing him persistent, unrelieved pain. His oncologist suggested a pain pump, a little device the size of a small paperback book that continuously delivers small doses of highly concentrated medication through an IV tube directly into a vein. But Frank refused, because he felt certain that the pump would restrict his activity and remove the last vestiges of his independence and privacy.

Frank chose to remain at home under the care of his wife, Doris, and resigned himself to living out his days in pain, despite his increasing reliance on pain pills. But the pain debilitated him, sapping his energy and limiting his ability to enjoy life.

Somewhere near the beginning of his illness, Frank had also decided he would have to forgo his secret dream of attending the fiftieth anniversary of D-Day in Normandy, France, where he had fought as an Allied pilot during World War II. The effort traveling would involve seemed just too much for him.

Frank's primary care physician recommended hospice, which both Frank and his wife resisted. "We weren't ready to say, 'This is the end,'" Doris told me later.

One night when Frank's pain was excruciating, however, Doris called the phone number the doctor had given her. She explained her husband's condition to the nurse on call, who arranged for Kelly, a hospice nurse, to come as soon as possible.

When she arrived, Frank was not able to get out of bed; the pain in his legs was overwhelming. He also had terrible constipation due to changes in his diet, diminished activity, and the side effects of some of his medications. The constipation had decreased his already poor appetite. Now he was eating hardly anything, which caused him to feel weak and exhausted. Without enough physical activity, his poor circulation had worsened and his muscles had started to waste away.

Frank had been an energetic "doer" all his life, and he understandably felt depressed and withdrawn. "The pain is horrible," he confided to Kelly when they were alone. "But worse, I feel as if I am running out of time, and there is one last thing that I really wanted to accomplish." Frank admitted his Normandy dream to her, uttering it aloud for the first time.

"Let's relieve the discomfort. Then we'll see if we can work on your dream," Kelly told him. She suggested the pain pump, promising him that if he tried it for a week and didn't like it, they could go back to using the pills. Frank agreed to give it a try. She also assured him that the pump, with its aggressive pain management, did not mean he was "giving in" to his disease, but instead taking control of its side effects.

By the time Kelly left that afternoon, Frank was sleeping soundly for the first time in a week. The next time she visited he was walking unaided from room to room. His steps were slow and careful, but Frank was walking—and he was elated about it.

The following week, Frank asked Kelly to join him in the living room. With determination and excitement in his eyes, he announced, "The celebration is in three weeks. What are the chances my wife and I could make it?"

"Well, this is a challenge!" Kelly replied. She was delighted that so much had changed in only two weeks, but even with his pain under control, fulfilling Frank's wish would take a lot of creativity and planning. "Let me discuss this with the other members of my hospice team," she said. "I can't promise anything, but I'll try."

I was a member of that team, which is how I became acquainted with the details of Frank's case. The social worker, chaplain, doctors, other nurses, and I pooled our energies. Not only would Frank be traveling across international borders with narcotic pain medications, but his pump would certainly set off metal detectors and attract suspicion along the way. Letters explaining Frank's illness, his need for narcotics, and the pump had to be written. And what if he became sicker during the trip? We compiled a list of phone numbers of international hospice contacts, English-speaking doctors, and hospitals on the proposed route. In addition to our list, the American consulate or embassy could help the couple find English-speaking doctors and nearby hospitals. We also put together a travel kit of other medications Frank might need if problems arose in France.

Frank was giddy with excitement when Kelly told him a few days later that she thought it could work. But he had not yet talked about the trip with his wife, and he asked Kelly to join them as he broached the idea to her. Doris had many justifiable fears. "What if I make a mistake with the medications?" she asked Kelly. "What if something happens to Frank while we're so far from our doctors and hospitals? We know them, we feel comfortable with them, we speak the same language, and they have all his records."

Kelly assured her that they could always reach a hospice nurse by phone—even internationally—and she would make any calls necessary to doctors and nurses in the hospices abroad. "I cannot guarantee the trip will go off without a hitch," Kelly said. "But it seems to be a very important priority to your husband. Wouldn't it be wonderful to grant his wish and share the experience with him?"

Doris looked at her husband lovingly. "Is this really so important to you, Frank?"

He nodded and reached for her hand.

"Well, it certainly will be an adventure!" Doris said, seeming surprised by her own enthusiasm. "Kelly, could you come with us? It would certainly relieve some of my fears."

"I wish I could," Kelly said. "But with other patients to care for and family responsibilities...I'm sorry."

In the end, their grown daughter, Laura, accompanied them to serve as an extra pair of hands with the baggage, wheelchair, and portable oxygen tank. Kelly provided all the training the two women might need.

We all eagerly awaited news of their trip and then vied for visits as soon as they returned. Frank had become a celebrity to us! We all deeply admired his courage and determination. I met the family at their home on the fourth day after their return.

"I saw some of my old buddies!" Frank exclaimed, his eyes brilliant with excitement. He passed a stack of photos to me.

"And the three of us hadn't taken a family vacation since Laura was little."

"It was great! Dad was amazing!" Laura chimed in. "I saw him in a new light. His war stories carry a new meaning for me now."

"I can't believe we were so afraid to make that initial call to hospice," said Doris tearfully. "We thought it meant losing hope, giving up. We never dreamed it might allow us to have such a rich experience. Thank you."

THE BOTTOM LINE

Choosing hospice does not mean "giving up hope"; it can be about help with living your dreams.

5

"ONLY THE BEST FOR MY FATHER"

Have you ever heard anyone say, "I love my father and I'd do anything for him, but mediocre or bad medical care would be acceptable to us"? Of course not! We are willing to spare no expense and tolerate any inconvenience to provide for the people we love. This is especially true when someone we love is dying.

Sometimes, perhaps subconsciously, the price paid and the difficulty endured are seen as measures of the depth of our love and devotion. Perhaps, too, searching out the "best" doctor and medical center is seen as a measure of the value of the sick person's life. The best people *should* be treated by the best!

Yes, it is sometimes necessary to go to a distant medical center to obtain specialized treatment for rare and unusual illnesses, but top-notch care is often available in or near your own community. A local specialist may have successfully treated your illness hundreds of times. In addition, many doctors today have a research nurse on staff, and information and advice from experts around the world are available on special Internet sites with the click of a mouse. Even if you obtain your treatment plan at a major medical center, your local oncologist or hospital may be well equipped to follow that plan in a convenient, familiar setting.

Medications are the same everywhere as well. The penicillin in New York is identical to the penicillin in California or Iowa, and the same is true for chemotherapy drugs, powerful painkillers, steroids, and other treatments for the seriously ill. So traveling long distances to get the "best" care may actually become a detriment to everyone involved.

Mr. Kim

Lee Kim was sixty-five years old when he was diagnosed with prostate cancer that had already spread to his bones. He and his wife had moved from Korea to the United States only eight years before, and they still had difficulty with English. His daughter, Amy, a young widow with two small children, worked as a pharmacist and was the sole support of the entire family now that Mr. Kim was too sick to work. They were barely managing financially.

Mr. Kim's prognosis was bleak, but radiation therapy was strongly recommended by his local oncologist, whose office was a ten-minute drive away. Radiation could not cure his cancer, but it would help relieve his bone pain. Amy had also sought a second opinion at one of the top-ranked cancer centers in the United States. The oncologists there agreed with the diagnosis and treatment planned by the local cancer specialist.

On my first visit to the Kims', I climbed the steps of a Victorian-style house in a typical American suburb, rang the bell, and was greeted by Amy, a slender, attractive woman in her thirties. Enticing smells drifted from the kitchen.

"Who does that wonderful cooking?" I asked.

"My mother," said Amy, and called toward the kitchen in Korean. The door swung open and a tiny woman stepped out. "Mama, come meet Ms. Callanan," Amy said, and then repeated the phrase in her native tongue. "My mother hasn't learned English yet. She stays at home with my kids, minding the house, while I work."

As Mrs. Kim approached us, I noticed the deep lines in her face that seemed like a road map of her grief.

"Please tell her that I am sorry that this tragedy has befallen your family," I said.

Amy translated, and her mother bowed deeply to me.

I spent a half hour or so with Amy, discussing her father's condition. She told me that five times a week he received radiation treatments at the cancer center where she had asked for the second opinion. The fifty-mile trip took an hour and a half each way.

"How do you manage that?" I asked, knowing that most insurance plans wouldn't pay for such transportation.

"I've had to hire a car and driver," Amy said. "I work, and so I can't drive my father myself. We can barely afford it. But he's being treated at one of the top facilities in the world—and I want only the best for my father."

Amy then led me to her parents' bedroom. The shades were drawn. On the bed was a frail, slight form curled in a fetal position, facing the wall.

"Papa," Amy whispered, "please turn over. Ms. Callanan is here to see you." Mr. Kim turned slowly toward us. "How are you feeling, Papa?" she asked. He nodded halfheartedly and forced a smile. I greeted him, then checked his blood pressure and pulse, listened to his lungs and abdomen, and asked how he was feeling.

He indicated that he had severe pain in his thighs and ribs. This is common with advanced prostate cancer that has metastasized to the bone, and I knew it might take some time for the radiation treatments to have an effect.

I called Mr. Kim's oncologist to get an order for increased pain medication and asked Amy to explain the new protocol to her father. As a pharmacist, she understood very well.

"All the time tired," said Mr. Kim. "Hospital is hard. But Amy thinks it's best...." His voice trailed off.

"Papa, they *are* the best," said Amy, holding her father's hand. "I know it takes a long time to get there, but I think it's worth it."

Mr. Kim answered her in Korean. In any language, this conversation is the same: I could tell by his tone that he clearly loved his daughter and appreciated her care. He also wanted to make her happy and carry out what she believed to be the right decision regarding his health. She did have some medical training, after all.

If Mr. Kim had had a rare type of cancer, it would have been understandable to seek treatment from a specialized cancer center. But Mr. Kim's cancer was very common, and the long drive five times a week took an enormous toll on his body and spirit. He traveled alone with a driver who didn't speak Korean. I pictured him in the hospital being ushered through the halls and into treatment rooms like a mute child.

One day when I arrived, Mr. Kim looked particularly exhausted. "If you took a blanket and pillow with you in the car, could you sleep on your way home from the hospital?" I asked through Amy. He adamantly shook his head.

"My father would never do that," Amy said. "It is not his—I should say *our*—way. It is not dignified!" She went on to explain that Mr. Kim's cultural mores did not allow him to show weakness or discomfort.

Again I pictured this proud man sitting up straight in the backseat of his hired car, worn down by pain, exhausted from treatment, forcing himself to stay awake, locked in silence after trusting his failing body to strangers in a country that was not his home. The image broke my heart.

Later, Amy admitted that her father returned home from the hospital disoriented, exhausted, and in pain. "Yet he hardly ever complains," she said. Her voice trailed off, and she wept behind her hands.

At this point I felt I had enough information to intercede. I suggested that the family transfer treatment to the hospital near their home. "It might help relieve a lot of your father's stress and discomfort—not to mention the financial burden," I said. Amy considered my suggestion, but she remained convinced that the prestigious cancer center would bring about better results for her father.

"Make sure you are not confusing greater financial and emotional strain with better and more successful care, or with proof of your love," I said quietly.

The next time I visited, I found Mr. Kim severely depressed. He refused to eat or get out of bed. He was in the same position as on my first visit, but this time he was much slower to rouse. "Please, Papa, it's Ms. Callanan," Amy pleaded, but her father whispered something in Korean and remained facing the wall. Mrs. Kim came in with a tray of delicious-smelling small dishes, but he did not even acknowledge her presence. When we left the room Amy took away the untouched food.

"Depression is not uncommon with someone who is terminally ill," I explained when we were out of earshot. "The doctor can prescribe an antidepressant, but it will take about two weeks to be fully effective. The steroids and pain medications your father is taking might also be causing mood swings."

"I can't bear to see him like this, Maggie," Amy said. "I can see that these long trips are taking a lot out of him. I'm starting to wonder if they *are* a mistake."

"What does your father want? He needs to feel he has a say in what's happening to him. But I know he'll get comparable care in your local hospital. It has a very good reputation. There's no reason to put him through added stress. He needs to be home as much as possible right now. I think that will be his best medicine," I said.

Three days later, Mr. Kim refused to continue treatment at the distant cancer center. He became sicker and weaker as Amy frantically tried to switch his care, midstream, to the local doctor who had originally diagnosed him. The change was accomplished as quickly as possible, but Amy had only limited time with her father, as she spent her evenings copying documents, calling doctors, mailing in forms, and making sure the transfer went smoothly.

When I next came to visit, Mr. Kim was more relaxed, responsive, and alert. His pain was much better. He even said to Amy and me, "I like this new hospital better than the one far away," but valuable time had been lost, both with his treatments and with his family.

Mr. Kim died a few weeks later, and his family was left not only with their grief but also with too many what-ifs.

What-Ifs

When I visited the Kims after Mr. Kim had died, I did my best to validate how hard they had tried and how well they had worked together. They were a devoted family, and it was clear that they had honored him in the best ways they could.

I don't want the families I visit to feel guilty about the what-ifs, because they are a given and often the most difficult part of losing someone you love. In one house I hear, "What if Mother had agreed to the chemo [or radiation or surgery]? Maybe she would have had more time." Then in the very next house I hear, "I keep thinking that if Father hadn't agreed to the chemo [or radiation or surgery], he wouldn't have been so sick before he died." Particularly with cancer, there are many more what-ifs than guarantees.

I know how difficult these choices are. More often than not, they are made with the best of intentions and with a lot of love and concern. We all want to know that the person we love is receiving the very best care.

THE BOTTOM LINE

Save time, money, and stress—the best care may be close to home.

6

"I DON'T KNOW ... MY DOCTOR HAS MY RECORDS"

When I started in nursing more than thirty-five years ago, if a patient questioned what medication I was handing him or her, I was not to divulge that information. Rather, I was to direct the patient to ask the doctor. Many patients never asked and so never knew what medication was prescribed for them or why. Those days of blind, trusting innocence are over, or at least should be. Medical professionals have found that the more involved and informed patients are, the better they will fare.

And yet when I question patients—particularly older women—about the medications they're taking or the medical procedures they've had, I still sometimes hear, "I'm on two of those little white pills and one yellow." Or worse yet, "Oh, I don't know, dearie ... my doctor has my records."

Today, of course, we face a very different reality than we did three or four decades ago. My last employer switched health care insurance coverage three times in six years. In most cases, this meant I had to change not only physicians but also radiology and laboratory companies in order to remain covered. Remembering where last year's mammogram was done so those films could be compared with this year's became a difficult and confusing task. Maintaining continuity of care became nearly impossible even for me, a nurse who understands the system. *Not* following my insurance company's exact protocol could mean that I'd incur staggering costs.

This lack of continuity of care can be especially dangerous for people facing a serious illness. That is why I urge every
patient—or a designated family member—to keep accurate doc-
umentation of all treatments and procedures in one readily accessible place. When people who are newly diagnosed with a
serious illness ask me for advice, the first thing I tell them is to
get a small spiral notebook, about five by eight inches, and start
keeping notes: dates of doctor visits, lab work and medication
prescribed, and important contact names and numbers. Always
get business cards and keep them in the notebook, which
should be with the patient at all times.

I grew up with my family in the diplomatic corps of the
State Department. Since we moved every two to three years, my
mother kept records for the entire family and hand-carried them
to each new place we were assigned. She had an inexpensive com-
position book for each of us, in which she noted all illnesses, allergies, and broken bones with dates and treatments. Copies of
our immunization records, X-rays, and other documents were
kept in large manila envelopes. From Japan to Brazil, they were
always safely with us. Military families usually do the same. I
carried on this tradition for my own family, even though we
didn't move around.

When the terrorists of 9/11 struck, my friend Louise was
several weeks into her chemotherapy for ovarian cancer. Louise
lived in Washington, D.C., only seven miles from CIA head-
quarters, and the whole city was under red alert in anticipation
of further attacks. I reminded her: "You can get the same
chemotherapy treatment in Delaware, where your beach house
is, or any other state. It's often available abroad as well. Let's ask
the nurse practitioner to write out your treatment protocol and
give you prescriptions just in case you have to get out of town
fast. Wherever you decide to go, a good oncologist will have access to the same drugs you would be getting here."

As it turned out, evacuation was never necessary, so she
was able to successfully complete her therapy with her own

oncologist. But having her protocol, prescriptions, and a copy of her medical records in her car gave her great peace of mind.

In my experience, those patients who have kept accurate, concise records of their health histories, treatments, and medications have contributed greatly to the continuity of their care. Original medical records are often located in various medical facilities or offices. In an emergency, a particular doctor may be difficult to reach, or the facility where the lab work was done may be closed. Not having that pertinent information could be harmful.

On the other hand, a patient or caregiver who has easy access to a written medical history feels informed and empowered. Rather than being handicapped by a lack of information, that person is able to work with the medical team to decide *together* what is best. Patients feel a greater sense of control, and in turn, trust that they are receiving the most appropriate care. Having the records also reduces guesswork and prevents duplication of tests that have already been done. It is crucial to help a doctor avoid prescribing medications that have previously caused adverse reactions or allergies or that will interact adversely with medications another doctor may have prescribed.

Today, patients (or the people appointed to be their health care proxies) are almost always asked for a signature to acknowledge the medical information they have received and to give consent for any procedures. If you have emergency information such as a do-not-resuscitate order, carry it with you always, as close to your driver's license as possible. If you are unable to speak for yourself, this is where the emergency room staff will look first for critical information.

Remember, if it's important enough to draw blood, do an X-ray or treatment, it's important for you to have a copy of the results in your folder. Ask your doctor's office or hospital to give you a copy. You may need to sign a release, but it is your right to have this information. In addition to the small spiral notebook, it's also useful to have a loose-leaf binder to hold lab and X-ray reports as well as doctors' letters and reports. A plastic page with pockets for business cards makes it easy to keep track of doctors' addresses and phone and fax numbers. Since your doctors may often need to share your medical information with one another, you will benefit by being able to provide contact information quickly and accurately.

THE BOTTOM LINE

If it's important enough to draw blood, take an X-ray, or have a treatment, you should keep a copy of the information and results. To get good medical care, you must become an active, assertive, and record-keeping consumer.

PART II

MAKING DIFFICULT DECISIONS

7

THE RIGHT TO BE
COMFORTABLE

Choosing Palliative Care

When I ask people what they fear most about dying, they often say, "It's not the being-dead part I'm afraid of. It's how much pain I'll have to go through to get there."

Today, thanks to huge strides in the field of hospice and palliative care, pain and other uncomfortable symptoms can almost always be controlled and relieved. We now have remarkably simple and effective ways to help people stay pain-free and alert, even during the last stages of a terminal illness.

Many people are confused by the difference between curative and palliative care. The goal of curative care is to cure an illness or keep it under control. The goal of palliative care, often called "comfort care," is to make the patient as comfortable and functional as possible, understanding that cure is not an option. It is now a mandate of the Surgeon General of the United States and of the Joint Commission on Accreditation of Healthcare Organizations (and other medical facilities) that patients be kept comfortable and free of pain. An institution's license to provide medical care can be in jeopardy if these mandates are ignored.

It has been standard practice for years to regularly check a patient's four vital signs: temperature, pulse, respiration, and blood pressure. Because of this new mandate, pain is now considered the fifth vital sign. A patient's pain or discomfort level has to be monitored, treated, charted, and reviewed at every visit.

You wouldn't ask a dentist to deliver your baby. Neither should you expect every doctor to be qualified to provide the best care for the unique needs of the dying. Hospice and palliative care are medical specialties, like cardiology and neurology. Surprisingly, most doctors are not trained adequately, if at all, in pain control or in the special needs of the dying. They may also lack expertise in aggressive symptom management. The main goal of traditional medical training is to conquer illness and disease; comfort is an issue but not the primary focus. But when survival is no longer an option, curative care ceases to be appropriate or beneficial.

This does not mean that treatment stops. Palliative care offers many options and must be expertly adapted to the unique needs of each patient. It often requires precisely prescribed and monitored medication. Radiology may be used to decrease bone pain from cancer or to shrink tumors. Surgery may be appropriate to diminish the size and pressure of a tumor or to place a stent to open a blocked passageway in the body (such as the bile duct to the gallbladder). Other treatments include physical therapy, massage therapy, aromatherapy, or meditation. The value of each option is determined by weighing its benefit against its burden to the patient. Since comfort is the goal, the most benefit is sought with the least possible burden. And since terminally ill patients are in a state of fairly constant change, these options are constantly being reevaluated, added to, discarded, or combined according to the comfort level achieved and, most important of all, in keeping with the patient's own wishes.

It takes physical, psychic, and spiritual energy to suffer. When a person's energy must go toward coping with pain, nausea, vomiting, restlessness, insomnia, anxiety, or depression, he or she is not free to focus on anything else, especially on taking care of unfinished business and writing the last chapter of his or her life in a way that is a fitting tribute to that life.

If you talk with a grieving family member about the

meaningful events that took place while a dying person was receiving palliative care, you will invariably hear about conversations and tender moments shared, rather than about the specific physical changes that occurred during that time. These are wonderful gifts that help all involved through the dying and grieving process. This is the goal of palliative care: respecting the dying person's right to be comfortable.

ROSE AND EVELYN

It was months after the deaths of both of their husbands that Evelyn and Rose attended the same grief support luncheon. "We've never officially met, but I remember you and a gentleman I assumed was your husband from the waiting room of Dr. Dooley's office," Evelyn said.

"I thought you looked familiar," Rose replied. "When did your husband die?"

"My Bill died seven months ago," Evelyn said. "Hospice cared for him."

"Harry died six and a half months ago at a cancer center out of town," Rose said.

Instantly engrossed in their shared journey, the widows compared notes. Both husbands had had lung cancer that had already spread to other organs before they were diagnosed. Both had had radiation, which slowed the disease but did not cure it. The doctor had been equally honest with each of them about their odds: even with more aggressive treatment, only 5 percent were cured; 20 percent were able to buy some time, but the amount of time and the quality of life varied.

Both Harry and Bill had started chemo and suffered from side effects: weakness, nausea, and vomiting with significant weight loss.

Rose's husband, Harry, had been committed to "going for the cure."

"He just wouldn't give up!" Rose said with pride. "He was such a fighter!" He didn't respond to the chemo, so it was stopped. But he insisted on trying a clinical trial at a major cancer center three states away.

Rose stayed in a hotel near the center's hospital but kept in close phone contact with their children and friends back home. The clinical trial failed, and the doctors suggested sending Harry home for hospice care. But one infection followed another, making him too sick to travel. He died in the hospital, so quickly and unexpectedly that his family was unprepared. Rose was at his bedside when he died, but he never saw his children or friends again.

Bill's story was different. After the first round of chemo, he'd had a long talk with Evelyn and the kids.

"I've heard the odds," he said, "and a bird in the hand is worth two in the bush. I feel well enough now to do some of the things I've planned, and I don't want to risk losing that."

The family was upset but supported his decision to stop the chemo and become a hospice patient. With hospice's help in providing symptom control for his shortness of breath and chest pain, Bill was able to take Evelyn on the cruise they had always dreamed of. Hospice helped them arrange for portable oxygen and a wheelchair to be available if needed. The hospice nurse also contacted the ship's medical unit to review Bill's needs and to provide the hospice phone numbers if problems arose.

These preparations were comforting but, as it turned out, they weren't needed. Bill and Evelyn had a wonderful "second honeymoon." "He was so enthusiastic," she said. "It was like a well-earned vacation from being sick!"

Energized by this experience, Bill planned two smaller weekend trips to visit his brothers because "today may be a better day than tomorrow, and I haven't finished kicking up my heels yet!"

Having comfortably accomplished these goals, Bill gently

deteriorated over a few weeks' time. His symptoms continued to be well controlled, but he became weaker, bedridden, and sleepy, with some confusion. He slipped into a brief coma and died peacefully with his family surrounding him.

After the grief support luncheon Evelyn called her daughter to tell her about meeting Rose. "They chose a different path than we did," Evelyn explained. "And I must say there were times that I wondered if we had made the right decision. You know, at the time I thought that I would have done *anything* to keep Dad with us for one more day. Rose's husband lived about two weeks longer than Dad did, but look at how different the quality of their last six months together was. I couldn't help feeling sorry for Rose and Harry. Now I know we made the right decision."

I don't mean to say that it is always a mistake to keep fighting. Each person has the right to make the choices that best fit his or her unique journey. But I do urge you to work with your health care team to clearly identify the balance of benefits and burdens in every option. This will help you make the right decision for you.

One of the most difficult things about caring for someone who is dying, especially of cancer, is the uncertainty. Because the patient gets worse no matter what you do, it can feel as though you made the wrong decision. The what-ifs are inevitable. This is actually an indication of how we grieve our own inadequacy and powerlessness over death.

THE BOTTOM LINE

The end of life does not have to be about suffering.

8

"I'M DYING! OF COURSE I'M IN PAIN!"

Expert Pain and Symptom Control

I was leaving the house after admitting my new patient, a seventy-year-old gentleman. His son, Robert, was outside, pacing up and down the driveway puffing furiously on a cigarette. Something was clearly wrong, so I went over to talk.

"Robert, I know this was a long visit with lots of paperwork to be reviewed and signed, and I'm sure you're tired of listening to me. I get tired of listening to myself!" No smile from Robert. "It's a lot to digest in one visit, but you seem angry. I wonder if you have any particular concerns or input that would be helpful to me as I get to know your father and your family."

"Well, since you asked, I think a lot of what you said in there is a bunch of hooey!" he snapped.

"Help me understand what doesn't make sense to you."

"Listen," he replied, "you can't pull the wool over my eyes with this 'being free of pain' stuff. I've heard enough about cancer from my friends and relatives. You get sick and have some pain. Then you get sicker and have a lot of pain. Then you die in horrible pain. That's the deal. That's the way it works!

"And I saw what happened in the hospital. All Dad did was stare at the clock, waiting for three hours to pass so he could have his next pain shot."

No wonder he's so angry, I thought. "How awful that must have been for you to watch," I said. "But I promise that won't happen here at home. We do things differently, and our plan does *not* include watching the clock. We will have plenty of medication available to him right here in the house, and I will show you and your mother how to give him what he needs for comfort, as often as he needs it, and as much as it takes." Robert was looking at me with skepticism.

"All I ask is that you write down everything you're giving, how much, and when," I went on. "I'll set up a medication sheet to make it easy for you both. And don't forget—if you have questions or concerns, or if he's not getting comfortable quickly enough, a nurse is just a phone call away twenty-four hours a day. We can change what we're doing in the middle of the night if that's what he needs," I assured Robert. "My job is to have everything here that you might need, before you need it.

"The information you or your mom writes down about the intensity and frequency of his pain will help me identify how much medication he needs. It's like justice with her scales—we need to balance the amount of pain with the right amount of medication to cancel it out. I will calculate how much medication he needs in the next twenty-four-hour period and then figure out the least intrusive way to medicate him. For example, instead of using lower-dose pills every two hours, we might prescribe a stronger, time-release capsule once or twice a day, or a skin patch with concentrated medication that lasts seventy-two hours." Robert's eyebrows rose slightly.

"It's depressing to have someone come at you with medication often during the day," I explained. "It reminds you too many times that you're sick and relying on drugs. That wounds the spirit and upsets most people. So we try to get away from medicating so often."

Robert was now leaning toward me, squinting slightly, and nodding thoughtfully. It seemed he was following my explanations.

"Give me two or three days and I promise you that not only will I have his pain controlled, but I will also fix his constipation and have him sleeping better at night. I promise! If not, you can fire me and ask for another nurse; maybe you'll get a younger, prettier one. " Now he grinned.

At that moment we became a working team. Believe me, much can be accomplished in driveways.

There are many reasons why terminally ill patients or their families may not seek out the best professional help to manage pain. They may believe that pain is an unavoidable symptom of dying. They may hate taking pills. They may think (mistakenly) that every doctor has been trained to treat pain, or that all pain is alike. They may fear doctors or hospitals, or a language barrier may keep them from communicating easily in such a setting. They may not have insurance coverage. They may have well-intentioned home remedies that simply do not work or that are inappropriate for the patient's particular needs. They may fear becoming addicted to pain-control medications such as morphine despite the fact that in good palliative care, such drugs are effective and safe. Finally, they may avoid getting relief because according to their cultural or spiritual beliefs, suffering has merit.

Pain has long been undertreated in this country. This has not been because of a lack of concern or compassion, but rather because pain was not adequately understood or taught to physicians. According to the *Journal of the American Medical Association,* only about 3 percent of all medical schools in the United States require a separate comprehensive course in pain control, and only 20 percent teach a course on death and dying—despite the fact that every single patient of every doctor will die.

We are now learning that inadequately assessed and undertreated pain not only leads to needless suffering but also carries a high price in lost productivity and increased health care costs.

However, things are changing because of hospice and the relatively new medical specialty called palliative care. These have put the focus on understanding the origins and progression of pain, new and innovative ways to control it, and better management of other symptoms of discomfort. Many hospitals now have pain clinics or palliative care teams available to consult with a patient's physician. Hospice and palliative care physicians have extensive training in the management and control of all types of pain and other distressing symptoms. They are the experts.

Pain warns us that something inside our body is going wrong and needs attention. There are many reasons why a dying person may feel pain, including:

Chronic injuries or illnesses such as arthritis

Pressure caused by growths or tumors

Organ secretions, such as the gastric acid that causes heartburn and ulcers

Cancer that has spread to the bones or nerves

Heat from fever

Side effects from treatments, such as chemotherapy and radiation

Pressure sores (bedsores) from inactivity and poor nutrition

But it's also important to pay attention to nonphysical factors such as stress, fear, and anxiety. Our spiritual, emotional, and personal lives have a profound effect on our bodies as well as our minds. Sometimes pain is the physical manifestation of emotional or spiritual stresses. That is why the hospice interdisciplinary team approach to comfort care has been so incredibly successful.

When people are allowed to suffer with pain and other discomforts, losses spread to every part of their lives. They will experience loss of pleasure in living, loss of participation in family life, loss of appetite contributing to excessive weight loss, loss of sleep, and loss of hope. They suffer from depression and from the distress they see in family members who feel helpless to relieve their suffering. All of this damage is now avoidable with simple, readily available treatments.

The key to pain control is to identify its source. The words that patients use to describe their pain often point to its origin. For example, "constant ache" usually signals organ or soft tissue pain. A complaint that "it increases when I move" makes bone or joint pain a possible suspect. "It increases when I take a breath" most often indicates lung or pleurisy pain. "Pins and needles," "burning," or "stabbing" is typical of nerve pain. And a patient who speaks of "cramps or spasms" probably has muscle pain or spasmodic pain from an internal blockage such as a kidney stone or extreme constipation.

There is no single medication that will provide relief for all types of pain. Doctors who have not been trained in pain control often have a favorite, relatively mild narcotic, such as Tylenol #3 or Percocet, which they give for all pain. These are good and effective medications that address specific symptoms, but when used inappropriately, they will constipate and possibly sedate the patient without giving adequate pain relief.

My intention here is not to blame physicians. In addition to inadequate training in pain control, they often are fearful of being accused of improperly dispensing narcotics and being reprimanded or stripped of their license to practice by the state medical board. So it is understandable that they are reluctant to prescribe more than a small amount of these legally controlled drugs. The answer is to seek care from doctors trained in hospice and palliative care. They are recognized experts in properly prescribing and monitoring controlled drugs, and medical boards know that their patients have unusual problems with pain control, often requiring more medication than is usually prescribed.

Different medications are effective for different types of pain. For example, the family of medications called nonsteroidal anti-inflammatory drugs (NSAIDs), such as Motrin (ibuprofen) or Aleve (naproxen), may be more effective for bone pain than a narcotic such as morphine. Nerve pain may respond better to certain antiseizure medications or antidepressants than to narcotics. And since many patients experience more than one type of pain at a time, medications are often combined. One medication may also be used to potentiate (strengthen the effects of) another.

Medication timing is another important area. Some drugs are used on what is known as a "p.r.n." or "as-needed" basis, when the problem occurs. Others, particularly long-acting or time-release medications, must be given on a regular schedule to provide continuous, effective relief. For the most part, if pain is constant, medication should be given regularly *before* the pain is experienced, and then continued even after the pain is relieved to prevent its recurrence. The earlier the pain is treated, the more easily it can be controlled. It is unnecessary and counterproductive to make people in pain "watch the clock" until the next scheduled dose. And by hospice standards of care, it is also cruel.

Being able to swallow is not a requirement for achieving good pain control. Drops of pain medication can be put under the tongue (as can medications for nausea, shortness of breath, insomnia, anxiety, and so on). Certain medications are given through skin patches or ointments, or rectally, in suppository form. Still others are inhaled. Medications can also be continuously given through a fine, tiny needle under the skin that needs to be changed only every few days. And with the advent of central venous access devices, which are surgically implanted intravenous catheters or tubes, giving medication by IV is simplified enough to be managed by family caregivers at home. All of these methods can be used even if the patient is unconscious.

I have treated many, many hospice patients who, because of good pain and symptom control, lived much longer than their prognosis and were able to use that extra time to achieve some important last goals. Seek out the experts; the help is there. I want all my patients and their caregivers to enjoy their time together for as long, and as comfortably, as possible!

THE BOTTOM LINE

With hospice and palliative care available in today's world, you don't have to die in pain or with other suffering.

9

CHOOSING TREATMENTS—

And Knowing Which Are Optional

Ten years ago I was privileged to care for Jimmy, who was dying from a malignant brain tumor in the prime of his life, age thirty-four. He had been married only ten years, and he was anguished about the welfare of his young wife, Debbie, and their two sons, who were eight and nine.

Jimmy was an engineer. He was an intensely practical person, an expert at collecting, processing, and successfully applying information. He approached his illness in the same way. "Give me the facts!" he would say. But his tender heart showed through his efficiency when he talked about his wife or when his sons came into his room for their "cuddle time."

Shortly after his admission to hospice, while Debbie was out of the room, he told me, "I want to know *everything*. Just exactly what should I expect from this illness and what can I do about it?" I took a legal-size sheet of paper and drew a line lengthwise down the middle. At the top of one column I wrote FIXABLE / WORKABLE. Under this heading I listed symptoms such as pain, constipation, and sleep disturbances. I also noted concerns about the family's future and about the children's fears and grief issues, help for his wife as his care needs increased, and grief support for the family after he died. His hospice team could offer expert, effective help to alleviate all these symptoms and concerns.

Above the other column I wrote NOT FIXABLE / NOT

WORKABLE. This list included his increasing neurological decline: his right arm and leg would become weaker, he would become sleepier, and he would spend increasing amounts of time in bed until he was there full time. He might get an infection or slip into a coma that would lead to his death.

I explained that we would help him cope with the problems that were not fixable or workable, and that we would use medications to minimize them as much as possible, but that we would focus primarily on the things in his life that *were* fixable or workable. We would strive to maintain a good quality of life so that he could enjoy being with his family and use this important time as creatively and meaningfully as possible. We would also give him as many choices and as much control over what was happening to him as possible.

Jimmy thought about all this for a long moment. Finally, with resignation in his voice, he said, "Dying from this illness is not what I would choose, but it sounds like there is a workable plan. If that's what's involved, I think I can do it!" The analytical engineer had reviewed the information and come to a practical decision. I was touched to the core by the poignancy of his summing up—not "I want to," but "If I have to, I can."

I asked if I could review these lists with his wife, and he agreed. There was much more to be discussed, but I knew Jimmy would ask for that information when he was ready.

I-95

On my next visit, Jimmy said he had a few questions for me. "Last time, you suggested that I could have some choices about my illness and treatments. Go over that with me, would you?"

And so I began. "Most terminal illnesses are like a journey down I-95. You can choose to stay on it from its start in Maine until it runs out at the tip of Florida and the journey is over. Or you can choose to take an earlier exit and end the journey sooner." I could see that Jimmy was hanging on every word.

"The complications and problems created by the illness are like the exits off I-95. Some of them are little problems needing only small interventions to keep you on your journey. Some are more serious. They require bigger interventions if you want to continue on. Exits are really opportunities. You can choose the treatments that will allow you to continue, or you can choose to allow the journey to end on *your* terms."

Jimmy's face lit up. "I get it!" he exclaimed. "On some level I can control this disease rather than let it completely dominate me." Then he continued more slowly, "With an illness like this, I never thought I could do it on my own terms. This really helps me deal with my fears and the feeling of being so helpless."

I asked him what he feared about his illness.

"That my sons will be traumatized if they see me having seizures," he said. "And I'd rather not be alive if I can't think and respond to my family."

I assured him that we had good medications to control his seizures. He would be on steroids to decrease swelling in his brain, and that should help keep his mind clear as long as possible. The steroids could be decreased or stopped if and when he wished, and we could keep him comfortable, but without those medications he would quickly deteriorate and die. We could transfer him to our hospice inpatient unit for his last few days if it became too difficult or upsetting for his wife and sons.

"Well," he said, "that gives me a lot to think about. But I want to go back to what you said about exits. Tell me more about how that works."

"An infection such as pneumonia is one. You can choose to treat it, or you can let it take its course. Bleeding into your brain, as happens in a stroke, is another. Not eating and drinking—either by choice or because you become too weak to swallow—is a third. Stopping the medications and letting the seizures take over is a fourth. That's an exit I probably would not recommend, because even though you wouldn't feel anything, it can be very upsetting for your family to see," I explained.

"That's a lot to think about," Jimmy said again. "I want to talk this all over with Debbie. If we have questions, can you go over everything again with us?"

"Of course!" I replied. "As many times as you need. And remember, no decision you make is set in stone. You can try a course of action, then change your mind and reverse it. But it's important that you understand what's happening, the available interventions, and the benefits and burdens of your choices.

"My job is to give you as much information as you *want* and need," I went on. "Some people don't want any information, so I wouldn't be having this conversation with them."

"Well, I meant it when I said I want to know everything. Please let me know if you see any exits coming along."

I promised I would be vigilant and keep him informed. He seemed relieved.

Accustomed as we are to traditional medicine, many people—especially family members—are shocked at the concept of not treating or trying to cure every complication that occurs. "What do you mean, we don't have to treat an infection?" they ask me. "Isn't that *murder*?"

This is a difficult concept for all concerned, but there are some very important distinctions here. Doing anything to a patient that hastens his or her death, *even at the patient's request,* is called active euthanasia or mercy killing, and it is against the law throughout North America. Physician-assisted suicide, in which a physician knowingly prescribes medication that a patient takes to end his or her life, is legal only in the state of Oregon, under very tight regulation. Neither is acceptable practice in any hospice or other palliative care program.

What I discussed with Jimmy is quite different. It is choosing *not* to use interventions that will artificially prolong the process of dying; instead, we allow a natural death to occur. While this is sometimes called passive euthanasia, it is not illegal in any state. It is often an opportunity for the dying to control the difficulty and duration of their journey.

Why do some patients choose an earlier exit, even with all the support we offer them? This is what they tell me:

"I'm tired and I don't want to do this anymore."

"The harder I try, the worse it gets. I've had enough."

"Why continue to go through this when it's definitely killing me, but it seems to be hurting my family, too?"

"What good is to be gained by continuing to fight?"

"I want to spare my wife and children any more anguish."

"There is no quality of life anymore."

Many patients, like Jimmy, are deeply comforted by the possibility of choosing how long to continue down this road on their own terms and for their own reasons.

An Exit

Months later, Jimmy was in bed full time. He had periods of confusion and was getting very sleepy. He was losing his ability to interact clearly with Debbie and the boys, and he needed more and more help with bathing, toileting, and eating. I also noticed that he had started "squirreling" food and crushed pills in his cheeks. This is a common behavior for patients with advancing brain disease, but I was concerned that he might breathe some of this material into his lungs, which could cause aspiration pneumonia.

I sensed a change in Jimmy's emotional journey as well. When he was mentally clear, he talked more about dying, and he told me that he was having very vivid dreams about his beloved grandparents, who both had been dead for many years.

"They're waiting for me," he'd say with a dreamy smile. He seemed to be detaching and drifting away from the here and now.

During each visit, I listened to Jimmy's heart and lungs with my stethoscope. One day, I heard the extra mucus and the fine distant rubbing sounds of a possible early pneumonia in one lung. When I called Jimmy's doctor with this report, he asked me to find out what Jimmy and Debbie wanted to do—or not do—about treatment. He would support whatever they chose. I went back to Jimmy's room.

"Jimmy, I'm picking up some changes and have reported them to your doctor," I told him gently. "Would you like to know what they are?"

Although early on Jimmy had clearly stated his desire to know everything, I always check, *every single time,* just in case a patient changes his mind or is too frightened to hear bad news. Jimmy nodded, squinting and blinking as if to clear away cobwebs in his head.

"I hear the kind of congestion in your lungs that we worry about," I said, "the kind that can become pneumonia. This is a big change." I softly rubbed his arm as I spoke.

"An exit?" he mumbled.

"It could be," I said gently.

"Oh, good ... I'm so ... so tired," he murmured. "I want to be done with this. . . . Talk to Deb ... she okay if I stop fighting?"

I spent a long time in the kitchen holding Debbie as she wept on my shoulder.

"We've talked a lot about this," she said. "It was fine as long as it was next year or next month or next week, but now it's *right here* and I'm *not ready*."

"I know, sweetie," I said, "I know."

"I can't bear to see him go downhill, and I promised I would support his choice to stay in charge. But it's so hard. Is there really such a thing as being ready?"

I sighed. "Intellectually, I suppose it's possible," I said. "But the loving heart is never *really* ready to let go and say good-bye."

Later Debbie and I sat together next to Jimmy's bed. I reviewed how we would keep him comfortable so he could have an easy, peaceful death. I offered to transfer him to the hospice inpatient unit if that's what they wanted and if a bed was available.

"No!" said Debbie emphatically. "I want him here with us. We've shared this journey so far, and the seizures he was afraid of never happened. The boys and I are proud of our teamwork, and my parents are on their way to help us. It's *important* for our family to do this together. We *want* him here!"

"Okay," Jimmy murmured dreamily. "We have a plan." He drifted off to sleep holding Debbie's hand.

Jimmy died four days later, as peacefully and comfortably as he had hoped. His hospital bed had been placed right up against his and Debbie's bed, and he died with Debbie and the boys all tangled up sleeping in their "cuddles," touching him, and dreaming with him as he breathed his last.

At the funeral Debbie told me, "It's so unreal that he's gone, but I'll never be as afraid of dying as I was before we took this journey together. Jimmy taught us so much, and the boys and I are so grateful to him."

Minor Complications Can Cause Major Problems

Many people are surprised to learn that the dying rarely die of their actual disease, such as cancer, but rather succumb to some problem caused by the ravages of their illness combined with their weakened state. Common complications include infections, changes in blood chemistry that can cause internal bleeding or inadequate oxygenation, and an imbalance in electrolytes or other body chemicals. For a healthy person, some of these problems would be a discomfort or an inconvenience, but they could be resolved by medical treatment. For the dying, these complications can be fatal.

A few years ago I developed pneumonia, which meant that I had to take five days off from work. After two days, the antibiotic kicked in, and I felt so much better that I decided to paint one of my bathrooms. I was a healthy person who had a case of pneumonia. It was an inconvenience, but a simple, direct treatment cured me.

Pneumonia for a dying person, however, is another story, and it can be caused by problems that healthy people don't have. The dying person's ability to swallow efficiently is often decreased by weakness, and tiny amounts of food or fluids can be inhaled into the lungs as the patient eats or drinks. The bacteria that cause pneumonia are often in the air around us, and the disease can develop easily if the lungs contain fluid, bits of food, or mucus—all of which offer a good environment for bacteria to grow. Add to that an immune system already compromised by illness or by treatments such as chemotherapy or radiation. This is why pneumonia in a seriously ill or dying person is a common cause of death.

When complications such as infection and internal bleeding occur, patients (or their designated health care proxies) are faced with a choice. They may decide to aggressively treat such problems in hopes of curing them, or they can consider *not* treating the root cause of these problems. For example, antibiotics may be used to fight a bacterial infection, or blood transfusions may be given to treat the anemia that results from ongoing blood loss. But both are temporary reprieves at best. These problems will continue to arise because of the progressive illness and the increasing debilitation of the patient. On the other hand, those who choose not to treat see these serious complications as an opportunity "to be done with this illness." Then comfort care is the most logical and compassionate choice.

It's surprising to most people that a patient can die peacefully and comfortably from pneumonia (and most other infections) or internal bleeding if good, aggressive comfort care is used. I'll describe how the two choices can play out in a case like Jimmy's.

The discomforts from pneumonia are caused by fever from the infection and by increasing mucus in the lungs that leads to difficulty breathing and anxiety from a sense of "air hunger." This is often followed by general respiratory deterioration and death, since not enough oxygen is being carried to the body's vital organs.

Curative care might involve hospitalization, frequent needle sticks for blood work, multiple X-rays, continuous oxygen in the nose, anti-inflammatory medications to reduce fever, IVs, antibiotics, and inhaled medications given through a nebulizer. If these treatments fail, the patient is put on a respirator. The decision to discontinue these extraordinary means will have to be made by the family or by the person who holds the patient's medical power of attorney (see Appendix A). Making this decision is traumatic for most people.

In terminally ill patients, pneumonia is frequently stubborn and often can't be controlled even with aggressive interventions. More often than not, the patient deteriorates and dies regardless, but in the hospital rather than in his own bed at home.

Palliative care for terminally ill people with pneumonia is vastly different and significantly more compassionate. We use anti-inflammatory medications as well as cool cloths and bathing to remove the discomfort of the fever. We can give the patient oxygen through a nasal cannula (short, tiny tubes in his nose) when and if he wants it. Medications to dry up lung secretions and ease breathing can be administered by mouth, by suppositories, or through skin patches. A few drops of liquid pain medication under the tongue can slow and strengthen the breathing. Medications can also be given under the tongue to eliminate the anxiety caused by "air hunger." No needles, no IVs, no blood work, no strangers providing care, no hospital. These easy treatments can all be given at home.

Since antibiotics aren't used, the infection persists and most often leads to death. But it is a peaceful and comfortable death. The patient begins to sleep more and more. There may be some confusion, which is followed by a brief coma and then death, usually within a few days. Often a death like this is so quiet and gentle that the people sitting around the patient's bed don't even know that it has occurred until they realize that a few minutes have gone by since the patient took his or her last breath.

THE BOTTOM LINE

Dying, like a highway journey, has potential early exits you can choose, to control the length, duration, and comfort of the journey called dying.

10

IT'S HARD ENOUGH
TO DIE ONCE

Deciding About a Do-Not-Resuscitate Order

One of the most difficult choices facing a dying person is whether or not he wants to have cardiopulmonary resuscitation (CPR) if his heart or breathing stops. Some people choose not to deal with this issue, or delay too long making this decision; in either case, it must then be made *for* them by their spouse or family. This is an upsetting choice at best, but it is even harder if we have to make it for someone else, and in the midst of a crisis.

If a do-not-resuscitate form is not signed, or if the doctor does not know the patient's wishes, *CPR will be attempted*. One of the kindest gifts a terminally ill person can give his or her loved ones is to make this decision early, sign the form, and let everyone know it's been done. This spares the patient's loved ones from being forced to make this frightening and potentially guilt-ridden decision themselves.

Because of cardiopulmonary resuscitation, many people with terminal illnesses today have to experience dying a second or even a third time, often without ever having regained consciousness. This causes undue trauma for the patient and the family. It is a death without comfort, peace, or dignity. And typically the family is excluded from being there with the one they love.

CPR is an attempt to restart the heart and lungs after they have stopped. It assumes that these critical organs *can* be restarted and kept working well enough to sustain life. During my first decade in nursing I worked in emergency rooms and intensive care units, initiating and participating in CPR more times than I can count. You have the right to want CPR, but because I believe in true informed consent, let me tell you what you would be choosing.

Time is of the essence when a person's heart stops: there is a critical window of opportunity—about four minutes—to restart the heart before irreparable brain damage occurs from lack of oxygen. The lifeless person is placed on a firm surface like a wide board. An IV is started anywhere a vein can be found. A large breathing tube is inserted down the throat to provide an airway so that a respirator can force oxygen into the lungs. Someone pumps down firmly with the palms of both hands on the patient's sternum or breastbone in a rhythmic pattern that forces blood from the heart to the other organs. This helps the chambers of the heart fill and empty again and again, artificially duplicating the heart's rhythm. It is not uncommon to break some of the patient's ribs while bearing down on the breastbone. Although this is a concern, it is not an important focus: the intention is to save a "savable" life.

In an attempt to shock the heart back into pumping on its own, the patient will be given one or more strong shocks by electrical paddles placed on either side of the chest. The shocks are so strong that everybody present must step back so as not to receive a shock from the bed as well. Simultaneously, medications are pushed through the IV tubes or injected directly into the heart muscle. Machines beep and hiss. Medical personnel often must shout their orders to be heard above the din. Meanwhile, the terrified family members are forced to wait in another room.

If ineffective, CPR is stopped and the time of death recorded. If successful, the patient and all the attached life support machines are sent to the intensive care unit for close monitoring, with hopes that at some point the patient may improve, regain consciousness, and be able to sustain life without the respirator. Some do, some never do, and some have CPR a number of times before they die, never having regained consciousness.

When CPR was introduced some forty years ago, it was intended as an emergency intervention to save a person whose dying was *reversible:* in cases such as life-threatening allergic reactions, near drowning, or heart attack. It was never intended for people with terminal illnesses, whose dying is inevitable and irreversible. In a terminal illness, CPR prolongs the dying, not the living.

Many people have a distorted or inaccurate view of what this intervention involves and what the outcomes might be. I've had patients say to me, "I just want a little CPR—maybe a few thumps on my chest," or "I want you to do it for a little while, but I don't want to go to the hospital," or "I'll let you know when I've had enough."

As technology advances, our expectations of what we are able to do to keep a failing human body alive increase. CPR is now the expected intervention in *all* situations unless a do-not-resuscitate (DNR) order is signed by the patient and a physician. A critical reason to have a living will and a medical power of attorney is to have your wishes known and legally documented *before* you and your family become victims of this situation. (See Appendix A, "Your Strongest Tools Are Made of Paper.")

DELPHINIUM

Delphinium's serene smile was a poignant contrast to the long and difficult course her disease had taken. Diagnosed fifteen years earlier, her breast cancer had been driven into remission several times, only to return. Now she was clearly dying. But with her sweet expression, she seemed to bob above the devastation her losing battle had caused.

"What a pretty and unusual name you have," I said upon meeting her.

She chuckled. "It was my grandmother's favorite flower. But please, just call me Della."

"You seem at peace with what's going on with you," I said cautiously, not entirely clear whether Della's serenity masked denial or was truly typical for her.

"I've fought this as long as I want to and I know that the good Lord is calling me home, so I'm ready to go and I don't want to slow this journey down. My husband, Dwayne, is the problem. He thinks we need to keep pushing the doctors for a cure. After all this time, he still won't get it. Lord, the man is thickheaded!" She rolled her eyes and sighed.

"I see here on your chart that you have already signed a do-not-resuscitate order. I also see that you have appointed Dwayne to hold your durable medical power of attorney. Does he understand your wishes and will he follow them? Will that be a problem for him?"

"Better not be, or I'll haunt him from the grave. He was right here sitting with me when Martha, the hospice social worker, explained all the forms. He knows how I feel. I don't want to be brought back or kept alive with machines. I'm ready to go home to Jesus! Enough is enough!"

I spoke to Dwayne about my concerns.

"Whatever Della wants, Della gets!" he said with a big, jovial smile.

Della's course of care with hospice went very smoothly for seven months. We were able to provide good symptom control for her occasional nausea and for the bone pain where her cancer had spread to her spine and ribs. Even though she became increasingly weaker, she enjoyed time with her children, foster children, and impressively large extended family. Hers was a busy, happy home, and she was content and peaceful there.

She had been in bed full time for about two weeks when it became apparent that her final days were approaching. Sleepiness turned into a semi-coma that wrapped itself around her like a big, fluffy quilt. She'd periodically drift awake with a sweet smile, then peacefully drift off again.

Then I received a call from Dwayne. He wanted to talk about Della's condition. I drove to their home with Martha, the social worker on my team.

When we walked in, Dwayne announced, "Okay, Della's out of her head now, so I make the decisions."

His words and his new assertive attitude made me nervous.

"I want to have everything done to save her," he went on. "I don't think she was in her right mind when she signed that form, but no matter—I'm in charge now!"

Martha had been a witness to Della's DNR form, and she told Dwayne that Della was clearly mentally competent when she signed it. Entrusting him with power of attorney showed that she expected him to carry out *her* wishes. I further explained that Della's life expectancy was now probably measured in days. If he insisted on resuscitation and life support, we'd have to transfer her to the hospital, nearly twenty miles away. CPR cannot be properly done and continued without the machines and people on the critical care team. We could not provide that at home.

I reminded him that with the cancer in her ribs and the bones of her spine, the CPR itself would probably cause multiple fractures. Even if it was successful, she would probably die again within minutes or hours—the disease was so advanced that continuing to live was not possible.

We also pointed out that with the distance to the hospital, it would be hard for her children and other relatives to spend time with her. Even though she was in and out of consciousness, she would miss their loving presence.

But there was nothing we or the very concerned physician could do to dissuade Dwayne. So an ambulance was called to take Della to the hospital. She was in the hospital for five days before her heart stopped. The team worked for thirty minutes to resuscitate her and finally regained a heartbeat, but she lived in a coma for only about forty-five minutes, then arrested again. Dwayne was there and demanded a second resuscitation attempt. After forty minutes it failed, and Della was pronounced dead.

I saw the doctor a few weeks later when I was at the hospital visiting a patient who had broken an arm in a fall out of bed. When I asked how it had gone with Della, he shook his head.

"What a sad way for such a sweet lady to die," he said. "She'd been so careful to make sure her wishes were known. But she should have chosen someone to hold her medical power of attorney who shared her philosophy." It is a sad fact that once the patient can no longer speak for him- or herself, the person with medical power of attorney can override the patient's previous written orders, and there is nothing the medical or hospice team can do about it. So choose that person carefully, and share your living will with as many people as you feel would support your wishes.

Out-of-Hospital DNR Orders

For people who are seriously or terminally ill at home, the issue of unwanted treatment has an added twist. Suppose the patient slides off the side of the bed and lands on the floor. Instinctively, the caregiver calls 911 for assistance to get the patient back into bed. But by dialing that number, the caregiver has set into motion a legal process that is beyond the patient's or family's control. The paramedics who arrive *must* do everything in their power to save the patient's life. They are legally mandated to do so. If their assessment indicates that the person on the floor needs an IV, resuscitation, or other treatment, they *will* provide them and take the person to the hospital, regardless of the patient's or family's wishes.

GREGOR

Back in the early 1980s, I had a delightful German gentleman, Gregor, as my patient. He had colon cancer that had spread to his liver. He was rail thin and jaundiced, with a yellow cast to the skin and eyes. His abdomen was so swollen with fluid (a condition called ascites) that he appeared pregnant. Despite his sickly appearance, Gregor was still able to function quite well, and his solid, rosy wife, Gerta, was determined to maintain the rituals he enjoyed for as long as possible.

Gregor had had a lifelong seizure disorder, unrelated to his cancer, that had been well controlled with medication. He rarely seized, and when he did, Gerta knew just what to do.

One of Gregor's favorite rituals was to go for a car ride each afternoon. On a particularly balmy spring day, just as they pulled into the driveway after a nice outing, Gregor had a strong seizure. Gerta calmly made sure he was safe and wouldn't get hurt and waited for it to end by itself. When it did, Gregor was typically disoriented and groggy, and he had somehow gotten wedged in an awkward position between the dashboard, the front seat, and the gearshift. Afraid that she would hurt him if she tried to pull him out, Gerta called 911 for help.

The paramedics arrived quickly with sirens screaming, noted how sick Gregor looked, pulled him from the car, put him on a stretcher, and loaded him into an ambulance. Greta protested loudly: she'd only wanted to get him into the house. Gregor had made it quite clear to her that he never wanted to go back to the hospital. She had *promised* him that he would stay at home.

The paramedics had already started an IV and were preparing to leave for the hospital when I returned Gerta's frantic page. I explained Gregor's status: he was a hospice patient who didn't want to be hospitalized again. The paramedic responded, "I'm sorry, miss, but without a signed order from a doctor, we have to take him. It's the law."

Situations like this were the basis for the creation of the out-of-hospital do-not-resuscitate (DNR) form, which is available through your doctor or hospice organization. This form enables patients to get quick and selective help as needed, without the risk of having interventions they don't want or won't benefit by. It does not take away any of a patient's power to choose the treatments he or she needs and wants. It simply puts the control firmly back into the patient's or caregiver's hands.

Some people are afraid to have a do-not-resuscitate form in their homes. Will they be denied care if their injury is fixable, such as a broken arm? Any fixable injury will be fixed, DNR form or not. The DNR form is for resuscitation and life support treatments only.

You don't have to worry that the DNR order will override you if you change your mind and decide you want aggressive life support after all. In that case, just put the DNR form away and don't show it. Your verbal wishes always override your written wishes, but to date, the form is the only way you have control over the 911 system. It does not take anything away, but it ensures that you won't go to the hospital if you don't want to go.

THE BOTTOM LINE

You have the right to choose CPR, but before you make this choice, be sure you really understand its benefits and burdens.

"WE CAN'T JUST LET HIM STARVE TO DEATH!"

Deciding About Artificial Nutrition

The first event in life, often only moments after birth, is to put the infant to the mother's breast to nurse. And so, consciously or subconsciously, food begins to become the symbol of love, nurturing, caring, and concern. It is virtually impossible to name a family or social event where food is not present.

Understanding this, it's easy to see why the loss of appetite and loss of weight experienced by a dying person are perhaps the most emotional and difficult issues with which families and caregivers struggle. As the family watches the dying person become gaunt, their anxiety level increases. They feel that they are failing as caregivers.

"If I could only get him to eat and put on some weight," I hear them say, or "The doctors and nurses will think I'm neglecting him," or "We can't just let him starve to death, can we?" And so they offer more and more tempting treats to entice the patient to eat.

"How does some chicken Florentine sound?" the caregiver asks. "Okay," the patient replies, usually just to please the family. Immediately the kitchen goes into a Florentine frenzy, only to have the patient take one bite and reject the rest. The family is crestfallen and devastated, while the patient feels bad for letting them down.

"How about turkey and stuffing?" And on and on it goes. When so many other pleasures have already been lost, meals and snacks that should represent a shared pleasure are now a source of conflict.

Weight Loss Is Normal

Diminishing appetite and weight loss are nearly universal symptoms of terminal illness. To expect a dying person not to lose weight is as illogical as expecting a woman to sustain a pregnancy and deliver a healthy child without gaining it.

Cancer cells, much like babies, have a greater metabolic rate than their host body. (Metabolic rate measures the pace at which food is broken down into nutrients and then delivered to the hungry and demanding cells.) If a pregnant woman does not take in adequate nutrition, what she does take in will go to the developing baby first, simply because the baby is growing and has a much faster metabolic rate. The mother will get whatever is left over.

It works much the same way with cancer, which is an illness of abnormally rapid cell division and growth. In many advanced cancers—when the cancer has spread beyond its original borders and invades other tissues or organs—the tumor has a higher metabolic rate than the rest of the patient's body, so the nutrition taken in will feed the cancer first and the patient will continue to lose weight.

This is sometimes referred to as "irreversible wasting syndrome." There are two components that cause this syndrome or process: anorexia and cachexia.

Anorexia is loss of appetite or inability to eat. Food no longer tastes good, or it may even taste bad—some types of chemotherapy, for instance, make everything taste metallic. Eating may cause discomforts such as pain, bloating, nausea, or vomiting. Or food may simply no longer satisfy. This is different from the anorexia of an eating disorder, which includes emotional and cognitive components. There are a few medications, such as steroids or hormones, that can increase appetite temporarily, and there are many effective medications to relieve nausea and vomiting. But even using these medications does not reverse the weight loss.

Cachexia is a destructive metabolic process that breaks down normal tissue and is nearly inevitable for patients with advanced cancers. It is caused largely by inflammatory proteins that are released in response to the underlying disease.

Advanced heart and pulmonary diseases, among others, also release these destructive proteins into the body and produce the same irreversible wasting syndrome. This happens regardless of how much nutrition is given to the patient or whether it is delivered normally by eating, through tube feedings, or parenterally.

Many people think that IVs are used to provide nutrition. This is not true. IV fluids, which are delivered through a needle in a vein, are made with the equivalent of a teaspoon of sugar or salt in a liter of sterilized water. Although vitamins and electrolytes such as potassium and sodium can be added to IVs, these fluids do not provide adequate nutrition. IVs are used to combat dehydration, to quickly deliver important medications or electrolytes, or to keep the vein open in case medications need to be delivered rapidly.

Tube feedings consist of liquid nutrients carefully poured down a tube inserted through the nose, down the esophagus, and into the stomach. These tubes are uncomfortable and can erode the membranes of the nostrils and the esophagus over time, so they are considered a temporary intervention only. As helpful as they can be, there is up to a 70 percent chance that some fluid will be aspirated, or washed back up the throat and down into the lungs. This can cause a deadly pneumonia. If long-term tube feedings are determined to be appropriate, the patient usually undergoes surgery to insert the tube directly into the stomach; still, aspiration pneumonia is a risk for this type of tube feeding as well.

The third option, total parenteral nutrition (TPN), is also known as hyperalimentation. A milky-looking sterile solution, not unlike baby formula, is delivered through a catheter (similar to an IV tube) that has been threaded into a major vein, usually in the chest. This nutritional formula also contains vitamins and electrolytes and must be carefully and frequently monitored by blood work to make sure the organs of the body are tolerating it. The catheter runs through a preprogrammed pump that usually delivers the feeding over a twelve-hour period, whether the body is tolerating it or not. Blood sugar tests must also be done regularly to make sure the patient has enough insulin to balance the sugars being given; otherwise the patient is at risk for insulin shock or diabetic coma. Nurses are particularly vigilant to be sure the patient's body is not being subjected to fluid overload, which can lead to fluids in the lungs and congestive heart failure.

In 1989 the American College of Physicians published a position paper stating its opposition to aggressive nutritional support, such as TPN, in patients with advanced cancers and other terminal illnesses. The statement indicated that it is the duty of the physician to review with the patient and family the lack of benefits and the increased burdens from using TPN: it does not overcome wasting syndrome, and it increases the risk of life-threatening systemic infections. Indeed, it is possible for this intervention, which many people see as lifesaving, to actually cause death.

The Kind Solution

The right and compassionate thing to do in most cases is to recognize that eating should be a source of pleasure rather than sustenance for the dying. Weight loss should not be a major focus; it should be on the NOT FIXABLE list. I typically suggest to the patient: "Eat what you want, when you want it, and as much or as little as you want. If you don't want to eat, try a little bit, but don't worry about it if you don't want to eat more."

Often, once the family understands what's really happening and why, they are relieved to give up the role of nutrition police. They continue to have available a good selection of small portions of foods that appeal to the patient. But if the patient refuses to eat, backing off is the compassionate thing to do.

GEORGE

George had a tall, slight build. His wife, Hattie, said he had always looked like a "long drink of water." He was seventy-three years old and by his own account starting to "slow down a bit." He had retired from a government job, enjoyed a happy marriage of forty-five years, raised two successful, independent children, and adored his two toddler grandchildren, who lived nearby. All in all, George felt that he had a good life.

His family quickly noticed his early signs of weight loss, since George didn't have anything extra to lose. Surgery had removed the intestinal obstruction caused by a large cancer in his colon, but it left him with a colostomy bag on his side. Sad to say, the cancer had already spread to his liver, and his prognosis was terminal. His family refused his oncologist's suggestion to call hospice because Hattie saw that choice as "giving up."

They sought second, third, and fourth opinions from physicians as highly recommended as their oncologist was. All made the same diagnosis, prognosis, and recommendation. So Hattie and George traveled farther and farther away from their home, seeking an opinion that was more acceptable to them. In the meantime, George became sicker, thinner, weaker, and more exhausted by the efforts involved in driving to see so many doctors.

I visited in response to George's daughter asking if hospice could "just stop by and tell my folks about your program." She hoped her mother would change her mind about hospice care.

George told me,"I know I'm dying, and I just want to enjoy my time holding my grandkids and reading to them as long as I can." With a twinkle in his eye he added, "I'd also love a bowl of crab soup from Captain Jack's Restaurant." Then he quickly added, "But if I give up on treatments, I know I'll be letting my family down."

Clearly Hattie and George wanted to continue aggressive care, so I promised to keep in touch. They weren't ready for hospice yet.

The fifth physician they consulted, a hundred miles away, initially said the same thing as all the others. But in response to Hattie's angry challenge, "You're not going to just let him *starve* to death, are you? Look at how thin he is already! Are you refusing to care for him?" this doctor reacted defensively.

"Well, maybe he'd benefit from some TPN," he suggested reluctantly.

Hattie felt they had found the answer. But George insisted on staying at home rather than go to a nursing home to receive this treatment. "I want to die in my own bed," he said. Their insurance wouldn't pay for twenty-four-hour in-home nursing, so with no other option, Hattie reluctantly took special training to prepare the syringes of vitamins and other additives for the TPN, hook it up, and remove it when it was done. She was overwhelmed by this responsibility and terrified that she would do something wrong and hurt him. Boxes and boxes of solutions, syringes, dressings, and other equipment now took over their dining room. An IV pole with a special pump was needed to ensure that the sterile feeding would flow into George's body at a monitored rate, so it stood by the bed.

A visiting nurse drew blood twice a week to make sure George was not developing an infection or receiving too much sugar from the TPN. The blood work would also indicate whether or not the additional fluid and nutrition were overloading George's already weakened kidneys and liver.

George and Hattie's home was beginning to look and feel like an intensive care unit. And although their insurance covered 80 percent of the cost of the TPN, which was more than $200 a day, the co-pay was becoming a financial burden on top of all the other medical bills. Weeks passed and their debt increased. The grandkids visited every day but were too frightened by the IV pump and other equipment around George to climb on the bed and cuddle with him.

The feeding was to run for twelve hours overnight and stop in the morning, so George could enjoy his day without being tethered to the pump. But during the night the pump kept beeping with alarms, sometimes false, and Hattie had to get out of bed to try to correct the problem. Changing the colostomy bag took time as well. Both she and George were exhausted, and more and more often the feeding got off schedule and ended up running during the day.

Having boisterous toddlers visit now seemed to irritate George or interrupt one of Hattie's stolen naps. They requested that the grandkids come less often. George developed a thrush infection—an overgrowth of yeast in his mouth, not uncommon while receiving TPN—so *nothing* tasted good to him now. His yearnings for crab soup were a thing of the past.

Meanwhile, George's abdominal tumor was benefiting from this artificially enriched nutrition. His stomach grew visibly larger each day, like a pregnancy on fast forward, and as it grew, George became more and more uncomfortable. His increasing girth made moving around in the bed difficult, and he started developing bedsores. His pain increased, and the resulting escalation in the use of medications for comfort burdened his failing liver. He became confused and sedated, and Hattie was afraid to let him out of her sight.

Her fear was reinforced when one day, while she was dozing in the recliner in George's room, he climbed out of bed and fell. He was badly scraped and bruised, but fortunately he didn't break any bones.

Hattie was now afraid to sleep at all—and as exhausted as she was, her own previously controlled symptoms of congestive heart failure started to recur. Her ankles became swollen with fluid and she was bothered by shortness of breath. She refused to leave George long enough to see her doctor and get the tests he would have requested. The family worried that George's illness would kill both George and Hattie. George was often too confused to recognize the grandkids when they did come. This distressed and bewildered the children, and they were afraid to go into his room at all.

At this point the family finally agreed to call hospice. I was his nurse and was immediately struck by where the energy in the house was focused. It wasn't on George—it was on the TPN. I sat with the family and asked them to describe the decisions that had brought them to this point. What did each of them think the doctor had meant when he said that maybe George would benefit from the TPN?

Hattie thought the doctor had meant George would gain weight and get stronger again, so that he could tolerate more treatments that might lead to a cure.

The daughter thought he'd meant that George would gain weight and get strong enough to be able to enjoy trips with the grandchildren again, even though he would eventually die of the cancer.

The son felt the doctor had been implying that it was morally, ethically, and medically wrong to let a person "starve to death." But he was now concerned about the toll the TPN was taking on the entire family, especially his mother.

George was too confused to participate in this discussion.

I called the doctor to explain the situation. He had not seen George for six weeks, since George was too sick and weak to make the two-hour trip. The doctor said, "His disease was very advanced when I last saw him. I never intended for the family to think that the TPN would cure him or significantly improve his condition. Maybe it would just slow the weight loss and buy a little time."

He continued, "It probably would have been a good idea to have a specific time frame in mind. For example, try TPN for a month, to see if George gained weight and was able to function better. If that didn't happen, we'd discontinue the TPN. Since he hasn't gained weight and is barely functional at this point, we should stop the TPN. It's not benefiting him at all, he's at high risk for infection and aspiration, and in fact it seems to be a burden for all of them."

When I repeated this conversation to the family, Hattie was outraged. "It's George's lifeline! It's the only thing that's keeping him alive! How can we possibly stop it now? If we did, I'd feel like we killed him." Her understanding of George's illness had become so distorted that she now believed his death would be caused by starvation rather than by the organ failure brought on by his terminal cancer.

My attempts to gently reinforce reality failed and only caused Hattie more anxiety. She demanded that the TPN be continued, even though the insurance would no longer cover it since there was no proof that it was helping George. Now the family was responsible for the full cost of more than $200 per day.

Ten days later, Hattie was taken off in an ambulance and hospitalized for congestive heart failure. While she was in the hospital, George rapidly deteriorated and died, still tethered to the TPN. After all her hard work, Hattie never got to say goodbye. And although it hadn't been a lot to ask, George had never again held his grandchildren or had his bowl of crab soup.

Did the TPN extend George's life? Perhaps for a few days. Were his final months spent the way he would have chosen? Not according to what he had told his daughter and me. When George talked of dying at home in his own bed, I doubt he had intended for his entire home and family to be so stressed and burdened by the treatments. One day of TPN melted into another as they all waited for the nutrition to kick in. It never happened, and George ran out of tomorrows.

Quality versus Quantity, Benefits versus Burdens

It is important to acknowledge the difference between *quality* of life and *quantity* of life. It's equally important to understand the benefits and burdens of the decisions you make regarding treatment. Ask specific questions. Ask more than one person. As caring and knowledgeable as they may be, physicians are rarely involved in giving the treatments they order, and they seldom observe how they are handled in the home. Instead, ask home care nurses, such as those from the Visiting Nurse Service, who have the most hands-on experience when it comes to such issues and questions. Also understand that if you choose an aggressive treatment such as TPN, some hospice programs will not accept you, as such treatments are viewed as futile.

And remember, no decision is set in stone. You can try a treatment and change your mind if the burden outweighs the benefit. Try to be clear about your goals, and regularly assess whether they're being achieved. Above all, remember that the last few weeks of life can be a wonderful time of memory making for both patient and family. *That* may be the nourishment that's needed most by everyone.

THE BOTTOM LINE

To expect a person to die of a terminal illness without losing weight is as illogical as expecting a woman to deliver a healthy baby without gaining weight.

MAKING ETHICAL DECISIONS

Imagine someone who lives alone and insists he or she can continue to do so despite medical or family concerns. All offers of help are refused. Friends' and family members' fears about safety and adequate care are increasing and are shared by the medical team. All attempts to hire someone to monitor the safety issues and provide care in the home are rejected by the patient, who is suspicious of strangers. Should the patient be *forced* to accept help?

Or consider a smoker who refuses to stop smoking when alone, despite repeatedly falling asleep with a lit cigarette, as shown by the burn marks in the bedding and carpets. The problem of *his* safety is compounded because he is often on oxygen, which is highly flammable, and because he lives in an apartment building, where other residents would also be at risk if a fire broke out. As the hospice staff is bound to guard patient confidentiality, is it legal and ethical for them to inform the building manager of this potentially dangerous situation?

Many difficult decisions and conflicts arise as we try to meet the special needs of the dying while still respecting their human rights. What one person considers "right" or "best" for all involved may differ substantially from the choices others would make. The patient, the family, the friends, and the medical team may be in conflict. Family members may become antagonistic and argumentative, and if the conflicts are not resolved, relationships may be permanently damaged. All of this adds stress to an already complex and painful situation.

Some typical end-of-life issues include when to use or discontinue artificial nutrition (tube feedings) and hydration (IVs), whether to request or refuse CPR, the patient's choice of care versus the family's wishes, choosing curative care or palliative care, breaches in patient or family confidentiality, and the patient's mental competence and ability to make his or her own decisions versus the need to appoint a legal decision maker.

What can a patient and family members do when faced with differing opinions or seemingly irresolvable conflicts? How can they find workable and ethical solutions to such complex problems?

Ethics Committees

Patients and families often don't know that most medical facilities have an ethics committee available to them as well as to medical personnel. These committees are usually multidisciplinary, drawing on the expertise of doctors, nurses, social workers, chaplains, and lawyers, all of whom volunteer their time. The great strength of this mix is that the knowledge, skills, and experience of the group provide a comprehensive basis for making sound decisions. All information is kept in strictest confidence.

Anyone can contact the committee and ask for an ethics consultation. Committee representatives might visit, review the patient's records, and interview those involved. The committee then recommends solutions that address the ethical, moral, and practical dimensions of the problem while respecting the patient's and family's beliefs and values and while remaining in accord with good legal and medical practice. Recommendations made by an ethics committee are not binding. It is the patient's and/or the family's ultimate right to accept or reject that advice.

This valuable resource is widely available. Most hospitals and many hospices and other health care facilities have their own ethics committees. Some smaller facilities consult with larger facilities as necessary. For example, a small rural hospice program can request support from the ethics committee of a larger neighboring program or from its state hospice organization. Whatever facility it is based in, an ethics committee is a neutral assembly of volunteers. They should not be loyal to any one institution to the exclusion of others. That in itself would be considered unethical and questionable professional practice.

Every situation is examined by using the following core principles of ethical decision making: (1) autonomy, (2) beneficence, (3) non-maleficence, and (4) justice.

Autonomy

The principle of autonomy implies the duty to recognize and respect every individual's right to self-determination as long as he or she is mentally competent. Following are some examples related to this principle.

- A reclusive patient hoards papers and other items, stacking them ceiling high. Only narrow passageways to the bathroom, refrigerator, front door, and bed are open. The family is concerned about cockroaches and rats. The hospice staff is worried about being exposed to germs that might be carried on to the next patient visited. Everyone is concerned about fire.
- A forty-five-year-old patient diagnosed with a terminal illness refuses all types of treatment, even though the family feels strongly that improvement or cure is possible.
- The parents of a six-year-old leukemia patient refuse to seek medical care or blood transfusions for their child because such

treatments go against the family's religious beliefs. Other relatives fear the child will die unnecessarily without the recommended care.

Beneficence

The principle of beneficence involves the duty to promote good for the patient and others. The benefits of any course of action should outweigh the burdens.

• A caregiver is certain that the artificial nutrition given by tube feeding into the stomach will restore health to a terminally ill patient. However, the patient's doctors and nurses warn that this treatment should be discontinued because the patient's severely weakened body can no longer tolerate the fluid overload. Out of love for the patient and refusal to accept that death is imminent, the caregiver also ignores the medical team's warnings that the feedings are being aspirated—washed up the esophagus and inhaled down the trachea into the lungs. Despite the caregiver's good intentions, this may cause a tenacious and life-threatening pneumonia. The ethics committee might raise the question of whose needs are being fed here—the patient's or the caregiver's.

• Adult children move their mother out of her retirement community against her will, to a nursing home closer to their work so they can visit more often. She misses her friends and the care she received at the old facility, and though she loves her children, she wants to return there. She prefers they drive the extra forty-five minutes to see her, especially since they only visit once a week as it is. The ethics committee might pose the question of whose convenience is being prioritized here.

Non-Maleficence

The principle of non-maleficence involves the duty not to inflict evil or harm on any patient or to allow it to be inflicted.

• The hospital nurses are uncomfortable administering the high doses of narcotics that have been ordered for the terminal pain of a drug addict. They fear that the high doses ordered may cause him physical harm and that by medicating him, they are facilitating his illegal behavior. However, good symptom control dictates that the needs of the addiction be supported *before* providing additional medication for pain control. The nurses raise this dilemma to their ethics committee: how does a clinician handle a clash between personal and professional ethics?

• A dying young father has stated many times, "I want to die at home." However, as he becomes less conscious and closer to death, the tumor on his neck is in danger of eroding his carotid artery, which would cause dramatic and heavy bleeding. Wouldn't his three small children be traumatized by witnessing a lot of blood? The wife needs help deciding whose needs are more important, the patient's or the children's.

Justice

The principle of justice involves the duty to provide care and comfort to all patients fairly, equally, and legally. This principle also includes cases where what's best for the patient may not be best for society as a whole.

• A patient, exercising his right to confidentiality, insists that his close friends and family caregivers *not* be told that he is HIV-positive because he fears rejection, discrimination, and abandonment. The medical team is concerned that without this information, the friends will not realize that they are being exposed to this life-threatening illness and the caregivers will not use the precautions necessary to protect themselves. Can you breach the patient's confidentiality to protect the safety of others?

Of all the cases presented to ethics committees, problems with justice are the fewest, primarily because most institutions have policies already in place to deal with fair and equal treatment of patients regardless of gender, age, race, ethnicity, religious beliefs, or sexual preference.

Other Ethical Principles

Ethical reasoning is a dynamic process, and many other values may be weighed and balanced alongside the core principles. These include the *sanctity of life,* the *quality of life, veracity* (the duty to tell the truth), *fidelity* (the duty to keep one's promise or word), *reparation* (the duty to right a wrong), *confidentiality* (respecting the patient's and the family's privacy), and *utility* (the greatest good or least harm for the greatest number of people).

Organizational Ethics

Most hospitals, home health agencies, hospices, and other medical facilities put a great deal of effort into developing a mission statement—a document, readily available to the public, that guides the organization in its practice and assures the public of the organization's dedication to delivering the highest quality of care. A truly ethical organization is also willing to be ever vigilant regarding its business practices and making sure these are true to its mission statement.

In today's world of managed care and waning public trust, we daily see major corporations toppled by illegal and unethical practices. Our deliverers of health care must be willing to hold themselves to a higher standard. If any patient, family member, or employee has concerns that an organization's mission statement is not being fulfilled, he or she should have the ability to take these concerns to the organization's ethics committee.

THE BOTTOM LINE

Ethics guides us to do the right thing. Experts can help us determine the ethical course of action in any given situation.

PART III

SHARING THE JOURNEY

"I LOVE YOU, MOM,
AND I WANT TO HELP,
BUT I'M NOT MOVING TO MIAMI!"

How much must you pay emotionally, physically, and financially to prove you are a loving daughter, wife, husband, son, or friend? Should you quit your job and assume the role of caregiver 100 percent of the time? If you can help only on the weekends because you have young children at home and a job you need to keep, does that mean you only love your mother 30 percent? If your sister is there more than you are, is she a better daughter than you are? If you are the caregiver, must you change every one of your mother's diapers if she becomes incontinent? Or even change any of them? Can you love your parent without bathing her? How exhausted must you become to prove your devotion?

These are difficult questions. When someone you love is dying, the care you give *never* feels like enough. It is normal to feel inadequate. Every caregiver feels this to some extent, whether it's acknowledged or not. Often these feelings mask the true issue: you are soon to lose someone you love, you feel powerless, and you are already grieving that loss. This is called anticipatory grieving—grieving for what lies ahead—but it does *not* mean you are providing inadequate care.

Caring for a dying person can be—and most often is—a powerful and tender experience. A daughter once said to me, "It's the hardest job I've ever loved. I wouldn't have traded a minute even though it was difficult and sad. My mother and I had a good relationship, and it ended in as positive a way as possible. I feel that both of our lives were enriched by the time we spent together in those last months of her life."

To be able to say, as this daughter did, that you would not change a minute of the experience is a wonderful goal. But there are many challenges on the way to that goal, and one of the most daunting is that people's personalities and character traits become more pronounced as they're dying.

As I often tell the families I work with, people generally die as they live. Quiet people usually become quieter, caring people show increased concern for those around them, and busy people get busier, even if it's only in their dreams. Controlling people often attempt to stay in charge, even more so as their bodies fail them, by issuing a stream of what seem like unreasonable demands on the caregiver's time and patience. Angry people may become more abrasive and difficult. When the caregiver quite understandably becomes frustrated or impatient, that feeling is quickly followed by guilt.

As we progress through life, our behavior patterns and reactions become the very personalized crutches that hold us up in times of stress. These crutches get stronger as the stresses do, sometimes ten times stronger. If you ask yourself, "How did this person react to stress in the past when he or she was healthy?" you will be able to anticipate what lies ahead. Once you have identified his or her way of coping and imagined it multiplied by ten, you can free yourself of the sense of being at fault for the patient's behaviors, and therefore be less puzzled, or even angered or wounded, by them.

It's also helpful to remember that physical changes can contribute to mental and emotional changes. Decreasing liver or kidney function makes toxins build up, resulting in unpredictable behavior. The spread of disease to the brain can impact every aspect of the personality. When the lungs no longer supply adequate oxygen to the brain, the patient can experience confusion and anxiety, among other difficulties. The same thing can happen with an imbalance in the body's fluids, blood chemistry, or electrolytes. Dementia and mental illnesses can worsen dramatically.

Regular, professional monitoring is essential to help you anticipate and plan for these changes even before they occur, and also to provide guidance for managing them *before* they become unmanageable. At the very least, professional support can help you understand why the patient may be behaving so differently and lighten what might otherwise seem an unsupportable load.

How to Know When Enough Is Enough

Dying of a terminal illness is usually not a momentary event, like flipping a light switch. It's a series of losses: of our customary role in the family and on the job; of many of life's pleasures, such as golfing and taking trips; of physical function and sometimes mental abilities. It's very hard for the dying person to give up so much, and it's very hard for the family and friends to witness this process.

And so the wishes of a dying person can come to seem more important than our own needs simply because we are in awe of the fact that the person is dying. We struggle to meet those wishes even when they override basic logic.

A caregiver may say, "I know that staying in her home alone is not the best choice for Mom, but it's what she wants," or "He's afraid to be alone and won't let anybody stay with him but me. I'm getting exhausted, but it's what he wants, so I guess I should do it."

Even if they usually are comfortable setting reasonable limits and boundaries, loving people often have difficulty refusing the wishes of someone whose life is limited. To do so feels like a betrayal of the patient and of your love for him. It feels irresponsible and unfeeling.

If you're dealing with such a problem, ask yourself four questions:

1. Is the patient thinking clearly? Would the dying person have made this request of you when he or she was healthy?
2. Is the request reasonable? Would it be reasonable if the person was ill but not dying?
3. Is it possible to meet the patient's wishes?
4. Is it safe?

If the answers to all four are yes, consider responding to the request. If not, reevaluate and set appropriate limits. Reasonable boundaries define love and fairness. If the caregiver falls apart, everything falls apart. Then the patient will have no choices at all. It's important that caregivers care for themselves. *You don't have to sacrifice yourself because someone you love is dying.*

Laura

Laura's ninety-five-year-old mother, Harriet, was dying slowly from a chronic respiratory illness. She had moved to a nursing home two years earlier, but she insisted that Laura visit her five times a week. This was quite a burden for Laura, as she was aging herself and maintained a hectic work schedule to support her own family. A visit to Harriet involved a cab ride into the city and travel on two train lines to a distant suburb. But Laura felt she had no choice: her mother needed her, and she wouldn't be around much longer. Laura loved her mother very much and felt guilty on the days she was unable to visit. Those feelings were quickly followed by resentment and frustration.

One day as Laura was mulling this over, she realized that what Harriet really needed was more one-on-one attention and a familiar face. So on the days Laura couldn't make the long trip, she hired one of the young aides from the nursing home to visit with Harriet for an hour after her shift was over. The young aide was eager for the extra work, and she was able to report to Laura each day on her mother's progress. This arrangement dramatically decreased the intensity of Harriet's demands, and it made the time Laura *was* able to spend with her mother much more fulfilling and less resentful for Laura.

Get Help, as Much and as Often As You Can

It's important to have a good, licensed, accredited agency helping you find the assistance you need. It's really too much to figure out all by yourself. If the dying person is counting on you for emotional support, make sure you have the energy to give it. There are trained people available to assist with the hands-on care, but your presence as a loving family member or friend is something only you can provide. Get help with other areas such as yard work and grocery shopping as well. Then, instead of becoming exhausted or frustrated, you will have time to simply sit with your loved one and enjoy fond memories. These remembrances help the dying person review his or her life in a positive manner, and they can significantly soften your grieving both now and in the future.

I was actively involved in the care of my father, uncle, and mother as they were dying, but in each case the amount of involvement varied according to the situation and to the needs of my own family. My children were young when my father died, and my parents lived in the next state. My mother was my dad's primary caregiver, and I helped on weekends, when my children were being cared for by their father. My mother hired a wonderful part-time home health aide, Sela, for my father's personal care. This additional help made my father's care manageable for my mother and me. We were freed to be with him emotionally as a loving wife and daughter.

When my uncle, who lived alone, was dying many states away, I was writing *Final Gifts* and my children were in college. My mother, my computer, and I moved in with him for the last two months of his life. The local hospice assigned a home health aide to give him regular assistance with bathing and other personal care. This support enabled my mother and me to just be with my uncle and focus on the emotional and spiritual work we all needed to do in order to end this long, loving relationship.

By the time my mother became fragile and ill at age ninety-three, my children were independent young adults. I had a full-time job, so I found a marvelous private-hire home health aide, Thelma, who worked for us forty hours a week providing the vast majority of my mother's care. When it became clear that my mother was dying, I was granted family medical leave from my job and moved into her apartment. To my delight and amazement, without being asked, so did my son, daughter, and son-in-law, each bringing a sleeping bag. We all pitched in and took care of her until she died three weeks later. This is what I call "parent payday," not only for her but also for me—I was grateful for and proud of my kids. She died peacefully with all of us around her bed.

I didn't feel that my love as a daughter or as a niece was measured by my exhaustion or by the number of diapers I changed. I did feel that my primary responsibility was to my own family, and that continued to be paramount even though my parents and uncle were dying.

Being a hospice nurse has taught me a key lesson in surviving this life challenge: *get as much help as you can, as early as you can, for as long as you can.* I loved my parents and uncle so much that I made sure their care needs were taken care of with the very best resources available to me and to the very best of my ability. I personally was with them and did as much as I could, given the limitations of my own family's needs. And I wouldn't trade those "hardest jobs I ever loved" for anything.

Granted, it was a blessing for us that the money was there to hire private help. Many families assume they can't afford this luxury, but they may be unaware of potential financial resources such as borrowing against a life insurance policy or using a reverse mortgage to access some of the value of the dying person's house. Helping you to find the appropriate people (an attorney, financial planner, and insurance company representative) and to fully utilize your Medicare and Medicaid benefits is another important role played by your hospice or hospital social worker. If you don't have the support of an organization such as hospice, can you do all this on your own? Of course you can—it's just harder and more time-consuming if you have no professional help.

Many people diligently save for a rainy day, only to resist spending that money on the care they need when they are dying. They often feel that having something to leave their children in their will is an important measure of success in life. Dying, however, *is* the rainy day they've saved for. Help the dying person to see that the best gift to leave his or her children is the good example of planning ahead, having resources, and then having the good sense to use them when they are needed, so as not to overburden family and friends. Being able to pay for help with personal care can free the family to participate in the more important tasks of emotional and spiritual care. Preparing ahead for this is truly a loving legacy.

THE BOTTOM LINE

One person should not be sacrificed for the dying of another. Get as much help as you can, as early as you can, for as long as you can.

LISTEN TO YOUR BODY

If you want to observe people who are truly attuned to their needs, watch babies and toddlers. They fall asleep when they're tired, even in the middle of the living room floor during a party. They wake up when they're rested. They cry when it hurts and stop when the pain abates. They eat when they're hungry and stop when they're full.

This unhindered responsiveness to the needs of their bodies begins to change when we start teaching them how to delay, overlook, and ignore their body's signals. We potty-train them, put them down for naps because *we're* tired, and push food at them when they clearly don't want it. They start to learn to react to convenience and other people's expectations rather than to their own needs.

By the time we mature, we're experts at denial. An alarm clock jars us awake in the morning. We're rushed, so we skip breakfast. Caffeine, not protein, is the fuel we expect to start our engines. We eat large, rich dinners late in the evening. Bedtime comes only after the chores are done or the TV movie of the week is over—often too late for an adequate amount of sleep before the alarm clock jars us awake again and the cycle repeats.

When someone we care for is sick, we need to recognize the illness as a stress on the body—an extra burden, a battleground. Throughout this battle the body keeps talking: *I am weak, don't push me to do things. Let me rest awhile to try to get some strength back.*

All of my energy is being spent trying to fight this illness and its assault on my body. Let me rest often.

Think of energy as if it were a modest savings account in the bank. Every demand on our energy is a withdrawal. Deposits of energy are rare and small—usually the result of resting. If we continue to make withdrawals without making deposits, the account will be depleted quickly. So it makes sense for the sick person to spend his or her small amount of energy wisely. This includes resting before important company comes to visit, using a wheelchair to get from the car to the doctor's office instead of walking, and alternating activities with periods of rest. "Pushing past the pain" may work when you're training for the Olympics, but not when you're seriously ill.

Listening to the body is enormously important for the patient, and it's important for the caregiver as well. Caregivers can easily overlook their own needs. Providing care for someone who is seriously ill is often exhausting and stressful. It can easily make *you* weak and ill. Stress does that.

Don't be afraid to change the message on the phone to say something like "We unplug the phone when we're resting. Please leave a message and we'll get back to you later." Sleep when the patient sleeps. Caregivers often ignore the early warning signs of their own illnesses because they're exhausted and totally focused on the person for whom they care. People at the end of life often tell me how anxious and guilt-ridden they are when they see their caregiver falling apart.

All too often I have seen two ambulances arriving at the house of a patient—one for the patient and one for the caregiver. I often say to the families and friends doing the heroic work of caring for the dying, "I only allow one patient per address." They laugh—but they get it.

STEVEN

Steven was beloved by both two-legged and four-legged creatures. He was a brilliant man, running a successful veterinary practice and teaching and writing articles in his field. He was also softhearted, a man who generously gave of himself until a malignant brain tumor struck him down in his forties. The tumor grew rapidly, and by the time I met him and his adoring wife, Donna, the tumor had robbed him of the use of his legs and nearly all of his speech.

Not wanting to accept what hospice represented any sooner than absolutely necessary, they had managed somehow—but I was hard pressed to understand how. Donna was clearly exhausted, as evidenced by the deep circles under her beautiful dark eyes.

Every day she got Steven out of bed and into the bathroom, where she washed and shaved him. Then she got him dressed. He was heavy and his body was swollen from his treatments. He didn't have the coordination to help Donna put his legs into his trousers or his arms into his shirts. After dressing him in comfortable but stylish clothes, she wheeled him out onto the deck, even though he could sit up only if banked by pillows. By the time he was out there, awkwardly propped, the morning was almost over and he, too, was exhausted from all the effort and activity.

Donna told me in our first meeting that she was dedicated to "keeping life as normal as possible" for her husband. But the reality was that her husband was a young man who was going to die soon. Valiantly retaining a semblance of normality was wearing *both* of them out.

One morning I walked in through the garage as usual for my biweekly visit and gasped as I entered the living room, which had become Steven's bedroom. Donna was struggling, red-faced, barely managing to hold him upright in a bear hug as she tried to move him from the bed to the wheelchair. They were both precariously close to tripping over the footrests of the wheelchair and crashing to the floor. Steven looked wide-eyed and terrified as she clung to him. I rushed to help and was stunned by how heavy he was. "We need to put him back in bed right now," I said. Somehow, we managed it, but we were both exhausted and aching when we were done. I looked over at her and saw that she was clearly overwhelmed and frightened by the experience.

"Listen," I said, trying to lighten the mood. "Remember my rule: one patient per address!" My ribbing elicited a weary smile.

"We need to talk about this," I said. We sat on either side of Steven's bed and each held one of his hands. He looked urgently at me with a look that said, *Do something*. "Steven, you seem scared," I said. He squeezed both of our hands (his sign for yes, as he could no longer speak) very tightly. "Were you afraid we might drop you?" Again a tight squeeze. I looked into his eyes. There was clearly something more. "Were you afraid that Donna might be hurt, too?" He squeezed and squeezed and squeezed our hands as he started to sob.

Donna's eyes filled. "Darling," she said, "I was just trying to keep life as normal as possible for you." She paused. "I guess I'm just not ready for you to be in bed full time yet." She put her head down on his thighs, and we all cried as he stroked her head tenderly, over and over. I couldn't find tissues, so I grabbed a roll of toilet paper from the bathroom, and we were soon laughing through our tears as we passed it around and helped ourselves.

"Okay, time for a new plan!" I announced. "Today we discovered that we need to adapt to Steven's abilities, rather than expecting him to meet our expectations. Right?"

He gave a thumbs-up.

"I will request more home health aide help," I said. "Maybe male volunteers will be able to get him up every now and then to a reclining wheelchair, but starting right now we need to listen better to what both your bodies are telling us. *Never* again should Donna try to do what she attempted this morning. Right, Steven?" He gave a double thumbs-up—this time with a big smile.

THE BOTTOM LINE

Pay attention to what your body tells you; it will be clear about what it needs and what it can handle. Respect those messages.

FAMILY OF BIRTH,
FAMILY OF CHOICE

In more than a quarter of a century of visiting people's homes as a hospice nurse, I have seen profound changes in our evolving concept of family. Gone for many is the 1950s notion of large, loving, involved families right around the corner. When a crisis struck, a single phone call marshaled all the help and support that was needed. Aging parents often lived with their grown children, a husband tended to the needs of his wife, an aunt was readily available to her niece, and parents cared for their children.

Our hearts may wish for this still, particularly when we are in crisis, but in today's world this is not the case for a great number of people, and for very many reasons.

Today gay couples adopt and raise children, grandparents bring up grandchildren, single working mothers live with other single mothers to help lessen each other's burdens, while other single men and women live alone but have a "family" of friends.

Where once relatives immediately assumed responsibility for an infirm loved one, today many individuals face the predicament of enlisting strangers to help or relying on acquaintances or family with whom they have never been close. This seems antithetical to all their notions of independence and is probably the toughest pill to swallow for many people, especially those who are independent or introverted.

In addition, many elderly people fear that their frailty makes them vulnerable to theft or abuse, so they are reluctant to ask for or hire help, even for routine tasks such as yard work. This same fear causes many to choose self-care until the eleventh hour, even if that means compromised safety or quality of life.

On the other hand, our changing concept of family also allows us to expand the kind of experience we will have in the last stage of our lives. If "family" now includes our best friends and co-workers, neighbors and fellow churchgoers, it is possible to allow our chosen family to play an active, participatory role in our care.

The infirm or dying person can give him- or herself permission to accept help from others. And caregiving friends can join together to become a new kind of responsible and loving family, providing an experience as profound, nurturing, and life-affirming as that of any family tied by blood.

JANE

Jane had been an independent woman her whole life. While in the army as a colonel in procurement, she simultaneously earned a Ph.D. in engineering and business. When she retired from the military, she began a successful construction company in Florida, fearlessly defying gender stereotypes. She built her own home, and then, right next door, a comfortable home for her sister, who was battling colon cancer. Her days were filled by her responsibilities at work, her role as den mother to her circle of close friends, and her care for her sister. She ignored the troubling signals from her own body.

What began as an irritating cough worsened into persistent shortness of breath. Occasionally she coughed up blood. Jane had been a caretaker her whole life, fiercely independent and perpetually healthy and active. Rather than complain or investigate her symptoms, she tried to brush them off—until the day her sister dragged her into the doctor's office.

Her friends had worried about her for so long that no one but Jane was terribly surprised when she was diagnosed with lung cancer. Her short prognosis of three months, however, was a shock to everyone. Her doctor suggested hospice, but Jane refused. She wanted to stay near her sister and eventually die at home. In her usual no-nonsense, efficient style, she started to make arrangements for each of her friends to play a specific role in her care. The colonel was once again in charge.

Durable medical and financial power of attorney was assigned to her closest friend, Jackie. Another friend took her to her doctor's appointments. A third coordinated the meals that were being provided by many friends, and still another took care of the lawn and yard. Music had always been a source of joy and comfort to Jane, and now she asked the choir she had sung with for many years to come by and entertain her now and again.

Just as efficiently as she did everything in her life, Jane had quickly gotten all these people in place and working well together, but there was still one thing she wanted. She asked our mutual friend Diane, a Ph.D. nurse who had served with her in the military, to check in on her. We humans have a profound need to be assured that what we are doing is right, especially when it comes to something we've never done before, and Diane's presence would make her feel safer.

Diane flew from Virginia to Florida as soon as she could. She entered Jane's room in her usual larger-than-life sort of way. She is commanding, authoritative, knowledgeable, and kind, a combination that makes her a powerful presence. She is also like a mother to her friends, a crucial element, perhaps, in completing Jane's sense of "family."

Diane looked around at the caring friends who had taken that shift, at the vases of fresh flowers and the many cards displayed on a dresser, and at Jane, who was nestled comfortably under layers of clean linens. She said, "Jane, you are so lucky to have such caring friends. It really is a testament to who you are and how you have affected others. I'm so proud of you and of how you are doing this together. Your work is done now, so you can just relax and rest."

Those words were as if she had given Jane permission to let go. Assured she had done everything well, Jane began to decline rapidly.

Jane's friends made sure she was comfortable and that there were two people with her at all times. As it became clear that death was approaching, the entire care group converged on her house. Her friends surrounded her bed and sang as she died. The singing continued as she was being carried out of her home by the funeral directors.

After the service, Jackie, who had power of attorney, found a note from Jane in her safe-deposit box. It thanked everyone involved for the gift of her last weeks and went on to make a request: "Now that you are all working together like a well-oiled machine, would you extend your loving care to my sister?" They all agreed to do so. As they acknowledged to one another, caring for Jane had been a gift to them as well.

A Word to Adult Offspring

The grown children of older people are often not fully aware of the vital role played by friends in their parents' lives. If they have lived at a distance or if they have been somewhat estranged, they may not understand how important these non-family members are to the dying person. It's understandable that the time left with a dying parent may be jealously guarded, especially by those who feel guilty about not having participated earlier and who realize that this is their last chance for reconciliation. However, in my experience, it is not uncommon for those who have previously neglected or ignored the parent to now swoop in and usurp the last days, denying the parent's need to say goodbye to loving friends.

Dear children, please know that your parents' lives did not go on hold when you moved out to start your new life. Their new life started as well, and they may have added many dear members to their "family." Family reconciliations are indeed a high priority, but honor these friendships as well, and do not deny your parents and their friends an opportunity for their own goodbyes.

THE BOTTOM LINE

Biological connection is not a requirement for having a loving, caring family.

16

HOW FRIENDS CAN HELP

The role of friend to someone who is dying is very special, and your presence can mean a great deal to someone in the last stage of life. But what is the best way to offer your comfort and support? First, it helps to try to understand what your dying friend may be feeling. She may welcome your help, yet need to stay involved in the decisions regarding her daily care. Sometimes her need for independence may be so strong that your ill friend would rather compromise her quality of life than rely on you. Your help may make her feel like she's being a burden, or diminish her dignity and pride. So it's important not to insist on providing a certain kind of help until you are clearer about her needs.

But it's also important to show how much you care, and not to let fear and nervousness keep you away. This can be an immensely enriching experience for you as well. It can help you dispel your own fears around death and dying. I have found that most of us are innately courageous, and what we know and experience around death is usually less scary than what we imagined death and dying to be.

Here are some snapshots from my personal album of helping friends.

CELEBRATION

Bonnie was in her late sixties when she was diagnosed with a rapidly progressing type of multiple sclerosis, an incurable, degenerative neurological disorder. The illness began as weakness and clumsiness in her right hand. Soon my vibrant, active friend had difficulty walking and severe muscle cramps. As thwarted as she was, her fiery spirit flared up in her final days a few years later.

Bonnie had been an interior designer; she was detail-oriented and creative. So it came as no surprise to me when she began planning her own farewell party, complete with food and posters displaying photographs of her family and friends. She'd taken particular care choosing the photos, perhaps because as her speech declined, she needed to express herself visually.

"My friends are so important to me," she said with the help of a voice amplifier. "Family is a given, but my friends represent the choices I've made. I want them to celebrate my life with me."

Her friends did just that, coordinating food for the party, arranging colorful bouquets, and having prints made of Bonnie's favorite images. I will never forget the best photo of all: Bonnie in her wheelchair flanked by her many friends, all of them laughing and talking excitedly as they reminisced over one photo and then another, enjoying the rich lives they had shared.

TAKING INVENTORY

Henry was a retired military officer and wanted nothing more than to have someone there to listen. At eighty-one, he had fought proudly in both world wars and loved educating me about military history and what the soldiers had had to endure. He also talked about heaven, a peaceful place where reunions were possible.

"It will be good to see my old buddy Al again," he said. "And my poor mother—she really didn't have an easy life. I hope she's really enjoying herself now!" He had a definite sense that love was immortal, and he anticipated feeling that joy.

Dying people often seem to feel that death is not the end. Again and again I have watched people near death become joyful at these reunions, unseen by us: mothers reach for babies they lost to miscarriage or premature death, husbands embrace wives again. People rarely suffer anguish as they die, nor do they tend to die in fear. By the time they are close to dying, they usually have reached an emotional state of acceptance and actually *want* to go forward into whatever awaits them. I have watched my patients realize that they are not alone in this journey, and that in particular has changed my life.

I've learned that most dying people want to impart what they've learned from living as well as from the process of dying. They often want us to realize how precious life is. They want to help demystify the journey for us and remove some of the fear. Finally, they are searching for affirmation that their life mattered to those who crossed their path and that they've made a difference by being here. It is our responsibility not only to tend to the physical needs of the dying but also to receive, appreciate, and validate their wisdom.

This kind of openness and receptivity is particularly important in the presence of someone who is at the end of life. It's natural to feel that we don't know what to do or say. *How terrible this is,* we think. *I wish there were something I could say or do to make it better.* Unfortunately, for fear of doing or saying something wrong, we tend to withdraw and do nothing. Often just listening is enough. Our presence may be sufficient. But withdrawing can hurt and isolate a dying person, even if our intentions were good.

HONESTY

Jill was thirty-one and a successful actress. She had flawless skin, high cheekbones, almond-shaped eyes, and finely tapered lips. Her superb memory had helped her career, allowing her to memorize scripts quickly. One day, however, her memory failed her: no matter how many times she tried, she couldn't remember her lines. She was baffled, but she didn't think anything was physically wrong until she was struck with terrible headaches. Tests showed that she had an inoperable brain tumor. Chemotherapy and radiation didn't stop her cancer from progressing, but they did veil her extraordinary beauty.

"So many people don't know what to say or how to act around me because I am sick," Jill told me. "Some of my friends won't call or come by. Those that do visit often avoid the reality of my illness completely. They pretend that I'm not losing my hair and gaining all this weight! 'You look so beautiful,' they say, which I know is a lie. Or they treat me like I'm a child who's not old enough to know what is happening. I know how sick I am. That kid-glove approach makes me furious! I just want my friends near me. They hardly have to say anything. I want sympathy but not pity. That's a useless emotion. And I definitely don't want my friends to *avoid* me!"

How Much Is Enough?

Friends often have trouble gauging how much they should be involved. A useful guideline is to recall how often you were in touch with your friend *before* he or she became ill. If it was once a month, then visiting twice a month now is more appropriate than twice a day. A very best friend might visit daily. And even with a close friend, it's always important to check first with the caregiver. Quiet and introspective people who are dying may need more alone time. Extroverts may want company. Sometimes people don't know what they want or need. Proceed cautiously and be sensitive. If your friend's illness is advanced, plan brief visits of fifteen minutes or so. Your friend can always ask you to stay longer if he or she's up to it.

Regular cards and notes of encouragement and support are often more appreciated than we realize. Express the qualities you especially like about your friend or reminisce about favorite shared experiences. We all appreciate learning the positive ways that we have affected others, most especially at the end of our lives, when we're reviewing who we are and what we've done with our time here on earth.

It's also important to be sensitive to what may be preoccupying someone at the last stage of life. Our friend may be thinking before the visit: *Will I feel embarrassed about the way I look? Will I know what to do? Will I be in pain and scare my friend? Will he think I'm afraid? Is it a mistake to allow him to share such a difficult time with me?*

Sometimes your dying friend may need to recede into a very private, quiet, internal space to come to terms with what is happening before he or she can deal with it publicly. Your friend may need time to consider the new identity that comes with no longer working or keeping the same role in a household, being forced to rest, giving up control, relying on the help of others, and accepting the natural changes that are occurring in the body. As a friend of someone in the last stage of life, it's important that you support the person in this process and not feel rejected if he or she doesn't always want to see you. The better you understand your friend's specific wishes and desires, the better you can respond to them. Be where your friend is mentally and emotionally as much as possible.

PRACTICAL HELP—WITH IMAGINATION

My friend Daphne was a flamboyant, unpredictable woman. She and her husband, Alex, had an interesting, passionate life, traveling extensively and filling their home with a wide variety of friends. Many of these friends wanted to be there for Daphne when she suddenly became seriously ill.

In the wink of an eye, a ruptured aneurysm at the base of Daphne's brain took her to the brink of death, where she lingered for weeks, then months. Finally she improved and, although quite impaired, was discharged from the hospital to continue a heavy regimen of physical, occupational, and speech therapy at home.

Her devoted family was delighted to have her back, but the amount of care Daphne needed depleted their energy for anything else. The yard was a shambles of leaves and other debris. The dining room table was covered with piles of junk mail, old newspapers yellowing in their plastic sleeves, and the ever-present medical bills. Daphne was so happy to be home that she didn't notice the mess, but her family felt overwhelmed.

Then, on a sunny, crisp, fall afternoon, Daphne's therapy was interrupted by raucous sounds from the front yard. Her husband wheeled Daphne to the window to see a surprising sight. Three friends had raked the leaves into piles that spelled WE LOVE DAF. When they saw Daphne at the window, they linked arms and sang a dreadfully off-key song about falling leaves. Then they did a series of clumsy pirouettes and collapsed in gales of laughter into the leaves.

Watching them, Daphne laughed heartily for what felt like the first time in months. Her friends then swept the leaves into neat piles, bagged them, and put them on the curb for pickup. Placing a gallon of fresh apple cider and a pot of colorful mums on the doorstep, they left.

"What Can I Do to Help?"

"What can I do to help?" is certainly a well-meaning question, but it can put a burden on the primary caregiver to come up with ways friends can feel useful and caring. One of the things that most impressed me about Daphne's friends is that *they* took the initiative. Here are other ways a friend might think of helping:

"If you can do without the car tomorrow morning, leave the car keys under the doormat and I'll take the car for an oil change and run it through the car wash. It'll be back by noon."

"I'm going to the grocery store in the morning. Stick your list on the front door and I'll pick up what you need while I'm shopping."

"I notice your inspection sticker will expire soon. How about if I pick up the car early tomorrow morning and get it inspected for you?"

"I'll bet you need some medical bills copied for your insurance reimbursements. Put everything in an envelope on your doorstep with the number of copies you need and I'll get them back to you tonight."

"You look exhausted. How about if I come over for four hours this afternoon and sit with your wife while you take a good long nap and a shower?"

"Wouldn't a massage, getting your hair done, and having a manicure and pedicure feel good? Tell me when to make the appointment for you and I'll come and stay in case your husband needs anything while you're gone."

"There's a new children's movie at the local theater. Would the kids like an evening out for a show and some pizza?"

"I'll stop by in the morning to walk the dog. Just hang his leash on the doorknob. If you like, I'll take him to be shampooed and groomed."

"An ice storm is coming; my husband will stop over tonight to turn the water off to your outdoor spigots."

"It's getting warm out; would it be helpful if the kids and I come over tomorrow to take down the storm windows and put up the screens?"

"Halloween is coming; how about if I took the kids shopping for their costumes after school? Next week I could take them to the pumpkin patch, then back to my house to carve their pumpkins. I'd bring them back after dinner. Would that be a nice break for you and the kids?"

"I know you and your husband enjoy Paul Newman movies, so I picked these up for you. No need to return them."

How to Keep Help from Becoming a Problem

Calling to check on how a patient and caregiver are doing, offering to help, and bringing casseroles are all wonderful things to do—unless nine other people are doing the same thing on the same day and all the casseroles are chicken! Oddly, this can become a time of competition and jealousy, as friends and neighbors jockey to be the most helpful and appreciated one. Caregivers have enough to do without being grateful and gracious traffic controllers as well.

I strongly suggest that the family appoint a manager or coordinator of helpers. They can then direct friends to call the coordinator, who will keep track of who's doing or bringing what and when. If the friends are linked by computer, the coordinator can send a weekly report to everyone at once. Friends can also send e-mails to be printed out for the patient and caregiver, so they can benefit from the messages of love and support without the phone endlessly ringing or disturbing a rest period. In this way, information is equally shared, and the concerned friends will know that they are actively participating and contributing without being intrusive.

THE BOTTOM LINE

Be present, show the dying person that he or she has mattered in your life, and just pitch in and help in practical ways.

17

WHEN LITTLE EYES
ARE WATCHING

Until my baby granddaughter, Ellie, was almost two, I had happily been a daily presence in her young life. Unfortunately around that time, the four herniated discs in my neck became so painful that I needed surgery. Bone grafts would be inserted and a titanium plate attached to the vertebrae to hold everything in place. After all, holding my head up *was* something I planned to continue doing.

The thought of baby Ellie crawling over me after surgery was not at all appealing, so my daughter and I decided that she wouldn't bring her to visit until I felt strong enough to hold her. But I would call her every day on the phone and sing and chat with her so she wouldn't feel that I'd abandoned her. We simply told her that Nana had a big boo-boo, was getting better, and would see her as soon as I could. After all, what could a two-year-old understand about discs or surgery, or why her nana couldn't snuggle and tickle her as usual?

About six weeks into my recovery, I felt well enough to see Ellie. I had missed her terribly, despite the phone calls. She timidly toddled over to the living room couch where I was propped up comfortably. I wore a large cervical collar for neck support, and I realized that this frightened her. So I unwrapped it to show her it was just a large "Band-Aid on my boo-boo." Her eyes widened as she saw the four-inch scar on my neck. She kept patting my knee with her chubby little hand, saying, "My nana, My nana," over and over. I kept reassuring her that I was all right, but she still seemed sad and reticent.

My daughter reported that during the next few nights, Ellie woke up crying with nightmares, and she was suddenly terrified of two sweet little neighborhood puppies who had always delighted her before. After much holding, rocking, and soothing, Ellie tearfully told her mother that an "arf" (her word for *dog*) "um um" (her word for *eat* or *bite*) "Nana." We were stunned. Because we had not explained *why* this "boo-boo" had happened to me, she came up with her own, more frightening conclusion: a dog had attacked me and bitten my neck. This could have been the beginning of a deep-seated fear of dogs for Ellie had we not figured it out.

In retrospect, she would have fared much better had she been able to see me regularly. The cervical collar would have just become an everyday thing to her.

The truth is not frightening to children if it is presented calmly and simply in what I call "information McNuggets." On the other hand, being excluded without explanation *is* frightening. Even children barely out of babyhood conjure up images and explanations in their young minds—often much worse than the reality.

Such fears, formed early in life, can become the foundation for lifelong problems dealing with illnesses, dying, death, and grief. When I hear things like "It terrifies my husband to go into hospitals!" or "Her thirty-year-old son won't come. He couldn't handle seeing her like this," or "I want the kids to remember Grandma the way she was, so we won't take them to the hospital," I wonder what happened to the *parent* in childhood that formed the basis of these abnormal fears. And too often, these fears are now being passed on to *their* children.

MR. CHAMBERS

The road sand from the last snowfall crunched under my tires as I drove into an exclusive gated community full of the rich and politically famous. The large white Dutch Colonial house was less imposing than the neighboring mansions, but it was meticulously cared for. It had probably been one of the original homes when this was still sparsely populated countryside.

Ronald Chambers, seventy-six, greeted me at the door. He was a handsome man, well groomed and dapper in a starched white shirt, tie, and V-neck sweater. Despite his warm welcome, the fear in his eyes was clear.

"Please come in. Let me take your wrap. My wife, Claudia, is sleeping at the moment and we mustn't disturb her. She's quite weak, you know. Please, let's talk in the kitchen."

Two placemats were neatly set at the table, as was a cozy-covered teapot with matching cups and saucers. Lemon slices circled a plate that matched the creamer and sugar bowl. It made a scene befitting the polished mahogany elegance of this grand old home.

"How lovely this is." I smiled. "Thank you." Then I watched and held my breath as he struggled to pour hot water into the delicate cups, his hands trembling.

"I apologize," he murmured. "I've heard wonderful things about your organization. I just never expected...We never thought...She's always been so healthy...gotten so sick...so fast." He sat across from me at the table and swallowed hard as his face crumpled for a long moment.

"Oh dear," he said, straightening up, "I do apologize. The papers...I imagine there are papers I should sign."

Each visit that I made to this devoted couple increased my concern for Mr. Chambers. He was doing a superb job of caring for his wife and had hired extra help for her personal care, the cooking, and the housework. But his fear and distraction were steadily increasing until it was difficult for him to sit still for even a few minutes. Following directions was becoming impossible for him. He literally shook. I'd never seen anything quite like it. He was constantly moving, dusting, rearranging magazines, picking things up and putting them back down. His silent frenzy increased as Claudia's health deteriorated. I had the constant sense that at any moment he would bolt and run. It was like watching a nervous breakdown on fast-forward.

Lesley, my team's social worker, requested a private meeting with Judy, the couple's forty-two-year-old daughter, and me at a local coffee shop. Our team was worried about her father, and as it turned out, so was Judy. She was very actively involved and stopped by every evening after work to visit her mother and have dinner with her dad.

"It's the only way I can be sure he has at least one proper meal!" she told us. "He's a pretty good cook and was always able to take care of himself, but now he's falling apart. Going every day also helps me keep tabs on the medication schedule and on how Mother's doing."

We shared our growing concern that as her mother was deteriorating, so was her father. We suggested she take him to his doctor for a checkup to make sure there was no underlying medical problem. We also suggested she look ahead and make sure he had enough help and support as his wife's needs increased. Judy then reported that she had just requested family medical leave at her job. She would be moving back in to help her parents, and she planned to stay "for the duration." We agreed that this seemed like the best plan.

Lesley explained to Judy that our primary concern for Mr. Chambers was the depth of his stress. It seemed more like intense fear bordering on terror. It's normal to be stressed when your beloved spouse is sick and dying, but his reaction was extreme.

"Could you tell us more about your dad?" Lesley asked. "Perhaps it would give us some insight so we can support him better."

"My father has never spoken about his childhood, except to my mother," Judy began, "but I'll tell you what she told me.

"He was the only child born to his parents. His mother, who he adored, nearly died during his birth and was never very strong after that, but she lavished love and attention on him. His father was very quiet and somewhat stern, not at all affectionate, but a hardworking man who provided adequately for his small family. They lived on a farm in Oklahoma, fairly isolated from other people, so my dad and his mother were each other's entire world.

"The summer that he turned five, he was sent away to his paternal grandparents' house in Idaho without explanation. He barely knew them, and they were as quiet and stern as their son. He was frightened and lonely for his mother, but he couldn't even talk to her, as no one had phones back then.

"He was sent back home in time to start school, but his mother was gone. She'd died of what I guess was a heart problem or something while he was gone. Apparently he was sent away because she was sick. To make matters worse, nobody told him a thing. All reminders of her were gone—not even a picture remained, and her name was never mentioned again. No one grieved in front of him. No one showed him that she was even missed! He had never even gotten to say goodbye. They acted as though she had never existed."

Judy's eyes became moist. "Can you imagine what that did to this shy little boy?" She handed a yellowed photo across the table to us. A darling towheaded six-year-old Ronald stood like a little soldier with his arms at his sides. His serious small face was cocked to one side and his eyes were squinted in a slight frown as though he was trying to figure out why anybody would want a picture of him.

"Doesn't it just break your heart?" she asked. "This is all we have from his childhood."

After a short silence, Judy went on. "So even getting him to go to a doctor is nearly impossible. It's irrational, and he knows it, but he can't stop the fear. He actually gets physically ill thinking about it. I'm not sure he'll be able to go to my mother's funeral," she said.

"My mother was the only woman he ever dated. They married later in life because he wouldn't marry her until he could provide for her properly. He adores her. She knew about her own cancer and how serious it was long before she told him about it, she was so concerned about how he'd react. Of course, not telling him was worse. It was too much like losing his mother."

Without ever having been resolved, this deep emotional issue was once again emerging. Once again this grown man was a terrified little boy, about to lose the only woman besides his mother and his daughter that he'd ever loved. Again, he was powerless to do anything to stop it or make it better. Again, he was going to be frightened and alone in the world.

After Judy left, Lesley and I sat for a while with our barely warm tea. "How cruel we can be to children in the name of sheltering or protecting them," Lesley said quietly.

"I'm going to request that our bereavement team meet with Mr. Chambers *now*, instead of waiting until after Claudia's death," she continued. "This poor man is not only grieving the upcoming loss of his wife but also grieving the loss of his mother—seventy years later!"

Imagine how different it would have been if five-year-old Ronald had been kept at home while his mother's health declined and if his sick mother or his father had held him and told him what a good boy he was and that it was not his fault. He needed to hear how much he was loved by his mother and by everyone else in the family. He needed to hear that he would not be alone, that his emotions were normal and mattered, and that his mother's memory would not fade, even though her physical presence did. His parents could have explained to him gently that his mama was sick and probably would not get better, but that he could help take care of her and do nice things for her—draw pictures for her room, bring her juice to drink, rub lotion on her hands, tell bedtime stories, cuddle her, and sing to her—and that would make her happy.

Then as his mother got sicker, they would hold him again and reassure him that he was doing such a good job taking care of her, but that she would have to die soon. She didn't want to leave him, but she was too sick to be able to get better, and she would go to heaven (or whatever was their belief) soon. She would tell him that he would still be safe, cared for, and loved by Papa and everyone else in the family. Even though she would no longer be physically present, she would always love him and watch over him, like his own special guardian angel, forever.

There is no way to make the loss of a loved one easy, but adults have more life experience to draw from in understanding sickness and death and in dealing with the grief of great loss. They need to share this understanding with their children. Keeping little Ronald involved and allowing him to see their own tears of sadness would have taught him how to behave when someone is sick and shown him that grief is not something to hide or to be ashamed of. Holding him and reassuring him that he had not done anything bad would have helped him to learn that he was not responsible for his mother's illness. Giving him healthy outlets for his feelings, such as art, writing, or sports, would have helped him to express his pain in beneficial ways. (Today, counseling or therapy would also be an option.) Finally, allowing him to participate in the funeral, even briefly and privately, taking the time to explain to him everything he would see and to answer his questions, would have helped him to understand that his mother did not simply disappear.

Once again: the truth, if presented in an age-appropriate manner, does not frighten or damage children. Being excluded and abandoned, emotionally or physically, does. Children shouldn't be expected to navigate a crisis of such magnitude on their own. They can't figure it out by themselves. They need their questions validated with supportive, age-appropriate answers. They need us to show them what to do and how to express the grief they feel. They need to share their tears and sadness with us. And just as we all do, they need lots of love and support on this life-changing journey.

THE BOTTOM LINE

As we teach our children to share, walk, and read, so should we teach them how to cope with loss and grief, as these are a necessary part of life.

18

PEOPLE DIE AS THEY LIVE—
INTENSIFIED

There is a pattern of behavior well-known to those who work with the dying and their families: *people die as they live—intensified*. Nice people get nicer. Busy people get busier, even if only in their dreams. Quiet people get quieter. Demanding people demand more. Manipulators will surpass their past controlling behavior. This is critically important for caregivers, family, and friends to understand, because to expect the behavior of a dying person to be significantly different from what it was earlier in the person's life is unrealistic and frustrating.

Most pregnant women have a growing sense of their baby's personality—how it reacts to movement or rest, how it responds to music or loud noises such as ambulance sirens. We are who we are, and we are wired that way at conception. Our unique behaviors will carry us through life's challenges, triumphs, and tragedies. Why, then, would we even imagine that any person's dying would be different from his or her living?

SAM'S WAY

Sam had been a full-time construction worker all his adult life, at least when the lure of fishing or hunting didn't call him to play hooky. Being a rough-and-tumble sort of guy, he overlooked the bruising that started to show without explanation on his arms and legs. But eventually the dizziness, weakness, and shortness of breath made climbing the scaffolding impossible, and even getting on a ladder was dangerous. Everyone was shocked when he was diagnosed with acute leukemia. At age thirty-nine, a stunned Sam took early retirement on disability.

Chemotherapy brought about a remission, but within months the disease was back. A second remission seemed harder to come by and lasted a shorter time. Monthly blood transfusions initially gave him a real boost of energy, but they now achieved diminishing results and were needed weekly. It seemed that the time was fast approaching when even daily transfusions would be inadequate. Sam was now spending most of his time in his lounge chair or in bed. Slowly it dawned on him that he wasn't getting better; he was dying.

His wife was devoted to him and tolerant of his rowdy ways, but she had described his parenting skills as "missing" on my first visit to the family.

"If it wasn't work, it was hunting, fishing, or hanging out in the bar with the guys. He just always seemed to prefer being with the guys more than being at home with Crystal and me," she said.

Twenty-year-old Crystal was a shy and soft-spoken young woman. She sat by her father's chair or bedside for hours, silently and desperately waiting for him to acknowledge her. As time went by, she became visibly frustrated and angry at his failure to connect. Her agitation baffled him—it was so unlike her—but he was just too exhausted to deal with it, so he would close his eyes and doze.

One day I asked Crystal what she was hoping for.

"You know, one of those heart-to-heart conversations," she said sadly. "Maybe there's something important I should know from him, sort of like that final wisdom from your daddy before he dies." Her eyes filled with tears.

"Did you have many heart-to-heart conversations when he was well?" I asked. She just laughed and shook her head.

No Hollywood Endings

Movies have made everybody think that deathbed scenes are times for openhearted sharing, with high emotions, secrets, and true feelings spilling forth. Crystal was waiting for her father to turn into the caring papa from *Little House on the Prairie,* when the reality was that Sam probably was not going to be more forthcoming on his deathbed than he had been in his life.

I gently explained this to Crystal and held her as her tears turned into sobs. She realized that Sam's absence from her life when he was well was a reflection of who he was as a person and a father, and that he was unlikely to change now and give her the fatherly recognition she so desperately desired.

After Crystal and I talked, the social worker on my team, Maureen, increased her time with her and was wonderfully supportive in helping her to deal with her double grief—because Crystal was not only losing her real father but also mourning the death of the little girl's dream daddy she had waited for so patiently all these years. Maureen was able to help Crystal realize that she was a good and loving daughter and a young woman with much to offer this world, even if her father did not tell her so. Her willingness to care for him and love him, without his approval, was itself a testimony to the wonderful person she was.

I suggested that the family and friends do a "roast" for Sam. They all gathered around his bed late one Friday afternoon and told outrageous stories about him. He had been a crazy, overgrown party animal, and he blossomed upon hearing the stories of his mishaps and poor judgment. "But somehow or other he always landed on his feet!" his best buddy proclaimed. Then he put a big burly arm around Crystal and said, "You know, missy, I remember the day you were born. Your pop was on top of the world! You would have thought no one else had ever had a little girl. And did we hear about every report card and every soccer game you ever won?" he asked his cronies.

"Oh, boy! Did we! Brag, brag, brag—that's all he did!"

"And he's so proud of you, too, Denise," he continued. "He knew how much you had to put up with, and you stuck with him anyway! None of us could ever figure out why, though!" Raucous laughter and the sound of knee slapping filled the room.

I could see Denise's face soften as her eyes filled with tears of love for her husband. Here was the validation she and Crystal had always yearned for. Maybe it was given to them in a backdoor kind of a way, but it *was* given to them—in Sam's way.

One of my favorite sayings is "Don't try to teach a pig to sing—it wastes your time and it aggravates the pig." It is not our job to expect, or try to force, someone to act the way we think is right. It doesn't work, anyway. It is our job to recognize the uniqueness in each person and celebrate it. If you can work with that uniqueness and be realistic in your expectations as you share the final journey, it will go much easier, and your relationships will strengthen, not splinter.

THE BOTTOM LINE

People die as they live, but more so. To expect something different is to set yourself up for disappointment and failure.

PART IV

AVOIDING
POTHOLES

TRIPPING OVER YOUR ROOTS—

And Crashing into the Family Tree

Everything I've said about the dying person's unique coping style is true for the family as well. Mom might be the busy one, always on the move, efficient, practical, no-nonsense, the true boss of the family. Dad, on the other hand, may be the quiet, steady, reserved dreamer who withdraws into himself when the going gets tough. Then there's the sister who is shy, easily anxious, hesitant, dependent, and needy. Perhaps the brother is boisterous and outgoing, a party animal, kindhearted, but usually too focused on his own life to be aware of others' needs. At ninety, Grandma's once vibrant personality has been dimmed by her physical compromises and by her failing hearing and sight. She has moved into a solitary world of old memories and dreams, cradled and rocked in her favorite chair. And don't forget Aunt Tillie down the street, whose image of what life should be is frozen forever back in the 1950s.

And now all these good people are thrown together on a journey none ever would have chosen, each contributing his or her unique talents, and each needing different things to sustain them. Imagine the many ways this might play out. Will they share a loving, bonding experience, or will the family splinter in turmoil, frustration, fear, anger, and rage (all signs of early grieving)? All this can be doubly confusing because the dying process brings out the best and the worst in people—often simultaneously.

How do you navigate this necessary but difficult interplay between relatives and the dying person? When I begin to work with a new patient, I often sit the family members or friends down and ask them to describe each other: their personalities, their strengths and their weaknesses, and their difficulties. What fulfills and nourishes them? How have they handled crisis in the past? How do they think they might handle this crisis and this upcoming loss?

Their responses are interesting—usually humorous kidding; sometimes touching validations; often a comfort in being understood, foibles and all, but loved anyway. And doing this exercise has already contributed subtly to their teamwork and support of each other.

Then I explain the behavior pattern we hospice workers know so well: people handle this ultimate life stress as they have handled other great stresses—but in an intensified way. Mom might now go into a frenzy of sterilizing the house and alphabetizing the over-the-counter remedies in the medicine cabinet, while Dad might become obsessed with the Learning Channel and taking long naps. A sister may become increasingly anxious and agitated and develop a vague rash and sleep disturbances, while her brother steps up his drinking and partying and is rarely at home. Aunt Tillie might become frightened about the pain pump and fuss about these "newfangled devices" and what they cost, while Granny, sensing the turmoil around her but unable to hear and understand it, increasingly withdraws into her dream world.

Helping all the participants to understand this behavior is very helpful, not only as a means of validating the uniqueness in each family member and working successfully with those differences but also in anticipating and preparing for the challenges that lie ahead. If some level of understanding and compromise is not attained, the players may come into conflict with each other as clashes of needs and styles occur. Imagine how long Dad, who is escaping into his solitary relationship with a show on animal cloning, will tolerate Mom, who is driven compulsively to vacuum under his feet, then polish and rearrange the furniture in the TV room.

Now put a dying person in the middle of such a scenario—maybe another son and brother. Perhaps he is silently raging against the injustice of a death too young, trying to understand what's happening to his rapidly failing body, frightened or concerned about how the family will get along without him. Perhaps in his well days he was a detail-oriented scientist, self-motivated, needing a lot of his own space, nourished by his voracious reading, intricate model building, and long solitary hikes. Now he is increasingly confined to home, often bored, more and more dependent on other people, but snappish or sullen when they try to help him.

Are any of these people or their reactive behaviors wrong? They may be unpleasant or uncomfortable, yes—but wrong? No. The rule of thumb is: *as long as no harm is being done to self or others, the behavior is acceptable.*

Everyone involved in this journey becomes like a planet hurtling around the family solar system, sometimes free to act as they need, but other times crashing into each other, causing more stress and upset. If for a moment each person could step back and see the whole picture, they would understand that no one is wrong for acting as they do. It's just the unique way they were wired at birth. So the key is to allow yourself to be who you are and react how you do. At the same time, do that for each and every person involved. Support each other, but be respectful and stay out of each other's way as well.

THE BOTTOM LINE

When dealing with major life stresses such as death and dying, families and friends cope as they usually do, only in an intensified way. Understanding this can prevent irreparable damage to or destruction of family relationships.

20

"WHOSE DEATH IS IT, ANYWAY?"

When someone we love is dying, all of our feelings, spiritual beliefs, and cultural expectations about death become emotionally charged and intensified. We may be so rooted in our own strong feelings that we're surprised and shocked when others don't share them. It is a particular challenge not to project our own hopes, fears, dreams, and expectations on the dying person's journey.

NICHOLAS

"Are those *diapers* you're carrying?" The young man suddenly filled the front doorway, barring my entrance. I recognized his face from the photos that proudly adorned Mr. and Mrs. Pennington's walls and bureaus. He was Nicholas, their only son, and as he pointed to the package in my hands he had such an air of authority that I suddenly felt I might have done something dreadfully wrong. He made no attempt to introduce himself or welcome me in. I looked down at the enormous package of adult incontinence briefs and waited for him to speak.

"One of the main reasons we brought Dad home to die instead of putting him in a facility was so he could die with dignity!" he said with indignation. "He would *never* want to be seen in *those*!"

"Please let me introduce myself," I said quietly. "I'm Maggie, your father's hospice nurse. Did your mom or dad tell you I was coming?"

"Yes, my mom did before she left. My dad's sleeping, and I wanted to give her some time to get her hair done and do some errands. I'll be here until five o'clock or so."

"I'm sure she appreciates that," I said. Neither of us said anything else for a moment, and then I eyed the mammoth package in my hands. "Can we talk about this inside?"

"Oh, sorry. Sure, come on in. I'm Nicholas," he said politely, taking the package and setting it next to the door. I followed him through the quiet house and into the kitchen. As we sat down at the table, I thought about how many of the most important and meaningful conversations happen at someone's kitchen table.

"Look, my dad is a very proud man," Nicholas said right away. "He's a *man*, for crying out loud, and I am sure he would feel humiliated if you make him wear one of those diapers! What he's going through is hard enough, and I won't have you or anyone else add to that burden." His anger was apparent. I sat quietly and listened until he had said all he needed to. I could see how much he loved his father and how difficult it was for Nicholas to see him getting weaker.

"I can hear your devotion and concern for your father," I said. "Is there anything else regarding his care that you're unhappy about?"

Nicholas thought for a moment before responding.

"No, I really think everything is going as well as can be expected. He's happy here, and my mother is far less stressed not having to go back and forth to the nursing home. It's much easier on her. And they both have said how nice they think you and your organization are."

I smiled and said, "Your father has told me how proud he is of you. He calls you 'a chip off the old block,' and now I see why. Your father's main concern is his family's well-being, and clearly so is yours. Nicholas, I think you'll be surprised to learn that your *dad* requested these briefs because it's taking him longer to walk to the bathroom now, and he was worried about having an accident. *That* would humiliate him and be a burden for your mother to clean up. With the briefs he maintains control, and having control actually protects his dignity. They afford him privacy and really don't show under his clothes or pajamas."

"I had no idea," Nicholas said quietly. "I guess it would have embarrassed him to tell me!" I was touched by his obvious respect for his father.

"I know it's hard having to shift the way we perceive those we love," I told him. "Your father is still a strong, dignified, and proud man. When we're healthy and younger, most of us are hung up on our ideas of pride and self-consciousness. It's nice that your father is putting practicality ahead of vanity. He's keeping his focus on what *can* be done. Otherwise he would just focus on how his body is changing, and resent it. Your concern is justified, but sometimes we have to ask ourselves, whose dignity are we discussing?

"It's hard to see the situation through the eyes of the dying person, particularly when we're so emotionally invested. But Nicholas, I promise you that we will continue to treat your father with dignity in all we do."

Our conversation seemed to restore a sense of calm. I felt grateful to have met Nicholas; even in this brief time, I came to better understand an important member of the family. As the only child, he knew he had responsibilities and a new role that came with his father's illness. What he hadn't anticipated was that his father would teach him in death as much as he had in life.

SPIROS

Spiros was the imposing patriarch of a large, loving Greek family. His strong, dark features would have seemed ominous except for his huge, dazzling smile. I couldn't look at his laughing face without smiling myself.

"Eat, eat, eat!" was the chorus I heard every time I visited over the six months or so he was in my care. The family simply would not let me refuse their offerings, and if I did, I would find them wrapped up in plastic containers on the front seat of my car. Every one of the four pounds I gained while I took care of Spiros was a delicious journey into some Greek delight: gyros, stuffed grape leaves, falafel, spinach pie, baklava. As his wife or one of his daughters heaped my plate with food, Spiros would hold court, recounting stories of the "old country."

I was a willing audience, and he offered up each tale as if it were some golden treasure. Back when there were few cars on his island and the oceans were still teeming with fish, he and the other village children would spend days freely exploring caves, diving for sea urchins, fishing in the aqua seas, and getting into some very entertaining mischief.

As Spiros spoke, one of his many relatives and friends would arrive bearing some new delicacy, and then they'd settle in on the couch or on the floor at his feet to listen, prodding him to retell one particularly entertaining detail or another. They slapped their thighs, threw their heads back in laughter, and shouted in delight, their eyes and ears always fixed on Spiros. And he delighted in having the lead role in this production, despite the cancer in his bones that destroyed his bone marrow, rendering it unable to produce the red blood cells needed to sustain his life.

Spiros became one of my favorite examples of someone who lived his life to the fullest until the very end. He was especially proud of his three sons, who were educated, married, successful, and had healthy, exuberant children of their own. They were a shining example of an immigrant success story, and Spiros rightly felt he had worked hard to create a good life for them all.

But the time came when Spiros was no longer mentally clear enough to tell his stories, and he spent more and more hours sleeping or lying quietly, as if he were floating off on a soft cloud. Meanwhile, the family was confident about carrying out his final wishes. He had spelled them out in a detailed letter, and although this living will had not been drawn up by a lawyer (Spiros didn't believe in paying lawyers), he had written and signed it with the input and agreement of his family, and given it to his eldest son for safekeeping.

Was the document witnessed? No, but who would ever question Spiros? The letter clearly stated what he wanted and what he didn't—case closed. No CPR, no artificial hydration or nutrition. He wanted to stay at home in the care of his family. He wanted to be kept as comfortable as possible, and he didn't want his wife or children to be involved in maintaining his personal hygiene. His wife and sons were committed to supporting his desires, as was Rosina, a highly skilled and compassionate nursing assistant.

This tranquility ceased when Spiros's younger sister, Athena, arrived from New York. She had not seen him for months, and now she became quite hysterical.

"He's out of it!" she wailed. "You're killing him with the drugs. Do something! I want him to go to the hospital immediately!!" Everyone panicked, and I received an urgent page to come quickly. I paged our much-loved chaplain, Carolyn, and asked for her help as I was driving to Spiros's house.

Athena was pacing up and down the driveway when I arrived. I spent about fifteen minutes pacing up and down with her, listening to her tirade and trying to calm her. She repeated the same litany she had given to her family: "He's out of it; you're killing him; I want him to go to the hospital." In her opinion I hadn't done anything right.

As we talked, I tried to validate the love and devotion that was hidden behind all of Athena's complaints, unreasonable as they were. I learned a long time ago that if you want to defuse someone's rage and anger, first validate that person's feelings. Resisting or arguing will get you nowhere—and it will only escalate the other person's anger.

After a while Athena confided that Spiros had looked after her like a father ever since theirs passed away when she was young. It was Spiros who had made sure she went to college, sending her regular checks as he worked night and day at his diner to make that possible.

Once she realized I was willing to hear her and take her worries seriously, she calmed down and agreed to come into the house to talk things over with the rest of the family.

We all sat around the enormous dining room table as I reviewed the course of Spiros's illness, the medications he was on and why, and how we were prepared to handle any situation that might arise. Everyone in the family besides Athena was already aware of all these points, since we had designed Spiros's plan of care together. But she seemed on the defensive about many of the particulars. The family had little patience for this. They were already irritated because she had visited so rarely, and now they felt she had just barged in with criticism and was trying to tell them what to do.

I asked Athena to clearly state her wishes and concerns. She rattled out what she thought should and should not be happening. Quite on his own, Spiros's eldest son, David, diligently wrote down everything his aunt was suggesting. Her list included hospital care and hyperalimentation (intravenous artificial nutrition) because she thought we were starving Spiros, even though the diminishing of his appetite was normal for someone at his stage of illness. David added her desire for high-tech interventions to "keep him alive as long as possible." This seemed to validate and calm her.

Just as I was about to address her issues, David produced his father's letter stating his wishes. With his huge dark eyes, black wavy hair, and broad shoulders, David was a commanding presence, and he knew how to get people's attention without raising his voice. I could see why Spiros had so comfortably passed his baton to him. David read his father's letter aloud to the gathering. He then handed his aunt the list of *her* wishes that he had carefully written down. "Be sure to give this to the hospice nurse when *you're* dying," he said quietly. "But we will continue to follow my father's wishes as *he's* dying."

The stunned silence that followed was broken by the ring of the doorbell. I was mightily relieved to see Carolyn, our team chaplain. She gathered everyone together around Spiros's bed and led the family in a nondenominational prayer that blessed everyone present for their love, devotion, and dedication to this wonderful husband, father, and brother, who was dying as uniquely as he had lived.

THE BOTTOM LINE

Our dying should be as uniquely our own as our life has been.

21

FINDING POWER IN
A POWERLESS SITUATION

My best friends know that when my life is a shambles, my house is spotless. If I can't control distressing issues in my life, I can jolly well vacuum like a madwoman or cover my fridge with crisp new Post-it notes. These behaviors make me feel that I can still control *something*—and even look better to the world for my efforts.

People under great stress feel powerless and out of control. This is such an uncomfortable and demeaning feeling that, consciously or subconsciously, they turn to behavior that empowers them in some way, makes them feel better and more in charge.

These coping behaviors are not always logical, and they may even seem strange to us, but they're normal for the situation. What is problematic is when the comforting behavior is harmful or destructive, such as drinking too much, using illicit drugs, or misusing prescription drugs such as tranquilizers. Being hostile or abusive to others or yourself is also the wrong choice of behaviors and will only compound the problem rather than relieve it.

There can also be problems when our choices collide with other people's ways of coping. Those who increase their sense of control by being busy can easily intrude on the family member who needs quiet to regroup. As I've said, under great stress, most busy people get busier, while most quiet people get quieter.

It's important for caregivers to remember that patients, too, need to find power in this powerless situation. What may seem to the caregiver or family as uncooperative, difficult, or manipulative behavior may in fact be an effort to regain some sense of control.

MATTHEW

Even in his well years, Matthew had been an alcohol abuser and a manipulative personality. Now that he was dying of cirrhosis, he was becoming even more of a challenge for his wife, Florence. She would bring water so he could take his pills, but the glass would be wrong, or the water too cold or not cold enough. Then the head of the bed was too low or too high. Then the order in which he would take his pills changed every-day...and on and on.

All these demands could turn pill taking, which should have been done in a few minutes, into an hour-long power play, and this routine was repeated four or five times a day. Florence was having a difficult time not taking this behavior personally, as it seemed intended to irritate her. She felt pun-ished for being well and for the occasional breaks she took from caregiving.

Our team social worker, Kim, came up with a workable so-lution. She saw that Matthew might not feel so powerless if he had more choices throughout the day. She suggested that Florence ask him for his input in as many situations as possi-ble. Did he want a hot breakfast or cold cereal? Did he want to be bathed at eight or ten in the morning? What did he want to wear? We ordered a reclining wheelchair so that he could go outside a bit when the weather was good. Kim also suggested that Florence share the medication schedule with a few friends and neighbors who had offered to help. The pills were poured out ahead of time into baby-food jars with lids, marked with the time to be given. Not only did this allow Florence her much-needed breaks, but it gave Matthew different people to interact with, and this helped decrease his resentment at being home-bound.

Even more important, Kim was able to help Florence understand what motivated Matthew's behavior so that she did not take it so personally.

"I used to think he was just being hateful toward me," Florence told me. "I wasn't sure I could keep taking care of him. But Kim helped me see how many losses he's already had and how important it is for him to feel some control."

EMILY

I did a mental review of Ethel's condition as I drove to visit her. She had lived with her daughter, Emily, and her retired son-in-law, Ray, for almost twenty years, and was a spirited and positive force in the family. She had been healthy until ninety-two, when her chronic heart failure started to become unmanageable. She had played a very active role in the lives of her three grandchildren, sitting on many soggy soccer fields, wrapped up in a down comforter and cheering like mad during scrimmages she was hard pressed to understand. But her Robbie or her Suzie or her Brad was involved, so she cheered and cheered and the whole team loved her.

In return for her love and involvement, the entire family now participated in providing exceptional care for her at home.

I grew alarmed as I parked at the curb and saw Ray's car in front of me. It had been backed up against a high pile of leaves, the engine was running, and Ray was sprawled motionless in the passenger seat. *Oh, no,* I thought as I bolted out of my car. *Carbon monoxide poisoning!*

I rushed over and tapped loudly on the window. "Ray, Ray—

are you okay?" I shouted. He startled and sat up with such force that his head grazed the rearview mirror.

"What? What . . . ?" he muttered as he looked around, disoriented.

"What are you doing? Are you okay?"

"Well, Ethel's not doing so well, so Emily's on a tear!" He rubbed his face. "This morning she cleaned the chandelier with Q-tips, and she's been vacuuming ever since. The vacuum nearly sucked the curtains off the windows, and when I heard the pocket change from the top of my dresser clatter down the wand, I figured I'd better get out of Dodge!" He laughed. "The racket was getting to me, so I decided to sit in the car and listen to NPR. I guess I fell asleep. What time is it?"

"You're a good guy, Ray!" I said. "I know you understand that all this cleaning is helping Emily deal with her feelings of powerlessness as her mother approaches death. There's no point trying to make her stop it. She would only be more stressed."

"You're right," he said. "We're all going to miss Ethel, but Emily's really taking it hard. The two of them have always been so close. Maybe I'll drive down to the market and get her some flowers. She loves flowers. Maybe I'll get some for Ethel, too!" He slid across the seats and gave me a big wink as he started the car, armed with a new plan to make things a little better for Emily.

Ray was a devoted husband who years ago learned his wife's style of coping, how to help, and when to get out of the way. He knew what she needed, he knew what he needed, and he knew that both of them could have their needs met without an uproar or conflict.

Understand that people may react in strange ways when under great stress. Recognizing and supporting that, rather than fighting it, demonstrates your caring and love. Later on, these odd situations can become the focus of humor and provide a refreshing balance to the sad days of grieving.

THE BOTTOM LINE

You can't control the dying process, but sometimes you can find other ways to feel more in control.

22

CAREGIVING IN
A WOUNDED RELATIONSHIP

Let's acknowledge the truth that not every relationship is wonderful and loving. It is not uncommon for mean and hurtful people to die in mean and hurtful ways even while someone is selflessly caring for them. So is it possible to bring closure and resolution to a wounded relationship, or one in which love has already died? Can healing still take place where turmoil, rejection, or pain still exists?

Yes, of course. Uncounted individuals choose to care for others even though the relationship is shadowed by pain or rejection. I have met more women than you can imagine who took in and provided care for an abusive ex-husband or a husband who'd left them years before with young children and no means of support. Typically I hear, "My kids are losing their father. I'm doing this for them."

I've also been moved by the many adult children who cared for alcoholic, drug-addicted, or abusive parents. "It's the right thing to do," they tell me, or "I'm doing this for me."

Such caregivers may act out of a sense of obligation and responsibility instilled in them by their culture, upbringing, or religion. They may want to set an example for their own children or desire to guide and support them through their loss. The hope of mending the broken relationship may motivate them, or they may simply feel sorry for a person who would otherwise die alone without care, or in the care of strangers.

Whatever the caregiver's reasoning, this choice takes a huge amount of courage, and the caregiver deserves an extra dose of love, support, and nurturing. To criticize the caregiver's choice— as happens too often—is to miss the genuine healing that can occur. It can also compound any feelings of rejection and insecurity the caregiver may already have.

Even though you may feel concern for a caregiving friend and worry that he or she may be hurt again, it does not help to say things such as "He was a bum! Why should you take care of him now?" or "You're crazy! Your hard work won't be appreciated." Instead, try something more supportive: "I give you a lot of credit for taking care of someone who hurt you so badly. You are very brave, and I'm sure you have your reasons. Is there anything I can do to make it easier for you?"

I have always believed that the measure of someone's value is not how that person handles the good times but what he or she does with the bad. To selflessly care for someone despite a history of diminishment, rejection, or even abuse is a job that few would choose. Give those who do this job the support they so richly deserve.

LEONA

One afternoon after our weekly interdisciplinary meeting, another nurse on my team, Leona, asked if I would have lunch with her. She looked frazzled, and over lunch she explained why.

"My mother is not doing well," she told me. "She is quite elderly, and for a long time I have been taking her to her doctor visits, helping her make sense of treatment options, and stopping by a few times a week to make sure everything is running smoothly. Now she needs help every day, and I recently found Theresa to keep her company and care for her. She's one of the best home health aides I know. I honestly don't know what I would do without her. My sister certainly isn't much help!"

"I'm sure you have everything under control, but you look tired and worried. Is there some way we can encourage your sister to help you?" I asked.

Leona laughed ruefully. Her sister, Elizabeth, lived only an hour away, but she claimed that her busy social schedule prevented her from visiting more than once every few months.

"I know it sounds like sour grapes, but after all I do for Mom on a regular basis, you'd think the queen herself was visiting when Elizabeth sweeps in. Mom brags to the neighbors about her visits. She even shows off the articles from the society pages about Elizabeth's latest charity functions, right down to the details of her gowns. There never seems to be any praise for *my* life or appreciation for *my* efforts. I know it sounds childish, but it gets so wearing."

As tears welled up in her eyes, Leona continued. "And it's always been this way, from as early as I can remember: 'Why can't you be more like your sister?' 'You're just not as pretty as she is.' 'You won't get into the school Elizabeth went to. You would never be accepted.' 'You want to be a *nurse*?' And the worst: 'You always have such bad taste. Look at that good-for-nothing you married. I knew the moment I met him he'd leave you high and dry. Now look at the mess you're in.'"

It was painful for me to hear. Leona was a down-to-earth, compassionate woman who had raised three great kids alone despite her low nursing salary. She was successful in her own right, respected by her peers and appreciated by her patients. Yet even now, one comment or disapproving glance from her mother could make her feel small and inferior.

"Now Mom has taken a turn for the worse. It's time for hospice, and I don't know what to do." She sighed and explained that she didn't want her co-workers involved in her mother's care. "I'm afraid she will just get too ugly. I know we hospice workers have seen it all and we don't gossip, but I just can't think of facing everyone at the office when they see what my family's really like. Destroying my professional confidence would be the final insult my mother could deliver. The trouble is, I've decided to protect my own reputation and not put her in hospice, but I'm just not sure I can do it alone. I know it is a lot to ask, but I trust you professionally and personally, Maggie. Would you help me?"

Leona wanted to make sure she was making the best judgments, and she recognized that being daughter, nurse, and primary caregiver would make this difficult to achieve, so she requested that I act as her backup nurse as she coordinated her mother's care privately.

In the months that followed, I visited her mother, Nancy, regularly and spoke to or met with Leona often to discuss her mother's medications, pain management, and general well-being. It was during one of my visits that Leona asked if we could take a walk into the garden behind the house. I could see she was very upset.

The door was hardly closed when Leona burst out, "I know I should expect this by now, but it gets to me all the same. For two months I have done *everything* for that woman. Laundry, shopping, garbage, bills, you name it! Every week I even take her out for her salon day and lunch at her favorite restaurant. Still, the only praise she has to offer goes to Elizabeth and her kids for their few small efforts. Is a thank-you for my efforts too much to expect?

"I've been brushing off her rejection for *forty-five years,* Maggie, but I'm not finding it so easy anymore. I don't deserve to struggle with complicated grieving after she's gone as well because we couldn't get closer while she was alive. I want to fix it *now!* And it enrages me that my sister can't even be bothered to miss a luncheon at the country club to be with her own mother! What I would give to know why we have always been treated so differently, Maggie. I never felt like she even *wanted*

me. When I bring it up, she flatly denies that there's any difference in the way she's always treated us. 'Are you never satisfied?'
she says. That just turns the blame on me!"

I thought for a minute before replying. "You may never get
her to admit the reason; she might not even be able to understand it herself," I began. "The important thing is that you find
a way to make peace with yourself now and recognize your own
value instead of waiting for her validation. Leona, when someone is dying, it feels like the sand is running out of the hour-
glass. While there's still time, though, you have to keep trying
to heal this hurt somehow. You know from your own hospice
work that grief is more difficult and complex when relationships have unresolved issues. I am sure you two can work
through this."

Determined to repair their relationship, Leona began sharing even more of her dreams, her memories, and her time with
her mother. With the help of a wheelchair, Leona took her on
regular outings, and because their "dates" had a consistent,
scheduled time, they opened an ongoing dialogue, a thread of
human experience. Over the next weeks and months, something began to shift between them. Leona found her mother becoming more open and even a little affectionate with her. She
began to tell stories of "the old days," and they grieved together
the loss of Leona's father so many years before. Their time together slowly transformed into something they both enjoyed.

Weeks later, as her mother's health began to seriously decline, Leona and her kids moved into Nancy's small apartment
to care for her, and everything seemed to be under control.

Then on my next visit, I found Leona pacing the room,
completely distraught. We took another walk through the
garden. Just hours before I'd arrived, Leona had come upon
a metal box her mother had hidden behind shoe boxes in
her bedroom closet. Receipts and a ledger confirmed what
Leona had always suspected: even beyond treating them differently emotionally, Nancy had spent thousands of dollars on

Elizabeth's family, including a down payment for her car, money for education, and generous loans with no repayment recorded.

"How can I find peace with this, Maggie? How can I not resent this? I've struggled to make ends meet all these years, while she's been helping Elizabeth. She's bought Elizabeth's kids elaborate presents for birthdays and holidays, even though she rarely sees them. My kids, who spend time with her regularly, are lucky to get an occasional card with a check for ten dollars! I thought we had come so far, but I'm not sure I can be in this house another minute," Leona exclaimed, sobbing.

"Forgiveness must come from within *you*, Leona. You're doing all you can, and your mother feels your love, even if she can't show it yet. Don't compromise your values. Your mother never understood that you earn love, you don't buy it. All that money and attention she gave Elizabeth didn't work, did it? Where is Elizabeth now?

"If she can't find a way to show love for you in the way you need it, you at least have to know you're doing your best. You're a wonderful person, Leona, and you may have to allow love to come to you through others, instead of through her, if that makes sense."

Leona wondered aloud if she would still be able to provide loving, quality care for her mother now that she felt such rage and disappointment. But before she made any rash decisions, I suggested that she take a few hours to herself. I would stay with Nancy until Theresa arrived for the evening shift.

Leona later told me that she headed back to her home, speeding down the highway with the windows open wide, blasting the radio to drown out the sound of her cries and sobs. And when the need overcame her, she shouted at the top of her lungs.

"I had a lifetime's worth of hurt, and I knew that if I didn't get it out, that pain would harm me. And so I screamed until I exhausted myself. I'd cry, and then scream some more," she said. "I cried in the tub until the water got cold, until I emptied myself, and then fell into bed.

"But I lay there and pictured my mother dying with someone she barely knew to care for her," she continued. "As much as I appreciate everything Theresa has done to help us, it still isn't the same as having family there. I thought of how well my children and I have cared for her. I didn't want to leave the kids to finish it without me now.

"I realized that in the end I had *shown* her the differences between my sister and me. And I was proud of those differences! I really had done the right thing instead of the selfish thing. And in that moment, I realized that I *was* more powerful and more honorable and had succeeded in my life, even without my mother's or sister's validation.

"And so I went back to my mother and whispered, 'Mom, I found the box, so I know everything, but I'm here for you *even though,* and we're going to give you the very best care we can. I hope by now you've learned that the love I have for you is real, as real as it has always been. I never wanted anything more from you than your love and respect in return. But it doesn't matter anymore, Mom. I realize now that I am bigger than all of this, and so I will stay.' "

Nancy seemed unsettled and restless for two days and then died quietly in the presence of Leona and her kids.

After the funeral I stopped by to help Leona tidy up. As we folded a load of laundry, Leona described to me the incredible sense of release and peace she felt because she had risen above her need to receive her mother's approval.

"I was no longer held down by something that wasn't going to happen in the way I'd hoped. It *is* possible to overcome such losses. Ultimately I learned through this experience that it matters less to me now what my mother thought of me, than how I think of myself. My children and I gave my mother exceptional, loving care. We did it because we loved her and it was the right thing to do. That feels really good. I'm so proud of my kids. They were here for me when I needed them—without even being asked."

Leona was smiling broadly, her face peaceful and open and so very proud.

THE BOTTOM LINE

Caregiving in a wounded relationship deserves extra support and concern from everyone, as providing care is more difficult and the rewards are harder to come by.

23

UNDERSTANDING
CULTURAL DIFFERENCES

The American doctor, trying to be honest and help his patient make decisions about her care needs, told an elderly Japanese woman that she had cancer. The cancer, he gently said, was very advanced, and although there were no known treatments to cure it, he would do everything possible to help her and keep her comfortable. His patients usually appreciated his honesty and compassion. So the physician felt confused when the woman's family seemed to be very upset with him, whisked the patient away, and indicated they no longer needed his services.

The two families had been next-door neighbors and friends for years. The Smiths originally came from the American Midwest, while the Rodriguez family had Latin American roots. When Mrs. Rodriguez's father was diagnosed with severe and aggressive liver disease, the Smiths wanted to be helpful. Mrs. Smith had recently dealt with the terminal illness of her own mother, so she felt she had a lot of useful advice to offer.

But Mrs. Rodriguez balked at Mrs. Smith's recommendation that she be honest with her father about the nature of the illness. She also refused to inquire about a hospice program or to treat her father's pain aggressively with the narcotic medications the physician had prescribed. Mrs. Smith left Mrs. Rodriguez's home dismayed that her very "Americanized" friend could be so "backward" when it came to dealing with her father's illness. Meanwhile, the Rodriguez family had their own negative feelings about their friend Mrs. Smith.

John, the hospice nurse, felt very uncomfortable. Things were not going well with his first visit to Mrs. Ariapour and her Iranian-American family. First, the family insisted that John join them at their table for tea. Then they instructed him not to talk about the seriousness of their mother's illness or to say that he was a representative of hospice. They did not want the patient to know she was terminally ill. When John explained that certain permission forms must be signed by the patient in order to receive hospice care, the family became upset and demanded to speak to John's supervisor.

Mr. Chee was admitted to the hospital over the weekend. His daughter had recently moved him from the Navaho reservation to live with her in the city because he was ill. The medical workup revealed end-stage renal disease, and the hospital nurses were concerned. He wouldn't even look at the advance directives form, let alone discuss a do-not-resuscitate order. He also refused the treatments the doctor ordered, including pain medication. The only thing he seemed to want was to light incense in the room. And he was so silent and took such a long time to answer their questions! The nurses thought perhaps he was very depressed, so they called the doctor for some antidepressants.

Mrs. Jones had advanced metastatic cancer. Her doctor recommended hospice care at home. But her African American family wanted her to remain in the hospital and for "everything to be done" to treat her. When one of the nurses said, "Mary, here are your pills," Mrs. Jones's daughter snapped at her. "It's 'Mrs. Jones' to you!"

. . .

Everyone knows that cultural patterns and beliefs influence our lives in significant ways. They shape our belief system, the clothes we feel most comfortable wearing, the foods we like to eat, the way we decorate our homes, and the activities we choose. We celebrate our unique differences by appreciating the foods, crafts, artwork, music, and dance of other cultural groups, but we often don't understand how important these differences become when someone is dying.

How do we communicate when the medical team has one cultural perspective and the patient has another? How do we celebrate diversity when an in-law, a friend, or a neighbor from another culture is dying and the person's attitudes and beliefs seem foreign to us?

Different cultures have very different views about the meaning of life and death, what a good death is, what respectful care is, and how best to provide that care for a dying person. Just as people have different spoken languages, which others can understand only if they learn the language or use an interpreter, their differing beliefs, values, and practices are a type of social language. They must also be translated if we're going to understand one another.

A person's culture of origin runs very deep. Even those who have become acculturated to an adopted country and belief system may revert to their traditional beliefs, values, and practices during life's major passages. Several conflicts recur repeatedly as people of diverse cultures find themselves ill and dying within the American health care system.

Decision Making

Americans and other health practitioners trained in Western medicine believe that people have a right to make decisions about their own health care. If the patient is a competent adult, clinicians are expected to consult directly with him or her about the diagnosis and treatment plan. The autonomy and privacy of the individual are basic values.

Many other cultures, however, focus on the family as a unit. They assume that relatives will be responsible for caregiving and, consequently, that they know what is best for the patient. They often see the eldest male or eldest son as the family spokesperson. Information is to be given to this person, who will share it with the family. The family makes the best decision for the patient, and this decision is reported to the health team by the family spokesperson. This isn't just what the family expects; it is what the patient expects and *values*.

Hope Versus Truth

Since autonomous decision making is so highly valued in Western medicine, being honest with the patient is also highly valued. We believe that a patient can't make informed decisions unless that person knows the truth about his or her situation.

However, *hope* is frequently more highly valued than *truth* in families who believe that they should make decisions for the patient. Hope—the belief that "everything is going to be all right"—is seen as so important to a patient's well-being that the family takes on the burden of knowing "the truth" while maintaining the patient's sense of hope. They believe that if the patient loses hope, he or she will lose the spirit needed to live.

In these cultures, maintaining hope by avoiding the truth is seen as the family's responsibility. Even doctors and nurses working in these cultures will lie to the patient, or avoid the truth, just to keep hope alive. In this ethical framework, simple respect and kindness require that a sick person be protected from the painful truth.

In some cultures, notably within Native American tribes,

what is verbalized is believed to become reality. In other words, to say that someone is dying can actually *cause* that person's death. Thus American clinicians who tell the truth can be seen as cruel and dangerous. People such as Mr. Chee are frequently offended by Western medicine's stress on advance directives and informed consent, which seem to invite and even induce death.

However, there is a culturally sensitive way to handle such situations that doesn't violate the ethical concerns of Western health care professionals. Patients can be asked to make an autonomous decision about who should be told about their test results and prognosis. They can be asked whether they want to make health care decisions for themselves or to appoint someone else. When patients assign the decision to the family, they have exercised their autonomy by giving that responsibility to someone they trust.

Comfort Care Versus Curative Care

Modern medical technology gives us powerful tools, but these tools are not always used wisely. Many health care practitioners have witnessed patients undergoing very stressful treatments with little chance of cure. Some feel guilty about causing so much pain when recovery is doubtful. This has led most clinicians to believe that there comes a time for comfort care (palliative care) instead of curative care. In fact, many clinicians—myself included—have seen medical treatments that actually hastened the patient's death. Families in denial may push physicians to continue useless treatments, and some physicians fear being sued if they refuse. It takes a courageous and compassionate physician to say, "When I became a physician, I took a solemn oath, the Hippocratic Oath. It mandates me to 'above all, do no harm.' It is time to change the focus and goal of this patient's treatment from curative care to comfort care."

Families like the Rodriguezes and Ariapours often see the decision to switch to palliative care as "giving up." This is believed to be inappropriate, if not sinful. Many cultural groups assert that no one knows the future but God and that it is our responsibility to "do everything possible" so that if God's will is a cure, we do not act against God's will. In their fervor and with good intentions, some nurses from foreign cultures or from different religious beliefs have refused to suggest palliative care.

There have also been cases where nurses in long-term-care facilities resigned, overrode a living will, or ignored the family's and doctor's orders to stop tube feedings. They believed they were being asked to starve the patient, which was against their own religious beliefs. Interfering in such a way is of course illegal, but it shows how strongly our cultural or religious ideas can drive our behavior.

The issue is further complicated, as it was in Mrs. Jones's case, when the cultural group has been victimized by racism and discrimination. The suggestion to switch from curative to comfort care can be viewed as a "cheaper" or "cost-cutting" solution—one that denies their loved one the expensive care the person deserves. Such situations require immense sensitivity.

Managing Pain

In Western medical cultures today, pain is usually seen as an unnecessary evil. Severe pain should be alleviated as quickly as possible. Patients should express their pain quietly and describe it succinctly by using a 1–10 point rating scale (or a 1–5 point scale for children, 1 being "mild discomfort" and the highest number, whether it's 5 or 10, being "excruciating"). This helps their caregivers know how to address the pain and determine whether treatment is decreasing it.

In other cultural groups, however, pain may be seen as a way to atone for one's sins, something that must be accepted on one's path through life, or as a way to build and manifest character. People who hold these beliefs may wish to tolerate more pain than their caregivers are comfortable with. They may be particularly reluctant to use narcotic pain medications, which may be even more stigmatized in the patient's ethnic group than they are in American culture at large.

Some groups are also more stoic or more expressive about pain than Americans typically are. So it's easy for caregivers to interpret the quiet of those in the first group as meaning that they are not in pain or the cries and moans of the second group as "overreactions." Unlike Americans, who have been trained to think quantitatively from an early age, these patients may also have difficulty using a point scale to measure pain. Instead, they may use metaphors or other terms to describe pain *quality*, and these may not be easily understood by their American caregivers.

Effective ways to manage pain in these situations may include obtaining language interpretation services, asking the patient to compare current pain with past pain experiences, and identifying past ways of coping with pain.

Taking the time to understand the pain experience is especially important when patients have difficulty using the 1–5 or 1–10 scale. If a patient is reluctant to use pain medications because of spiritual or ethical concerns about the purpose of pain or the use of narcotics, bringing in a pastoral counselor or appropriate faith leader can help caregivers understand and may also dispel the patient's concerns.

Appropriate Treatments

When you are sick, do you have a favorite soothing food such as chicken soup? Do you take vitamin C to ward off colds? Does a hot bath make you feel better when you feel like you are coming down with something? These are treatments many Americans find healing. However, studies show that much of their benefit comes from the *placebo effect*. This means that if you believe something is going to make you feel better, it usually does, even if there is no scientific reason why it should do so.

Everyone should remember this when they think that the cultural treatments patients choose are worthless. They may not cure, but the treatments patients choose are those that give them a sense of comfort and well-being, and they can be a helpful adjunct to more scientific treatments. The goal is to use whatever works!

Most home remedies or alternative treatments are not harmful if used appropriately, and many are now backed by some scientific evidence supporting their effectiveness. Therefore, health professionals and caregivers should tolerate and respect most natural therapies and rituals, such as the sage Mr. Chee wanted to burn. However, everyone must be informed of these treatments to avoid possibly dangerous interactions with the patient's prescribed medications or medical condition.

Some patients are reluctant to follow the recommendations of their doctors and nurses because the advice contradicts their own understanding of what is wrong with them and how it should be treated. Almost always, these sorts of problems can be resolved. Patients should be encouraged to tell their health care professionals about their concerns, and the health care team in turn should approach the situation with respect, flexibility, and creativity.

Nonverbal Communication and Etiquette

It's hard enough when patients and their health care providers speak different languages. But differing patterns of nonverbal communication and etiquette can cause even more trouble.

How much eye contact we have, the amount of space we keep between ourselves and the other person, whether or not we touch the person, our tone and the speed at which we speak—all these things relay our messages as much, if not more than, the words we use. Unfortunately, the same nonverbal behaviors carry very different messages in different cultures. For instance, in Mr. Chee's Navaho tradition, an important way to show respect is to keep silent for a time after another person has spoken. The nurses, however, misinterpreted Mr. Chee's slow speech, punctuated with silence, as a sign of depression.

In the same way, behaviors that are considered polite and friendly by some people can seem rude and offensive to others. When Mrs. Jones's nurse called her by her first name, she was trying to convey friendliness and caring. However, the patient's daughter was offended by the nurse's "disrespect."

What Can Be Done to Prevent Cultural Confusion and Conflict?

To truly help other people, we must first accept them. Unfortunately, when the person we are trying to help (or who is helping us) comes from a different cultural group, we have a strong tendency to judge that person's beliefs, values, and practices as "right" or "wrong." The first step in preventing conflicts is to remember that cultural differences are just that—*differences*. We can honor and respect them even when we don't agree with them.

We should be particularly slow to interpret nonverbal communication and etiquette as offensive. Did the person mean the behavior in the way we interpreted it, or does it mean something entirely different in his or her culture?

If you are providing care, take the time to understand the patient's cultural values or behaviors. If you are a patient or family member, tell your care providers about the beliefs, values, and practices that are important to you and the patient. If they are not respectful of your requests, discuss the problem with the supervisor or the facility's patient representative. Every professional health care organization has standards requiring care practitioners to respect their patients' cultural needs and preferences.

The best way to understand a seriously ill patient's cultural beliefs is to ask the right questions in the right way. A sensitive way to begin is by explaining why you are asking them: "When people are seriously ill, they draw on their cultural and spiritual beliefs to help them. Are there particular beliefs that are especially important to you at these times? Are there special herbs, foods, or treatments that you find helpful? Are there special things I should know about caring for your body? Removing your clothing for an examination? Helping you to the bathroom? Helping you bathe? I want to be polite and respectful to you and your family. Do you prefer to be called by your first or last name? Could you help me to know if anything I do seems rude or offensive, so I can fix it?"

You should then ask specific questions regarding decision making and care: "Some patients like to be kept informed about their test results and make their own health care decisions. Other patients prefer that their families assume this responsibility. Would you like to be kept informed and make your own decisions, or would you prefer that we discuss your care with a family member? Whom would you like to make decisions for you?" And finally: "Are there special rituals or customs I can help you keep?"

For instance, consider again the case of Mrs. Ariapour. Faced with the family's demand to keep the truth from her, the hospice nurse, John, first explored the reason for this request. He listened carefully as they explained that Mrs. Ariapour's destiny was in Allah's hands and that it was wrong to assume she was going to die just because the doctors said she would. Because they believed that the patient should not be burdened by "bad news," they felt the family should take responsibility for all necessary decisions and for the consent forms that needed to be signed.

John then explained that informed consent was necessary for hospice care to begin. He acknowledged that they both wanted the same thing for the patient—comfort and good care—although they had different ways of achieving that goal. John, the Ariapour family, and John's supervisor then negotiated how they could meet the family's cultural preferences as well as the hospice requirements. They agreed on a plan: John and an interpreter had a conversation with Mrs. Ariapour. She reported that she felt "too tired" to listen to the doctors or make decisions about her care. She said her son should take care of these things for her. John was able to document this in the chart, and the son assumed responsibility for informed consent.

When you are caring for someone of a heritage different from yours, *respect* is the operative word. The experience can be an opportunity for growth and mutual understanding in both parties.

THE BOTTOM LINE

Respecting the cultural beliefs of the dying person not only helps the patient but also enriches the caregiver's life.

THE IMPORTANCE OF
SPIRITUAL INFLUENCES

"Why me?" "Why now?" "What did I do to deserve this?" "Is God punishing me?" "What comes next?" We call on faith, religion, or other spiritual influences to provide us with answers for the unanswerable, especially in times of crisis. Spirituality infuses every aspect of our lives but intensifies greatly as death approaches, even for those who have strayed from their original faith. It is most often our spiritual beliefs that give strength, meaning, and direction during these ultimately challenging life events.

In my experience, people take great comfort in spiritual teachings that death is not the end. Their anguish and struggle seem to lessen. Spirituality also plays a powerful role in how they face illness, make health care decisions, and deal with suffering and pain. It is very important for friends and caregivers to recognize this.

DANCING SPARROW

I had stopped by the hospice inpatient unit to get some supplies when I saw one of my favorite former teammates. Sherry was having a coffee break in the dining room and waved me over to join her. Sherry is an Eastern Band Cherokee of Virginia, and she always wears her native headband. She's a highly skilled social worker and a bright, enthusiastic person, and patients and families just love her spirit. I let her know how much I missed working with her as we caught up with each other's life.

Later, as we walked down the hall together, she suddenly grabbed my arm and said, "Let's go in here. I want you to meet my *favorite* patient." As we entered the four-bed room, three of the patients started calling out: "*I'm* her favorite." "No, you can't be, *I* am." "You're both wrong, it's *me* who's her favorite." Everyone was chuckling.

Then we went over to the quiet little patient in the corner. You could see how beautiful she had been just a few years before. But now, at age forty-six, she was dying of ovarian cancer, and her face was chiseled into deep, sad wrinkles. She was tiny and fragile like a small bird, now dwarfed by the hospital bed that had become her home.

"Maggie, meet Darcy, whose real name is Dancing Sparrow. She's from the Hopi tribe, near the Grand Canyon of Arizona," Sherry said. "This is Maggie, one of the pushiest nurses I know."

"I'm so happy to meet you, Dancing Sparrow," I said, taking her hand. Despite our laughter, I could almost inhale the profound sadness that surrounded her. "Is there anything I can do for you?"

"Hold me in your heart and pray for me," she said as her eyes teared up. A bit startled by the intensity she expressed to a virtual stranger, I replied, "I surely will, Dancing Sparrow. I promise!"

As Sherry walked me to my car, she told me Darcy's story. She had left her tribe and family twenty years before, seeking opportunities in the big city. But she went from one menial job to another, sinking deeper and deeper into debt and depression. She had been in and out of a few relationships, but one partner had been abusive and the others took advantage of her. And as much as she wanted to be back home with her people, even a bus ticket was out of her financial reach.

Now she was just too sick to travel such a distance, and even if she could, there was no one to take her. She had resigned her-self to never seeing her homeland again. Sherry told me that Dancing Sparrow feared that her spirit would wander forever and would never be at peace if it was not returned to her native land.

"It really bothers me," Sherry said. "I just feel like I have to get her back home, and I don't know how." The following week she called me, very upset. Darcy had died.

A few months later I was honored and delighted to learn that I'd been named Clinician of the Year by the National Hospice and Palliative Care Organization, and even more ex-cited that Sherry was Social Worker of the Year. Both awards would be presented at the organization's annual conference in Phoenix, Arizona. I'm not a believer in coincidences, but my first thought as I called Sherry to congratulate her was of our promises to Dancing Sparrow. We both knew that somehow this trip would give us a way to fulfill them.

After the awards ceremony, our supervisor, Cinni, Sherry, and I rented a car and headed for the Grand Canyon. None of us had ever seen it before.

"What are we supposed to do when we get there?" I asked Sherry.

"I've brought some sacred tobacco for an offering," she said, "and I'm sure we'll figure out the rest. It just feels right to be taking her spirit home."

We drove around the East Rim of the Grand Canyon until we found an isolated lookout just a brief walk down from a small parking area. We walked to the rim and stood quietly for quite a few moments, awestruck. Then Sherry started to hum as she offered her tobacco to the spirits and the four directions. Her humming got louder and louder as she rocked back and forth. Cinni and I tried our best to follow her, and before you could shake a stick, we were all dancing and singing with the canyon spread out below us. It felt good getting swept up in this ritual.

"A gift from God is what he is," Mary told me on my first visit. "He was educated fancy-like here in America, at Harvard. But he came back to his homeland and married me, who had nothing more than a sixth-grade education. He saved me from a life of sorrow."

Her unabashed gratitude intensified as her life was drawing to a close. She was a timid, unassertive woman who seemed to need direction for everything she did, and Martin tenderly obliged.

The rheumatic fever that was inadequately treated in childhood had left her with a severely damaged heart and weakened kidneys. As the doctors had recommended back then, they never had children. And with Mary's unquestioning trust and adoration of Martin, their relationship seemed more like parent and child. He treasured her with a fatherly vigilance and respect that was touching to see.

As her heart slowly failed, Martin and Mary prayed together—not for a cure, but for comfort and trust in God's plan. Their religion was the backbone of their lives, and prayer threaded through each day.

One day I arrived for a routine visit with Mary to find Martin enjoying a cup o' tea with our chaplain, Jim, a priest who visited regularly and gave them great spiritual support. They both loved Jim, so Irish himself, and he and Martin were deep in conversation. After I checked on Mary, I joined them in the kitchen.

"I am stunned that Mary is still here with us," I told them. "You remember last week when we talked about all the signs she had of an imminent death?"

"Oh, indeed I do," Martin said sadly.

"She still does!" I said. "Could she be lingering for some reason? What do you think?"

Martin nodded. "I think you're right. I hate to see her hang on like this. She's barely conscious most of the time. She stopped being able to eat or drink two weeks ago, just after Father Jim gave her the Sacrament of the Sick. Just like you told me, I sat with her and told her that I'd miss her terribly, but I'd be all right without her, and I'd join her in heaven pretty soon— after all, I am eighty-seven myself! But she still just seems to linger."

"Let's go pray with her," Father Jim said. We gathered around Mary's bed and started praying. There was only a flicker of recognition in her eyelids. Father Jim spoke eloquently of what a grand wife, devoted member of her parish, and caring friend and neighbor Mary had been.

"You have lived a good life, Mary. Your work is done here on earth. Now it's time for you to go home to God. And as today is the Feast of the Queenship of Mary, your patron saint, I think today would be a grand day for you to go home to heaven."

I held my breath in shocked surprise at his forwardness. And then, together, we witnessed Mary take her last breath. I could barely believe my eyes. She died as peacefully and simply as she had lived. Certainly there were tears of sadness, but they were mixed with prayers of gratitude that she finally felt safe and free to go—not only with Martin's blessing but also with the guiding words of Father Jim. As simple as that, he gave her permission to go, and she went.

What we sometimes view as a physical problem may actually be an unfinished or unresolved spiritual matter. Again and again, I've seen the dying choose to leave when they are surrounded by the people they love, with their priest, minister, or rabbi in attendance, and all praying together. We waste our words on so many unimportant things in life—praying together with the dying (if appropriate) can be a very positive way to use our words.

THE BOTTOM LINE

Spiritual needs and influences intensify as death approaches. Addressing these needs appropriately is critically important in the holistic and compassionate care of the dying.

25

DON'T LET THE DYING

SEE YOU CRY—

And Other Myths

I like to tease my patients and families by telling them, "Emily Post hasn't touched the subjects of death and dying." However, our society does seem to have a list of dos and don'ts for the end of life. This unwritten list is composed of antiquated niceties handed down from earlier times. Sadly, these myths limit our ability to be truly caring and present during the final phase of life.

Myth: Dying People Don't Know They're Dying Unless Somebody Tells Them

Sometimes, especially early on, this may be true: the terminally ill may be unaware of or in denial about the seriousness of their condition. But typically, as they get weaker and sicker, they gradually become aware that they are dying. This realization usually starts with thoughts such as, *I might not get better.* Later on the patient will think, *I'm not getting better.* This is followed by the admission *I'm no longer able to get better.* If hospice care is the choice, this is typically the time it is sought. After that comes *I'm getting worse, and I'm going to die.* And finally the realization dawns: *I'm dying, and I'm dying* soon!

The dying person often keeps these thoughts to him- or herself. They're new and can be both painful and confusing. The patient has been heading off in one direction—toward getting stronger and getting better—and suddenly it becomes necessary to redirect and adjust.

Very ill patients often ask me, "Am I dying?"

"How do you feel?" I ask in return. "What do *you* think is happening?"

I almost always hear, "I think I'm probably going to die soon. What do you think?"

I usually hold my patient's hand and reply very gently, "I think that's possible. What are your concerns? What do we need to talk about so you're more comfortable with these thoughts? It doesn't appear to me that you're dying today."

I never use the word *kill,* which is so violent and victimizing. I would never say, for example, "This disease may kill you."

People are surprised to learn that more often than not it's the patient who tells me he or she is dying—even before I know it medically.

DAVID

David, a young man dying of AIDS, had planted bulbs around the house that he shared with his partner. He was so looking forward to spring, when they would blossom, but one day he said to me, "I don't think I'm going to be around to see those bulbs bloom."

"Are you sure?" I asked, surprised. He seemed to be doing fairly well, and spring was not far off.

"Yes," he replied.

Sure enough, a week or so later he got a raging infection and died within two weeks.

The bulbs he had planted bloomed on the day of his funeral.

Afterward, David's partner dug up six daffodils and gave them to me in a pot. I planted them in my garden. Every time I see them I think of David and how he knew more than we did.

We need to listen to people with terminal illnesses—they often have an uncanny sense of what is happening to them. I've seen and heard enough over the years to trust my patients' premonitions.

Myth: Don't Let the Dying See You Cry

Have you ever been overwhelmed by emotion and tried to stop yourself from crying? It takes a lot of energy! Sometimes it's even painful: you blink and blink, trying to stop the tears. You gulp and gulp, trying to swallow the knot in your throat, and take deep breaths to loosen the tightness in your chest. Your entire focus is on relieving your physical discomfort instead of on the patient's needs.

When you suppress your normal, natural feelings, you are also sending a powerful message to the dying person: "I can't handle your sadness or anger. Please spare me." You are not available to hear the patient share concerns such as "I'd feel better if I didn't have so much company all the time," or "I'd feel better if my wife didn't expect me to eat all the food she gives me," or "I need to talk about how my family's going to manage financially after I'm gone."

IRIS

I was the nurse assigned to Iris, a woman in her sixties, after her daughter, June, an old friend of mine, moved in to take care of her. June confessed to me that she was "keeping herself strong" so as not to unduly upset or depress her mother. "She has enough to worry about," June said. "I don't want her to worry about me as well."

One day I was in Iris's bedroom when June came in. She planned to go out that evening, and she was trying on clothes

and jewelry and asking her mother's advice about which en-
semble worked. I could tell this was a long-standing ritual between them, something they shared.

On this occasion, however, Iris was drained. She couldn't
offer her daughter her normal forthright opinions, and I could
see that June was getting more and more distressed and then irritated with her mother's vagueness and lack of response.

"Mother, pay attention," she said. "I'm asking you about
my necklace."

"It looks nice," Iris said weakly. After a number of these
weary responses, June blew up. "I don't know what I'm going to
do without you!" she said, bursting into tears. She cried and
cried, curling up in bed with her mother, talking deeply and
gently about what her mother's death would mean to her.

The tears allowed a meaningful dialogue to begin. I saw Iris
crying as well, and she began confessing to June her concern
that her daughter would be okay after her death.

"You've been acting as though this wasn't happening," Iris
said. "I've been so worried that you weren't *getting* what's going
on."

When we are brave enough to truly share our feelings with
the dying, that loving act gives them permission to share their
feelings with us.

Myth: Don't Let Anyone Talk to the Dying About What Dying Is Like

If you've ever been pregnant or spent time around pregnant
women, you know that one of the kindest things you can do
is to listen to a pregnant woman's fears and answer her questions about what it's like to give birth. Not everyone gets pregnant, but everyone dies. How can we as caregivers help the
dying if we won't talk to them about their experiences?
Denying them this causes them to feel isolated and lonely, and

your relationship may need such open discussions to achieve depth and closure.

One way into this conversation is to ask hospice caregivers or other clinicians to share their experience and information. Always be guided by the dying person. He or she may need to hear only a little at a time, or may come back to certain ideas over and over again.

To have the courage to listen and share your fears about the important life event of dying is as appropriate as discussing the fears and importance of another life event such as pregnancy.

Myth: Don't Talk to the Dying About What Your Life Will Be Like After They're Gone

We often avoid this kind of conversation, thinking that it will stir up feelings of futility and loss or force the dying to confront a reality they can't handle. But in fact, many dying people are deeply worried about how their dying will affect the lives of the people they love, and talking together about those concerns can relieve this burden and anxiety.

Reassure the dying that the people they leave behind will care for each other in the future. Tell them that their life and their memory will help the people that they're leaving behind— that they've imparted useful values and have been a source of inspiration, and that they will be remembered.

Myth: If a Widow or Widower Finds Another Love, It Dishonors the Dead Spouse

I've witnessed many dying women who acknowledged what a wonderful marriage they had, and that they loved their husband so much that the thought of him alone and lonely for the rest of his life caused them pain. And because of this, they hoped that he would find love and a good marriage again.

This loving act not only validates the husband's goodness but averts any guilt he might feel in the future if he does find another love. If done in the presence of the children, grown or not, it can also help avoid the guilt that the children can put on their father for going against their (I suspect subconscious) expectation that he should live forever as a widower. They see this as a testament to his love for their mother. This is a serious issue that often splinters families in grieving. And that is exactly what the dying mother fears.

These assurances will be deeply comforting. The dying need to know that their living *and* their dying have been meaningful to those they love and will fortify them as they continue on with their own lives.

Myth: He's Dying. We Shouldn't Set Limits. We Need to Put Up with His Bad…or Manipulative…or Demanding…or Demeaning Behavior. After All, He's Dying!

I can't tell you how often I've gone into a patient's room or pulled a chair up next to his recliner and said, "I've just spoken to your wife in the kitchen and she's exhausted and in tears. Do you *want* to be at home?"

The surprised patient replies, "Of course I do!"

"Do you want to have to go to a nursing home?" I continue.

"Absolutely not!" the irritated patient replies.

"Well, then, you're going about this all wrong," I say. "Until there's a line of people at your door who are waiting for your wife's job, I'd suggest you be nicer to her. You've been pretty demanding and mean, and if she falls apart, so do all your choices. Then you'll *have* to go into a nursing home. It's up to you."

In the silence that usually follows, I go on: "I know you're angry that this is happening to you, and I'm available, as is my team, to help you find different ways to deal with these terrible losses. But it's a mistake to take it out on the very person who is willing to care for you twenty-four hours a day, seven days a week, because there's no one else who would even consider taking on her job."

More often than not, the patient doesn't even realize how difficult he's been, and of all the hugs and thanks I get with my work, the ones I get from these relieved caregivers are the best.

Myth: If Someone Is Uncomfortable with the Process of Dying, It's Okay Not to Visit the Dying Person

Sometimes a friend or loved one won't come to visit the dying person and gives reasons such as "I don't to see him like that," or "I want to remember her the way she was," or "I hate hospitals." The message the dying person gets from this is: "Even though you're dying, you are less important to me than protecting myself from my own discomforts and dislikes." Imagine how that feels to a dying person. At the very time that he or she needs to be surrounded by the love of family and friends, you can't be bothered. Your discomfort is more important than the patient's final needs.

If you are one of these weak people, please pay attention. If it's someone else, this is what I suggest you say to the self-centered person who is behaving this way: "Who promised that you should never have to do anything you don't like to do? Who spared you from facing the pain, and often the guilt, of visiting someone who is dying? Grow up! Life involves painful and difficult things for everyone. Who determined that *you* should be spared?"

Facing your fears may very well diminish them. Regardless, you have a responsibility here. If someone has played a positive part in your life, that person deserves your attention now, as his or her life is ending.

You can tell I feel strongly about this. I've seen too many

devastated people dying too sadly waiting for someone who never came.

Myth: We Should Protect the Children and Keep Them Away. We Want Them to Remember Granddad the Way He Was.

Imagine a loving and trusting child whose grandfather is dying. One day the family's behavior changes, and this confused little one is left with sitters or neighbors for long stretches. The child knows Mommy's upset. She's crying all the time, but nobody explains why. Then the next time the child goes to Grandma's house, she's very sad and Granddad is gone—poof—just like that. And nobody talks about it.

Children in these situations are susceptible to feelings of abandonment and worry about who will disappear next—maybe Mommy or Daddy, or even the child! Children's minds are prone to imagine something far worse than what has actually occurred. With simple, clear explanations of what the child will see, the child is usually not afraid.

It's equally devastating to rob the dying person of the love and sweet attention of grandchildren. There is nothing in this universe more precious than this unique relationship. Grandkids offer us an opportunity to live life again through their innocent eyes full of love and delight, without the burdens or responsibilities of parenthood. What a comfort to be reminded that our genes, our heritage, and our hopes and dreams go forward when we no longer can. So don't keep the children away.

THE BOTTOM LINE

Old wives' tales about dying should have been buried with the old wives!

PART V

LONG ROAD . . .
GETTING WEARY

26

"I COULD DIE LAUGHING"

People often assume that dying should be a somber event and that any show of humor would be impolite and disrespectful. But my patients have taught me that if humor was part of a person's living, it should not die before the person does.

Jacob, a patient of mine, was talking with our new hospice chaplain, Tim. "My wife and I still have a good laugh together in spite of my condition, sometimes even *about* my physical changes. If I didn't keep my sense of humor, I never would have lasted this long."

"Laughter is really about living, isn't it?" Tim suggested.

"Yes, I miss having a good laugh with my friends," Jacob said. "I've got great fishing buddies, and we used to laugh our way through many weekend adventures together. Now when they visit, they walk in here like funeral directors. If I try to joke around, it makes them uncomfortable, like they're afraid to laugh. Don't they know I'm still living and would welcome the distraction?"

So why do we resist humor? Is it for fear of offending someone? Is it because we are so sad or distressed? Perhaps we feel it's irreverent. Whatever the reason, we miss an opportunity to buffer the challenges of dying.

One patient told me, "Dying can be very dull and boring. I just don't have anything interesting to offer anymore."

Bringing laughter to this negative situation is a good therapeutic intervention. Endorphins—the "happy hormones" that are your brain's version of the painkiller morphine—are released by laughter and help balance some of the sadness.

When Joyce, a hospice volunteer, asked one of my patients how well our hospice team was meeting her needs, she replied, "Very well so far. We work together, we laugh together, we cry together, and then we laugh some more."

Knowing that people die as they live, we see that funny people die with humor as they have lived with it. This leaves us with a legacy of laughter.

THE LAST LAUGH

Casey McNamara had been quite a character all his life. A cloud of laughter, like leprechaun dust, had followed him everywhere he went. His best friend and golf buddy of many years, Father Mullins, who was also his parish priest, was a stalwart support during Casey's illness. After years of battling lung cancer, Casey was now in and out of coma and seemed to be hovering near death.

His family asked Father Mullins to come to the home to say a last Mass at Casey's bedside. With his heart breaking, the priest somberly celebrated the first half of the service and then began a brief homily.

"God help us in our hour of need and grief. Casey has always been a good man, a wonderful husband and father, a dear friend . . ." He paused sadly, but then a twinkle came into his eye and he blurted out, "But not a very good golfer!"

There were giggles around the bed. Then Father Mullins became serious again.

"Help us understand how this illness could happen to one we love so, and now it's taking him away from us. Please help us understand why."

At that moment Casey opened his eyes, looked straight at his dear friend, and smiled his quirky smile.

"It's the putting up with your damn sorry jokes all these years that put me in this condition!" Then he closed his eyes and drifted back into his coma.

"Casey, I should have known the last laugh would be yours!" Father Mullins said as he and the family wiped away their tears of laughter. Casey died peacefully a few hours later, laughter having been his last gift to those he loved in life.

THE FRIENDLY NEIGHBORHOOD PHARMACIST

In the early days, hospice contracted with independent pharmacies in each of the territories we covered. These handpicked pharmacists typically went out of their way to respond quickly to our patients' special needs.

My patient Joan's husband, Stuart, had called to report that Joan was having pain problems, so I immediately went to visit her. Joan was unable to keep her pain pills down because of nausea and vomiting, so I called the doctor to update him. Together we decided to switch her to pain and nausea suppositories until we could control the nausea and vomiting. Then she could swallow her pills again. This change was the first order I called in to Joan's neighborhood pharmacy, which had just been added to the approved hospice list. The pharmacist said he would send over the drugs as soon as possible.

Just then I received a call that another patient was having a crisis, so I instructed Joan that two boxes would be delivered, and reviewed how she should give herself the suppositories. I told her I would call in a little while to see how she was doing, and could possibly return if need be.

A few hours later, I called to see how Joan was doing. The medicine had been delivered shortly after I left, but her exasperated husband said, "Heck no, her pain is worse, and now she's messing on the sheets!" I made a return visit to assess the situation. Her husband's report was indeed accurate, but there was a puzzling sweet odor coming from the bed.

I checked the pharmacy package. The box of nausea suppositories was there, and two had been used as ordered. The box of pain suppositories was also there but was still sealed, so none had been given. But why was there a third box?

Eager to please, and knowing how much his longtime patient Joan liked candy, the pharmacist had included as a treat a box of small, foil-wrapped chocolates. Two were missing!

When we finally figured out what she had done, we laughed so hard and so long that I thought both of us would need oxygen! Stuart, however, with arms full of soiled sheets and on his third trip to the laundry room, was not amused.

"Say Goodbye, Gracie"

Years ago I was called to the home of a retired postman and his wife, who suffered with Lou Gehrig's disease (ALS, or amyotrophic lateral sclerosis). I rang the doorbell and was soon greeted by a small, cheerful elderly woman with permed hair who seemed to defy her diagnosis even though she clung to a walker. She turned and gestured for her husband to introduce himself.

"I'm George," he said, "and this is my Gracie. Say hello, Gracie."

To this she replied, "Hello, Gracie!"

"George and Gracie?" I laughed. "Okay, I'm Maggie. Did you love the old George Burns and Gracie Allen show?"

"Sure, we practically lived it!" Gracie said.

It didn't take long to see that this good-natured couple loved to laugh. They both fully understood the severity of Grace's illness, yet they were committed to enjoying every moment they had left together. They also had no doubt whatever of the existence of a hereafter, and believed they would soon be reunited again in a place "without traffic jams, high cholesterol, or lines at the supermarket," as George put it.

The next time I visited, the front door swung open to reveal a face wearing Groucho Marx glasses, complete with a fake nose and mustache. The name tag read "Mary Anderson, Certified Nursing Assistant." I considered Mary a great friend, a wonderful CNA, and one of the most important members of our hospice team.

The CNA's job description included keeping patients physically comfortable, bathing them, changing the linens, tidying the patient's room, and fixing a meal. But to Mary those job responsibilities were really a conduit for bringing light, laughter, and silliness into people's lives. She was a legend in hospice, and her patients looked forward to her visits.

"You look just beautiful today, Mary," I teased, "but maybe George would lend you his razor. Why, you seem to have much more than a five o'clock shadow, and here it is only ten in the morning."

"Well, I'll just have to ask him," Mary said, stepping aside so that I had a clear view of the couch. There sat Gracie and George giggling, also disguised in Groucho glasses and mustaches. Laughing, I just shook my head.

With this couple, Mary and I played a lighthearted version of the old "good cop/bad cop" routine. When she wasn't ribbing me, she was helping them come up with new antics to surprise me.

"Why don't you just sit down and relax a bit?" George said one day, offering me a chair after I'd finished his wife's exam. Sure enough, they had put an old-fashioned whoopee cushion under the seat. I'll never forget the guffaws and giggles, with George and Gracie wiping tears of laughter from their eyes. They lived for these plots and distractions!

"You'd better watch out, Gracie. If you're not nicer to

me, I'm gonna put your bedpan in the freezer!" I joked. More laughter.

None of this negated the seriousness of Grace's illness. She was walking when I admitted her, but she would slowly lose neurological function from her toes to her nose. Two years later, she was a quadriplegic having difficulty breathing. This was hard for all of us to watch, but the laughter continued.

I arrived for a scheduled visit and noticed that George's car was gone. Finding no one around, I walked anxiously into Gracie and George's bedroom. I was shocked and embarrassed to see another person in bed with Gracie at two o'clock in the afternoon! Had I intruded on an intimate moment? The person on George's side of the bed was completely covered up by a blanket. Gracie was lying on her back with the covers pulled up to her nose. The blanket was moving to little puffs of air. Was she having trouble breathing? No...she was *laughing*! So was the other person.

Then I noticed the shoes sticking out from under the covers at the bottom of the bed. They were white sneakers—Mary's sneakers! Mary was in bed, fully clothed, with her patient, both of them shaking with laughter as I stood there with my mouth hanging open. They loved this surprise the best, and I never heard the end of it.

Through the sheer power of humor, Mary gave so many patients an extra dose of life at the end of their illnesses. She and I worked together in hospice for seven years, and she always stood out as someone who created vitality and joy, not only for our patients, but also for our sometimes loss-wearied staff. She is a true hero of mine, and one of my best teachers.

We can't control what happens to us in this life, but we certainly can choose how we respond. If we allow ourselves to embrace humor during times of tragedy as well as times of joy, our lives will be richer and more balanced.

THE BOTTOM LINE

Humor adds life to our days—and it may even add days to our life.

27

MEMORY MAKING

My eighty-eight-year-old mother sat me down one day and told me she had a "big problem." It turned out that she had been seeing blood in her stools for many years, but her sense of modesty had prevented her from telling anyone about this, even her doctor. So instead of having precancerous polyps detected and removed early during a colonoscopy, she was now facing a diagnosis of colorectal cancer.

We were all surprised and delighted that she had a positive response to a course of radiation therapy and did very well for five more years. When she eventually developed a bowel obstruction, however, we calmly talked about options.

"Surgery is the only way to remove the obstruction," I said gently. "But it probably means ending up with a colostomy bag on your side. No surgery means that it's hospice time."

It was not with great angst but rather in a matter-of-fact way, as I recall, that she told me how it was to be.

"No surgery, and that's that," she said flatly. "I'm not going back to the hospital, ever. I'm staying right here."

But this no-nonsense conversation failed to shield me from the poignancy of the question that she uttered next: "Who would have thought it would happen so soon?" By this time my mother was *ninety-three*.

We are *never* done. The inbox is *never* empty. The desk is *never* cleared. The dreams are *never* all realized, nor the projects all completed. And so I often listen to my patients and their families struggle as they rage against the injustice, inconvenience, and untimeliness of dying: "Why me?" "Why us?" "It couldn't have happened at a worse time!" Yet when was the last time you awoke and thought, *This would be a perfect day for a tragedy?* No one is *ever* ready. There is never a best time for dying, but it happens anyway. It happens to everyone; no one is spared. As my dying father pointed out, "One out of one dies."

To die is a given, but there are still choices to be made. You can spend your remaining time raging against the injustice of it all, or you can acknowledge the inevitable, mourn it, and then get down to the business of memory making. It's a difficult choice, but it's yours to make.

My "heroes of the highest degree" are those who have consciously chosen to use their remaining time to write a last chapter that reflects the glory of their life or the life of the one they love. In making their memories, they have also made mine. They recognized that it mattered that they walked this earth and that it meant something to others that they were here. They transcended being tragic victims of a terminal illness, moving on instead to celebrate the richness of their lives while becoming enlightened teachers for all who were touched by their journey. Let me share how one of my "high heroes" wrote her final chapter:

BRENDA

"The key is under the flowerpot on the front stoop," Brenda told me when I phoned to set up my first appointment. "Just give a shout when you come in, and head downstairs."

Within moments of our meeting, while my eyes were still adjusting to the darkness of the room, Brenda announced, "I need you to know, right away, that I have a lot to do and not much time left." She was barely thirty-six, tiny and gaunt, and despite her ovarian cancer, she was ferocious in her focus, her eyes gleaming with purpose.

I looked around the one-room world her older sister, Rebecca, had created for Brenda in the rec room of her home—everything within reach, everything Brenda might possibly need during the workday hours she was alone. A small dorm-size refrigerator held an assortment of her favorite snacks and drinks. It served as an end table for a large basket that was spilling over with squares of bright fabrics—the beginnings of a quilt. A colorful hand-crocheted throw discreetly camouflaged a bedside commode. Angled so as to see the small back garden of her sister's town house, Brenda's comfy double bed had become her "office with a view." She lay under the covers, propped up against many oversized pillows, surrounded by swatches of fabric, letters, and photos.

"There's less of me and more of everything else in this bed," Brenda pointed out with a smile. "It's my kingdom, and there's a great deal to do here."

The first conversation I have with a new patient quickly tells me which part of the journey she is focusing on. Brenda made it clear that her focus was not so much on the physical part of her illness but rather on "remaining comfortable and alert so I can finish some of these things I've started." She pointed to the makings of a quilt and a photo album that lay at her side.

So together we made a list of the physical problems that were slowing her down and distracting her. The list included constipation, back pain that was especially troublesome later in the day when she was tired, and sleep disturbances that drained her dwindling energy.

"This is easy," I assured her. "All of these problems will be smoothed out pretty quickly—typically in less than forty-eight hours. We will add a new medication or two and rearrange your current pain meds to better address your fluctuating pain needs. I'll get right on it!" I promised. "Now, tell me about your special projects."

"I don't want my kids to feel like I won't always be with them. And I don't want them to forget the things we've shared. I've always been pretty good about documenting our time together. I've taken so many photos since they were born, but I just never seemed to find the time to make more than this one album."

She handed me the huge photo album with page after page of shots of her two children: Jessie from birth to ten, and Adam from infancy to eight. The images were playful and sweet: painted faces with snaggletooth grins; Jessie lying in the snow-covered front yard, making an angel with her little arms and legs, surrounded by the boot-stamped message: "I love Mom"; Adam crouching with a bat for that dreamed-of Little League home run, his helmet wider than his thin shoulders; a large Brenda-pumpkin laughing with a Jessie-witch and an Adam-Batman at her side on Halloween. Every family milestone was documented and lovingly displayed.

My heart felt like a cinderblock had been dropped into it. I was struggling to swallow away the tightness in my throat when Brenda said, "I've had more joy than anybody deserves, for every minute since these two were born! Now I've got to make sure they have everything they need to go on without me."

"Where are they?" I asked.

"I'm really blessed with good choices for them," she replied. "Six months ago, when it became clear I wasn't going to beat this damned cancer, two of my best friends, Judy and Rich Meyer, came forward and asked to be their guardians. They were *eager* to welcome them into their homes and families. These are people I trust and who have known Jessie and Adam since they were born. They all helped me when I struggled as a single mom.

"They are really loving, dedicated parents, and we've shared more holidays and important events with them than I can count. Judy is a stay-at-home mom who's been the leader of Jessie's Girl Scout troop for some time. Adam never knew his father, so Judy's husband, Rich, became a kind of surrogate dad long ago."

As she spoke, my eyes scanned the numerous framed photos that decorated the room, wondering if there might be some evidence of the children's real father. Brenda had not mentioned why he was absent from their lives, and I didn't ask. My patients allow me to experience their lives layer by layer, in their own time, and I have learned to respect that. Sooner or later, I am told what I need to know. I made a mental note of all of this to share with my social work teammate, Maureen.

Brenda's eyes had filled with tears of gratitude, and she paused, deep in thought. Then she let out a giggle that broke her sadness.

"One morning Adam announced one of his main reasons for deciding where he should live." She changed her voice to imitate her son's and said, " 'The Meyers' dog, Wimpy, likes us and lets us snuggle with him for a long time when we're sad and don't want the other kids to know.' Aren't kids so real and smart?" Brenda marveled.

"I never thought of that—having a free grief therapist at home all the time!"

She went on, "They continued to live with me for the next month and a half, but spent two nights a week with the Meyers. Then everything sort of fell apart and I just didn't have the strength to take care of them. I was also in so much pain, and I didn't want my kids to see me that way." She was quiet for a moment, seeming again to remember.

"I really hope I can finish these books so they have a record of the many fun times we shared," she said at last, her voice trailing off.

"Where are they right now?" I asked.

"They're living with the Meyers in our old neighborhood.

They're still in the only school they've ever attended, so there is some continuity for them. They are with all their old friends. Unfortunately, it just wasn't an option for them to be here at my sister's until I . . ." She didn't need to say what we both knew was inevitable. "And there wasn't anybody closer to home who could take on my care needs.

"So here I am, fifty miles away, being treated like a queen by my sister and her husband. The Meyers bring the kids to me every weekend, and my boss has given the kids phone cards with *huge* amounts on them, so they can call me anytime they want from anywhere." She half smiled. "I think this is as good a transition as possible for them and for me." Her brisk, efficient tone had returned.

Then Brenda stopped and gazed off for a long few minutes as her eyes filled with tears. "But this whole thing stinks, doesn't it?"

I put my arms around her as I felt the sting of my own tears and murmured, "Yes, it does. It really, truly does."

We gently rocked back and forth for a while, holding each other. Not spotting any tissues nearby, I reached in my nurse's bag and produced two packaged four-by-four-inch squares of gauze. We laughed as we honked out our grief, and Brenda said, "Thank goodness for soft tissues! If I had to use this gauze all the time, I'd have a nose like Rudolph!"

I silently wondered if I had the emotional fortitude to hear any more that day, but I still wanted to know more about her goals and how I could help her with them. I asked, and she went on.

"Well, first of all, I sold our house and have just about finished setting up a trust for my children's care. My boss has been great. Did I tell you that I'm a paralegal? He refused to let me retire. I'm just out on disability, so I have some income and I can still use the company services. The lawyers at work have been helping me free of charge! Isn't there an amazing amount of goodness in this world when you allow it to happen by asking for help?" She paused for a few moments. "People can be so basically kind and decent," she murmured.

"So what's next on your list?" I asked.

"The next big project is the quilts. The kids said they would most miss my hugs, so I'm making the quilts so they can wrap them around themselves when they need my hugs and when they go to sleep at night.

"Jessie's will have me as her angel in the middle, and the words 'Mom loves me always and watches over me forever!' This will be surrounded by our favorite photos, which I need to have transferred onto the cloth squares.

"Adam preferred a superhero theme, so I'll be 'Wonder Woman Mom' in the middle, swooping down to help him, surrounded by our special pictures together and the same message. What do you think?" I was speechless, so she went on, "It occurred to me that they may get teased if they have these on their beds in college, so I'm doing the reverse side in various patterned squares of their favorite colors, just plain—so no one needs to know about our secret hugs!" She seemed triumphant.

"Then," she continued, "I need to divide this one family album into two and add the extra photos that didn't make it in yet, so they can each have their own. I doubt they'll live together forever!" She chuckled.

Suddenly I had an idea to help her hurry her projects into fruition, and Brenda was delighted with it. I picked up the phone and requested a volunteer who had experience in quilting, sewing, and photography. Of course my hospice had such a person, Barbara, who was willing and eager to start right then and there.

I never cease to be dazzled by the rich talents and kindness embodied by hospice's volunteers. These men and women contribute so significantly to making hospice what it is, and we couldn't do our good work without their magic and support. They handle many of the social needs of our patients.

Over the next weeks the chaplain and Maureen, the social worker, collaborated very closely with the hospice that serviced the area where the children were living, so that spiritual, psychological, and emotional support would be available to Jessie and Adam throughout the course of Brenda's illness. Brenda took great comfort in knowing that special grief counseling, specific to their ages and needs, would be continued for thirteen months after she died. They could even attend a summer camp, run by the hospice bereavement team, for kids who had suffered the loss of a parent. By the children's accounts, they were actually grateful that they could talk about their feelings openly and by e-mail with other kids who were having similar experiences and feelings. Oftentimes children feel so alone—to them it can seem as if no other child has ever lost a mother, father, or sibling.

It was during one of their sessions that the children said that they wanted to surprise their mom with some special outings. Together with Maureen, they decided on short excursions that would be of particular interest to them and not be too taxing for their mother. Maureen, with the help of a volunteer and others on our team, arranged brief excursions that the family could share once a week. A limo service was donated to pick them up, along with Brenda's wheelchair, and drive them into Washington, D.C., for a special, private White House tour. A local ambulance company donated a van ride to a pumpkin farm for Halloween pumpkin picking. Brenda's company sent tickets for a production of *Oliver* at a nearby dinner theater. And of course, many, many photos were taken as these memories were being made so that the children would have them to treasure forever.

Brenda reported to me later that both Jessie and Adam felt an enormous sense of grown-up pride that they had actually managed to surprise her with their special outings. And once again, I was reminded that there is room for great joy and pride in the face of great tragedy and loss.

Between outings, Brenda's days were spent continuing her work on her projects with the help of Barbara, the volunteer. After several weeks, though, the trips became too difficult to manage. Brenda was deteriorating and sleeping quite a lot. As her disease progressed, her strength started to decline, and double vision developed. She became frenzied. "I haven't stitched my messages, and now it's getting impossible!"

At this point, Barbara offered to bring her own sewing machine to Brenda's house so that the messages could be machine-embroidered under Brenda's watchful direction. Another volunteer scanned the photos from the family album onto a disc. When she told the copy center what she was trying to do for a dying young mother (the patient's and family's identity are never revealed), they printed the pictures on high-quality cotton fabric free of charge.

While the quilts were being completed, Jessie and Adam each received their own copy of the family album at a special family gathering. With great sensitivity, Brenda had asked the Meyers to start adding pictures of the kids with their "new family" into each album so she could see them. "Those albums shouldn't end when I do," she said. "It's so important for me to see them move into a good and loving future while I can still cheer them on. My dying will certainly wound them, but I can't let it cripple them forever." I was thunderstruck by her insight, courage, and amazing love.

The last weekend that Jessie and Adam visited their mother, it was obvious that Brenda would die very soon. She was comfortable, occasionally confused, but drifty-dreamy and sleeping most of the time. Despite all this, she awoke bright-eyed and mentally clear to present the children with their quilts and witness their delight as they wrapped themselves snug inside. They hugged her, tearfully said their goodbyes, and told her how much they would love her forever. They wished her a good trip "to heaven to be with other happy angels," and they promised to watch for the brightest twinkling star in the night skies, which she had told them would be her looking down on them.

She died peacefully in her sister's arms two days later, her work done.

It's impossible to count the hearts that were positively affected and changed by Brenda's creative and loving way of helping her children go on in life without her. The cancer may have caused her death, but it couldn't rob her of the spirit that continues to affect the lives she graced.

THE BOTTOM LINE

The dying can spend their precious time raging against and fighting their illness, or they can choose to celebrate life while making final and powerful memories.

28

"IT FEELS LIKE WE'RE LOSING HER BEFORE SHE DIES!"

The process of dying and losing life is the reverse of be-ing born and gaining it. As babies attach to their fami-lies and mature from dependency to independence, they move out into the world and add layer upon layer of abilities, skills, and interests to their lives. The opposite is true for someone who faces a terminal diagnosis, progressing illness, and ap-proaching death. The person pulls away and detaches from this life in stages, often very gradually.

Imagine dropping a pebble into a still pond and watching the rings go out from the center. As we die, the rings come back in. Interests diminish as the patient becomes less attached to the outside world. Professional achievements, social skills, physical appearance, the state of the household—all become less important, until they may not matter at all.

While such changes may be hard for the healthy to imagine, this acceptance of the dying process and release from these con-cerns can be a kind of freedom for the dying person. Finally the only things that matter are comfort, being with the people the patient loves, knowing that loved ones are doing all right and will continue to do so after the person has died, and dying "right." This detachment and withdrawal are normal parts of the process of dying.

To put it another way, it no longer matters to the dying what is happening in the world, even if they were always avid observers of the news. Those brisk dinner-table debates over national politics become a thing of the past. Soon news of town and neighborhood happenings brings just a vague smile; eventually even the interactions downstairs become unimportant. Only comfort and love from caregivers elicits a grateful smile or nod and a sense of peace.

The family and friends who want to please and entertain the dying person are often upset and frustrated by this pulling away and lack of response. So they try harder and harder, jumping through higher and higher hoops to find the gift, food, or conversation that might elicit a happy or enthusiastic response. They are often disappointed.

SHIRLEY

The door was always left ajar in anticipation of my visit, so I was surprised to find it locked. When I rang the bell a second time, I heard a frenzy of clattering pans from the kitchen.

"My goodness, Trudy, what in the world are you up to?" I called out. The smell of freshly made cookies was enticing. "And by the way, the door's locked, if you were wondering why I was standing on this side of it," I said, familiar with Trudy's ready sense of humor.

"Oh, fiddle!" she cried. "I didn't mean to lock you out, Maggie. Hold on. I'll be right there."

"Look at you," I chided when she let me in. "Sit down here! You look like you're ready to explode. Did you take your blood pressure medication this morning? Remember, I only allow one patient per address!" I teased.

She nodded breathlessly as she flopped into her mother's favorite wingback chair.

"You're a picture!" I laughed—she was usually the pin-perfect minister's daughter. I took her wrist as if to hold her hand, subtly checking her pulse instead. "Where's Shirley?" I asked.

"Mama's sleeping down the hall, as usual," Trudy said,

sighing and shaking her head. "Seems like that's all she does anymore."

I glanced around the antique-filled living room. Vases of fresh flowers from the garden sat on every doily-covered surface. "Is somebody getting married in here today?"

"Worse than that, I'm afraid." She sighed again. "The church ladies are coming for tea."

"So *that's* why you're in such a state!" I said. "Whose idea was this?"

"Ida Mae stopped by yesterday and was concerned that Mama's sleeping so much. She said she's depressed and needs some excitement and stimulation. Ida let me know that she's very good at diagnosing such things," she said, rolling her eyes. "I felt awful, like she was criticizing the care I've been giving my mother." A wave of exhaustion seemed to wash across her face. "By this morning, it seemed like she'd called every woman in the whole darn congregation! So the ladies' social club is coming for tea in three hours. Tomorrow evening the chorus will serenade Mama, and then the bell ringers are scheduled for the next day. I'm trying to clean the house and fix some cakes and cookies to pass around."

"That's very kind and thoughtful of your friends," I said. "You are blessed with so many caring people around you. But I think it's way too much for both of you at this point. Remember when we talked about how your mother would sleep more and more and gradually detach from everyone?" I asked.

"I do remember, now that you mention it," she said. "I've just been so busy with the day-to-day things that I didn't think much about the changes until Ida Mae came and seemed so shocked. Mama didn't even seem to care that she was here. Then I really felt awful."

"Well, the name of that syndrome is *normal*. You need to know that I think you're doing a fabulous job with your mother, especially because you're not making her try to keep up with your expectations," I said, patting her shoulder. "So let's think of another way for these good church friends to contribute."

After some discussion and a few diplomatic phone calls, the tea party was called off. Instead, a special prayer service would be held for Shirley at the church the following Sunday. The congregation would pray, the chorus would sing, the bell ringers would ring, and the social group would provide baked goods and tea after the service. One of our volunteers sat with Shirley at home so that Trudy could attend the service. A church deacon videotaped the entire service, with many of Shirley's friends sending love and greetings to her.

"The tape is wonderful," Trudy later told me. "When Mama is awake and clearheaded, we watch it together—she enjoys it so. When she gets tired, we stop. Then we watch the rest later. Their kindness means the world to both of us."

Just as a newborn baby becomes distressed by too much stimulation and needs lots of sleep and close family time, so Shirley's life had pulled back to the same simple needs she'd had when she was born. As she neared death, she simply did not have the strength to waste on a roomful of people vying for her attention, and she would have been too exhausted to make small talk or even listen to the stories exchanged. Once her daughter and friends were able to understand that this was normal and not take it personally, they could find other ways to express their love.

THE BOTTOM LINE

Know that the dying are not pulling away from you. To pull away and detach is normal. Be where they are, and know that love transcends all and never ends.

29

OUR PETS MAY KNOW MORE
THAN WE DO

A veterinarian once told me, "You'll never get close to a person until you first win their dog's trust." Dogs, more than any other pets, are very protective of their owner and family, and even more so when the one they are devoted to is ill. They pick up on the anxiety and grief in the home, and they are on high alert.

This can be a problem when darling little Poopsie decides the home care clinician is a threat. I would have significant damage to both legs were it not for the knee-high leather boots I was wearing the day Mr. Romero's three beloved dachshunds turned into Cujo 1, 2, and 3. And all I had been doing was innocently wrapping a blood pressure cuff around Granny's arm.

To prevent this, the home care clinician, chaplain, and volunteer should spend a little time initially with both dog and owner so that the pet understands they are friends, not intruders. During the rest of the visit, it's generally best to put the animal outside or in another room.

Of course, warnings aside, your pets also bring their ability to love unconditionally and devotedly to the very end. For many people it's calming and soothing to have a pet nearby. Much research validates what pet owners already know: that pets have a healing effect on humans both mentally and physically, from reducing anxiety and improving mood to helping lower blood pressure and cholesterol. Horses have provided therapeutic relief to disabled children and adults. Dogs have even been specially trained to anticipate seizures and maneuver their owner to protection before they occur.

Recognizing the therapeutic value of pets has led many nursing homes to offer programs in which pets and their owners make visits to sick patients. As another veterinarian explained to me, "The relationship between pets and humans is one of pure love. The affection received from a cat or a dog can only bring joy." Pets also have an innate sixth sense that can offer caregivers valuable clues about a patient's well-being.

SCOTT

Ten-year-old Scott had an inoperable brain tumor, but he had stayed in school as long as possible. Now, however, he could no longer muster the mental focus and physical energy required to get through a day of fifth grade, and he became my patient at home.

Despite what Scott had already lost, he remained cheerful and still had the playful attitude of a normal, healthy kid. Being at home meant he could delve into the academic subjects that interested him the most, be close to his family, nap intermittently, and get as much joy as possible out of each day.

On my second visit we played "indoor tennis" on the walls of the family room with a soft yellow foam ball and two large foam paddles. He wore an eye patch to control the double vision that plagued him, but he didn't let it slow him down.

"Isn't this fun?" he asked. "Mom would *never* have allowed me to do this before I got sick." He tipped his head to the side to have a better view of me despite his eye patch.

"Well, Little Dude," I said using the nickname he liked so much, "it's such a hard job being sick, and you're doing it so well. I think you deserve some extra privileges, don't you?"

"Guess so," he said, and slammed the ball with such force that it careened off three of the four walls. Despite his poor balance, he tried to dance around making the V-for-victory sign with his chubby fingers. His excitement roused his puppy from her sleep on the couch. She bounded across the room and wove herself between his legs, almost knocking him over.

"Couldn't you come every day?" he asked me. "I'm bored since I stopped going to school. My sister doesn't get home from junior high until four o'clock, so I don't have anyone to hang out with except for Mom and Missy, my one true friend," he said, hugging the little terrier. She was never far off, and whenever he rested, she nestled on the bed between his knees.

Besides his devoted puppy, Scott's great interest was aerospace and rocket ships. His mother spent hours reading to him everything she could find on this topic. His father bought him boxes and boxes of Legos to keep him supplied as he worked on building the large elaborate rockets they read about. Every shelf and windowsill in the house displayed his detailed efforts, and he was quite proud of what he was able to do "even with this stupid eye patch on!"

As the tumor in his brain continued to grow, Scott became weaker and dangerously unsteady on his feet. He spent a few weeks in a wheelchair, but eventually he was safe only in the hospital bed, which had now become the center of the family room. Missy rarely left her post between his knees, and as Scott got sicker, she left him for only a few minutes to go outside and relieve herself before yapping to come back in. Scott's sister, Tracy, would let her in and lift her up into his arms.

As the weeks went by, Scott seemed to become increasingly anxious. "I know I'm not going to get better, but I don't know anything about this dying stuff!" he said one day. "I'm scared of what it will be like. Will I feel lonely?" My team social worker, Joanne, and the chaplain, Laird, stepped up their visits with Scott and his family. I also suggested that Scott's mother read aloud to him a book called *Closer to the Light* by Dr. Melvin Morse, a pediatrician who cares for seriously ill and dying children. It is filled with stories his young patients told him about their near-death experiences and other visions that comforted them as they lay dying. Scott was noticeably calmer after that and started sleeping more.

His mother called one day and asked if the social worker and I could make a visit together.

"Scottie has something important to tell you." She sounded so upbeat, I was relieved.

"Of course!" I said. "I'll check with Joanne, but I'm sure she can come as well."

We arrived to find Scott sitting upright in the bed, eyes bright and cheeks so flushed with excitement I initially thought he might have a fever.

"Nana came to see me last night!" he exclaimed. His beloved grandmother had died four years earlier. "She said she was coming to get me and we would go to heaven together in a *rocket ship*!" He was bursting with excitement.

"Wow, Scottie, that's so great!" Joanne said.

"Oh, Little Dude, I'm so happy that Nana came to you. I was really hoping something wonderful like that would happen soon." I gave him a big hug.

"Yeah," he said. "Now I know Nana will show me how to do it, and it's going to be so cool! *A rocket ship!*"

We found his mother weeping in the kitchen. "He's worse, isn't he?" she asked with tears running down her face.

"Physically, yes, he's deteriorating," I said gently. "But emotionally, spiritually, and mentally he's *much* better. You can see that, can't you?"

She nodded and buried her face in her tissues. "I don't want him to be afraid like he was, but I just can't bear to lose him."

A week or so later, on New Year's Eve, the streets were still icy from a recent snowfall. I was hoping I wouldn't have to do much driving, but the phone rang just as I was finishing my breakfast.

"I know you'll think I'm crazy," Scott's father said, "but Missy is very agitated. She just won't settle down. Something seems different, but we just can't put our finger on it."

Uh-oh, I thought. Devoted dogs often seem to have a heightened awareness of what's happening to their owner. *I wonder what Missy knows that we don't.*

"How about if I come over and see what's going on?" I asked.

"Great!" he replied. "We were hoping you'd say that."

I was aware of a change the minute I walked into the family room. Missy was indeed out of sorts and looked at me as if to say, *Do something!* as she paced around Scott's bed and licked his face. There was an eerie feeling of unseen activity or busyness in the room, where the Christmas tree was still surrounded by Lego sets.

I was sure that Scott would die very soon. Something else was going on, but what? I stood by Scott's bed and stroked his hand.

"Hey, Little Dude, are you okay?" He gave me a dreamy smile as he struggled to answer me through the soft, thick fog of semi-coma, but then he sank back down into it. I stood for a long time just looking at him, watching his eyes dart back and forth under his nearly closed lids, trying to figure out where he was and what was happening to him.

"Scottie!" I gently called. "Is there anybody else here in this room with you besides Mom, Dad, Tracy, Missy, and me?" His eyes shot open and darted around the room, as if searching.

"Sweetie, is Nana here with us?" I whispered. I can only describe his face as beatific and full of joy and love as he nodded and looked from his mother to his father and then to Tracy. His gaze paused briefly on me, then swept past and settled for a long moment on someone unseen to us. Was it Nana?

Scott's smile slowly faded. We were all weeping openly as we said our farewells. Missy was softly whining as she walked up the bed to Scott's face and licked it many times. Then she jumped off the bed, never to return.

His final coma lasted about two hours, and the family and I sat by his side the whole time. At one point Tracy said thoughtfully, "You know, Nana was there for him, so he'll be there for us." She went on, "I'll never be as afraid of dying as I was before."

What a wonderful tribute, I thought, *and what a wonderful gift Scott has given us all.*

Later, Scott's father thanked me. "You must be very intuitive to have decided to come when you did," he said.

"I'd love to have you believe that about me," I said with a smile. "But as soon as you described Missy's behavior on the phone, it was a red flag. She knew that something important was happening. The thanks really go to her."

THE BOTTOM LINE

Animals can be helpful members of the caring team and sometimes can be aware in ways that humans are not.

30

THE "FINAL GIFTS" OF NEARING

DEATH AWARENESS

Sometimes hours, days, or weeks before a patient dies, he or she may say something or behave in a way that doesn't immediately make sense to us. Professional and family caregivers alike are quick to label this behavior as "confused" or "delirious."

Why are we so quick to label problems? It's because once they're labeled, we feel we know how to respond. It's as if the label gives us a recipe to follow; with clear directions, our comfort level and confidence increase.

Doctors and nurses have fancy medical labels: delirium, hallucinations, changes in sensory perception, encephalopathy, metabolic imbalance, hypercalcemia, dementia, confusion, untoward drug reaction, and so on. They may do X-rays and blood work. They might add, subtract, or adjust medications, call in a specialist, or order more tests.

Families have labels of their own: "Dad's out of it," "Mom's living in the past," "Aunt Tillie's losing her buttons," "Uncle Willie's in la-la land." They may react by ignoring the confused person, trying to reorient him, distancing themselves from him, or treating him like a child. Or they may simply decide it's time to consider a nursing home, "since he doesn't know what's going on anymore anyway."

All these caregivers are missing something vitally important. They are so busy labeling the person and dismissing his or her seemingly incoherent attempts to communicate as "crazy talk" or gibberish that no one is actually listening to the words and watching the behavior of the dying person.

Yet underlying this obscure and often symbolic language and behavior may be critically important messages—messages that the dying are trying to send us about what the experience is like for them. These can include such physical gestures as reaching out for someone or something unseen to us, waving the arms, or indicating a need to reach for someone who has already passed away.

This is a powerful opportunity to learn about a process that we ourselves must experience someday. As difficult as it is, and as much as we resist it, having this knowledge can increase our sense of control, diminish our fear, and provide us with great comfort.

In 1981, a colleague, Patricia Kelley, and I started to explore the fascinating and puzzling behavior we noticed in our patients. We collected our own stories and those of the other clinicians in our hospice program, and when we put them together, we were struck by what they indicated: rather than being confused or delirious, our patients seemed to have developed a special awareness of things we did not know as death approached. We named this phenomenon "nearing death awareness," and it became the inspiration for our book *Final Gifts*.

Nearing Death Awareness: "What I Am Experiencing"

Our patients' language and behavior fell into two very specific categories. In the first, our patients were trying to tell us what the experience of dying was like for them. They were telling us that they were getting ready to go somewhere not on this earth. They talked wondrously of seeing a place of great beauty or joy, a place unseen by us. They showed us with their behavior and words that they knew when their death would occur, even if we didn't know. In our presence, they often talked with and were comforted by people we could not see.

LALANI: "THAT'S GEORGE'S CHAIR"

After I did a presentation on nearing death awareness in Hawaii, the hospice clinicians were eager to tell me the story of one of their youngest patients, Lalani, who was dying with leukemia. Lalani was only five, so she didn't have a clear understanding of dying and the finality of death. She simply knew when she felt good and when she didn't.

Her widowed grandmother, Ula, had raised her from birth, as her mother was troubled and unable to handle the responsibility of a child. Ula adored this little girl who occupied the center of her universe and heart, and she worked very hard to hide the profound grief she already felt at the thought of losing her.

Lalani's hospital bed was in the center of the living room, and Ula slept in a big, reclining lounge chair pushed right up against it, so she could reach out to soothe the little one if she was restless.

But one day as Ula started to sit down, Lalani said, "No, Grammy, you can't sit there. That's George's chair!"

Ula, chuckling over this imaginary friend, said, "Oh, baby girl, I'd never want to take George's chair away. I'll sit over here."

As the week progressed, Lalani talked more and more about George. He would come and visit her, hold her and rock her to sleep, and stay to watch over her. She *loved* George!

Ula was becoming alarmed. Perhaps this wasn't just an imaginary friend; maybe Lalani was getting sicker and more confused. One night the child was particularly fretful and Ula's usual ways of easing her all failed, so, grabbing at any distraction she could, Ula reached for the large, multigenerational family photo album. Lalani always loved looking at pictures of herself as a baby and toddler and was mildly curious about the pictures of her mother, but she'd previously shown no interest in the older family members. This night, cradled in Grammy's lap, she was unusually attentive; she wanted to see not only her own pictures but also her mother's baby pictures and Grammy's wedding pictures. Ula kept turning the pages, going further back into the past, grateful to feel Lalani's small, frail body so relaxed in her arms. Suddenly, at the turn of a page Lalani had never seen before, the girl sat up and pointed excitedly at a yellowed picture of a mustached man, dapper in his pinstripe suit and top hat.

"There's George!" Lalani exclaimed, clapping her little hands. "George, it's George!"

Ula's heart started to pound. The man Lalani was pointing to was Ula's much-loved godfather, who had watched over and loved her deeply as a small child. There was no way Lalani could have known him. His name was indeed George, and he'd died sixty years before, when Ula herself was five years old.

Ula told me later, "I thought the hardest part of losing her would be knowing that I couldn't rock and hold her anymore. But now I know that she will go from my arms into George's. He is watching over both of us and is waiting to hold her and rock her as he did me when I was small. She will be in good hands. It helps."

Nearing Death Awareness: "What I Need"

Our dying patients also made requests of us to help them "get on with this journey." They asked us to understand, and be at peace with, their awesome ability to choose the moment of death. They asked us to help them reconcile their relationships with other people, with their Almighty, and with themselves. They asked for our help because something wasn't reconciled or something was unfinished.

Having worked with more than two thousand families of every race, class, and religious belief, I know better than to have any preconceived ideas about how a patient or a family will respond to me or what they will need from me. Each journey is unique.

I also cannot predict what a patient's unfinished business might be, but I can be pretty sure that there is some. It often emerges in the form of dreams or high emotions around relationships that don't have closure or resolution. As much as I wish a peaceful death full of reconciliations and meaningful experiences for each of my patients, it's not *my* dying. My job is to facilitate their journey and help them make it as uniquely their own as their living has been.

One of my patients chose to die in her barn, surrounded by her beloved horses, and her children respected her wishes. With their good care, she did so peacefully and without fear.

Another patient was a lifelong religious scholar, yet his every moment as death approached was filled with uncertainty, anger, and trepidation about what awaited him after death. And I have witnessed everything in between.

MRS. WASHINGTON: "I HAVEN'T GOTTEN ENOUGH CANNING DONE"

The second door on my left stood out in the bleak project hallway. It was painted a sunny yellow, and the plastic numeral 4 was surrounded by childish, happy paintings and the words "Welcome, Friends." I rang the small buzzer and was greeted by Mrs. Washington herself, who ushered me in with a warm "Come in, darlin'." More children's paintings adorned Mrs. Washington's narrow hallway, and the living room walls were nearly covered with framed photos of smiling faces, young and old.

"I appreciate you coming and checking on me, though I ain't goin' anywhere anytime soon, you can be sure of that! I still have too many little ones to look after!"

Mrs. Washington chatted easily and smiled often. She understood full well the nature of my visit, but she was too busy enjoying life to focus on the negative.

"Babysitting your grandchildren?" I asked, handing her a stuffed rabbit I'd found beneath the couch.

"Sweetheart, all the kids in this neighborhood call me Granny! I've babysat for more kids than I can remember," she reported with pride. "Now, I haven't taken care of too many babies since I got sick. They're a bit more to handle, but the older ones still come round and brighten my day. I just love kids. And I have plenty of my own, of that you can be sure!"

"Just how many is 'plenty'?" I asked, enjoying her spunkiness and spirit.

"Let's just say a lot. You'll see for yourself, anyhow. My front door gets as much use as a subway turnstile!"

In her seventy-nine years Mrs. Washington had clearly touched many, many lives. News of her illness had spread through the housing project and neighborhood. The prayers and constant attention she received helped to keep her spirits high, and perhaps even delayed the onset of more severe symptoms.

Mrs. Washington had colon cancer that had metastasized to her liver. I visited twice a week to check on her and inform her six grown children, who were all very caring, about the progression of her illness and what to do for her needs as they arose. Mrs. Washington's health declined gently, reminding me of the volume being gently turned down on a radio.

However, by the third month of my visits, Mrs. Washington not only could no longer babysit but also needed constant supervision herself because of the mild confusion and increased sleepiness she was experiencing. Even with the use of a walker, she had fallen twice, bruising a wrist and then a hip. This fiercely independent woman, who for so long had taken care of others, suddenly needed others to care for her.

Now I learned just how unusual this family was. They were gifted at understanding what was happening to their mother, and they accepted her physical changes without resentment or fear. They were often one step ahead of me, which is unusual! The weaker she got, the more they were there. Her three daughters and three sons were all employed and most had children of their own, but they seemed to turn up exactly when they were needed. I don't believe they ever talked about a schedule to care for their mother. Rather, it was a schedule of instinct. The son who was an auto mechanic would arrive to fix a leak in the kitchen while a daughter cleaned or cooked. One child would show up with new medications while another was bringing in groceries. They were so self-directed, I hardly ever had to make a suggestion.

With her bed in the middle of the living room, Mrs. Washington was able to monitor all these comings and goings, watch her favorite programs with whoever was reclining on the couch, and enjoy every meal with those sitting at the table while she sat comfortably in her bed only feet away.

As time passed, Mrs. Washington came to be in bed full time. When a liver is failing, toxins that are normally excreted are retained and build up in the body. The patient sleeps more and more and even when awake seems very drifty-dreamy. This is actually a compassionate process that happens naturally. It's as if the liver puts out its own anesthesia and the patient becomes very relaxed, peaceful, and pain-free.

As Mrs. Washington weakened, her voice became softer, almost whisper-like. This is not uncommon in the dying, and I have often reflected on how it forces the caregiver to lean in to listen, as if it were part of the plan to draw us closer to those who are dying. This allows an intimacy to develop that the caregiver may not have been comfortable with earlier on. It also forces us to listen with an intensity that the busyness of our day-to-day lives rarely affords us.

In her last weeks Mrs. Washington seemed as tiny as a newborn colt, her weight loss exaggerating every joint and bone. Numerous pillows, many hand-sewn by Mrs. Washington's loved ones, supported her tender places.

One day I walked into her room and was almost startled by her beauty—her face had become so defined that her high cheekbones seemed to be carved out of mahogany. Her granddaughter Addie was painting her nails bright red, while Addie's sister, Jewel, had undone her usual bun, so that her pure white hair hung straight down almost to her waist. She looked like a queen, and I said so.

Then I added, "I can see your girls are taking great care of you, Mrs. Washington, but is there anything else *I* can do for you today?"

She whispered, "I haven't gotten enough canning done for the winter." The girls and I looked at each other, puzzled, though for different reasons. I could see by the girls' expressions that they thought their grandmother had lost touch with reality. My puzzlement came from the fact that comments like this typically indicated unfinished business. But this sweet woman's every need and emotion seemed to be well taken care of.

"How much more canning do you have to do?" I asked.

Mrs. Washington flashed me a look that seemed to say, *I'm just too sick to explain such a thing to someone from the city. You clearly couldn't understand.* Then she said softly, "You don't think I'm leaving this family without making sure they've all got enough to eat, do you?"

I said, "Oh, Mrs. Washington, I understand. Let's see what we can do to help you finish up."

I walked into the kitchen, where Ruth, the girls' mother, and their aunt Naomi were preparing dinner. "Mrs. Washington seems to feel something's missing," I said, "but she isn't able to really explain what that might be. She said, 'I haven't finished all the canning. I can't leave my family without enough to eat.' What could that mean? Is there something unfinished, something the family needs before she dies?"

The two sisters started looking at each other with a loaded expression, as if they had been caught—or as if to say to each other, *Don't give it away.*

I had been in and out of that house for months, on very friendly terms, and had seldom witnessed such a complete, strong sense of family as I did with Mrs. Washington's relatives. But at that moment I realized that some family secret was rearing its head, and it probably would not allow Mrs. Washington to rest peacefully until it was resolved.

"No offense," I said, "but you two look like cats with mouthfuls of feathers and you expect that I'm not going to wonder where the canaries went." They started laughing but still said nothing.

"Come on, one of you—out with it, if you think it might help her." More looking back and forth, wondering who would spill the beans. Finally, Ruth, the eldest daughter, spoke.

"Okay, there's another sister, but she's done so many rotten things that the family won't speak to her anymore."

"You mean there's another one of you?" I couldn't believe no one had mentioned her. "Who is she? Where is she? What did she do that could have gotten this incredibly loving family to banish her from your lives?"

"Janella's just no good, believe me. Nothing could come of Mama seeing her. None of us has seen her in years," Naomi said flatly.

Ruth went on, "Janella borrowed money from us and didn't ever repay it, and then she stooped so low she just stole from Mama outright—her medicine, her money, a TV. She knew better. She was an embarrassment to us, and a threat."

I said, "But she's still your mother's baby girl, bad or not, and I think Mrs. Washington may need to see her before she dies. It might be holding her back."

"Well, that's impossible. Janella's in jail!"

"Oh, that's easy!" I said. "At least we know where she is! You underestimate the power of the hospice social worker!"

They shook their heads as if maybe I, too, was losing my faculties.

Lesley, the social worker on my hospice team, spent the

next day and a half locating Janella and receiving permission from the warden to allow her two visits to her mother's home. She would be accompanied by an armed guard and permitted visits of no more than one hour. A hospice representative would also be there to monitor Mrs. Washington and make sure her medications were kept secured. Since Lesley could attend only one of the visits, I volunteered for the second.

As Janella's first visit approached, I noticed how anxious the family was getting. They cleaned the house and practically locked up everything that wasn't nailed down. The idea that the neighbors would see the prison guard and one of their own sisters in the standard-issue orange jumpsuit and handcuffs filled them with mortification.

Lesley reported that on the day of Janella's first visit, the other six siblings crowded into that small apartment, watching over their mother like lions. They barely said anything to Janella as their sister walked over to her mother. Tattoos decorated both of Janella's forearms, and one of her front teeth was missing. The contrast of that streetwise, weathered woman with the tranquility of her frail mother seemed almost mythic. For a moment Janella stood over her mother, her head bent ashamedly, sorrowfully, and then the tears came.

Until Janella came, Mrs. Washington had been in that drifty-dreamy state I described earlier. Janella's presence seemed to return some light to her eyes. Once the rest of the family was able to see that Janella was not actually a threat, they awkwardly tried to look occupied, going into the other rooms to afford their mother and sister some privacy.

When I arrived for Janella's second visit, I opened the door to a remarkable scene. She was brushing her mother's long white hair in a slow, methodical motion and singing "Twinkle, Twinkle Little Star." It was magical, and I wanted to be careful not to disturb them. Janella sensed someone there and turned toward me. I could see that her eyes were full of tears. She was once again a vulnerable and tender little girl in the presence of her dying mother. She murmured, "She always sang this to us when she put us to bed at night."

At that moment, I thought of every person throughout the years who has ever said, "How can you take care of dying people? Isn't it depressing?" If every one of them could have stood where I was for one minute to see the beauty of what we do, they would never ask again.

After Janella's visit I could sense relief in Mrs. Washington. I guessed she would die soon after, having had that closure and healing. But she didn't, even as her body's systems shut down one by one. A week passed, and then another. She was peaceful and comfortable, and the family seemed at peace as well, yet Mrs. Washington couldn't seem to let go.

I said to the family, "What else is missing?"

I spoke to Lesley again. She thought that perhaps the two visits from Janella weren't enough. Her warden generously allowed another, this time for two hours, but he said, "This really will be the last."

This time when Janella came, the family seemed more receptive to her, acknowledging her presence and exchanging some tidbits of news. Finally, the eldest son, William, stepped out into the hall to ask the guard if Janella could eat dinner with them.

"It's just about ready," Naomi called from the kitchen. Janella nodded and grinned, trying to contain her gratitude.

They knew their time was limited, so they rushed to set the large table, pull up chairs, and bring the food. After a few nervous minutes, the stories started to flow and laughter went around the table, with Mrs. Washington sleeping peacefully nearby.

Before they knew it, the guard was knocking on the door to alert everyone that the visit was coming to a close. William leaned over his mother's bed to tell her Janella had to leave. And that was when he realized she wasn't breathing. She had gone while they were eating dinner together, only feet away. Her death was so quiet that no one had even noticed.

It hadn't been enough for Mrs. Washington to reconcile with her troubled daughter. She needed to see Janella folded back into the family before she could leave this earth peacefully. She had finished her canning. There was enough food for everyone, night had fallen, and her work was done.

THE BOTTOM LINE

Listen very carefully. You may be the one who's confused!

31

COMMUNICATING
WITHOUT WORDS

A young man dying of a brain tumor, no longer able to speak, clamps his teeth when his family attempts to feed him. An elderly woman, already nonverbal from the advanced stages of Alzheimer's, removes her dentures and throws them away. Both of these patients, easily ignored for being "confused" or demented, were actually talking to us without words. Had they been able to speak, they might have said: "Stop! I don't want it!" "Don't feed me anymore!" "I have no appetite, leave me alone!" "I don't need these teeth where I'm going." "Please stop trying to make it better and keep me here. Let me go!"

Speaking is only one way to communicate. Behavior, gestures, and expressions can be just as eloquent. Look how powerfully a baby or a loved pet makes itself understood by actions only.

Once again, however, we may be quick to label behaviors that we don't immediately understand. Consequently, we may ignore or dismiss these valiant efforts of dying people to connect with us when speech is no longer a tool for them. It is very important to be receptive and watch the behaviors of the dying, so that we recognize the messages they are trying to send.

REUNION

After I gave a talk as part of a Lenten series at a Protestant church, a heavyset, graying man came up to me and asked if I had time to hear a brief story about his mother.

"I never considered myself a religious man, and I really had no concept of what awaits us after we die. But watching my mother's behavior when she was dying convinced me that those we lose in life are waiting for us on the other side. I never would have believed it if I hadn't seen my mother reach out the way she did. But I'm getting ahead of my story.

"I am the oldest of five living children. There was another baby who died before I was born, who only survived a few days before pneumonia took him. The child was never even named. Anyway, every early January for the next fifty-six years, my mother mourned my infant brother, all the old sadness returning.

"Toward the end of my mother's own life, she became a brittle diabetic and went into a coma. She was in this state for a few weeks. We had her admitted to a nursing home. One day while I was sitting quietly in the chair, her eyes suddenly opened wide, she sat up, and the most joyful look washed across her face. My mother reached out as if someone was handing her a baby. She cradled and nuzzled it, crying joyfully, sank back on the pillows with great relief, and died.

"I was never the type to give much thought to this kind of stuff before, but it really felt good to know she and my brother would be together again. That's what she always wanted, and it made losing Mom a bit easier. I know she died holding my baby brother in her arms."

"LISTEN" CAREFULLY

My patient Allen was dying of a brain tumor. While this forty-nine-year-old former stockbroker remained very alert and clear-headed, speaking and writing became increasingly difficult for him as the months progressed.

It especially frustrated him when he had trouble communicating with Sandy, his attentive and loving wife of twenty years. I could see in Allen's expressive eyes how concerned he was for his wife, how grateful he felt for the care she lavished upon him, and simultaneously how worried he was about the toll it might be taking on her. He clearly did not want to be a burden to her.

One day he patted the bed for Sandy to sit near him. He seemed particularly tender, his mood serene. He then looked around the room as if he had an urgent idea and needed to find it. We followed his gaze until his eyes came back to the quilt that spread across their bed. He pointed to it, and Sandy and I said simultaneously, "The quilt?" He nodded. We each tried our hand at guessing his intention.

"Are you too hot?" "Too cold?" "Do you want us to bring you supper here on the bed?" "You want the paper?" "Do you want to nap?" "Are you comfortable?" To each of our questions, he shook his head. The more questions we asked, the more frustrated and agitated he became. Finally, Allen shook his head adamantly and closed his eyes, taking several deep breaths to regain his calm. Then he looked softly at his wife, who usually was so attuned to his needs and wishes.

It was clear he was trying to tell her something important, but what? He began again, pointing to the corner of the quilt. Allen picked it up and ran his finger across the rich pattern of flowers, tracing their shapes, pointing to various colors. This time we waited in silence, really trying to pay close attention and not impose an answer.

"It's very beautiful," Sandy said finally. He nodded enthusiastically, as if she was becoming his voice

"The quilt is very beautiful?" she asked again.

He nodded again, his eyes beginning to show relief. Sandy and I looked at each other, a bit puzzled. Why the sudden urgency to tell her how much he admired a flowered quilt?

"I'm glad you like the blanket, sweetheart," she said, taking his hand. But as soon as she thought she'd found the answer, he flipped the corner of the blanket over and pointed to the crimson and white stripes on the underside. He followed the lines, pointed to the various colors, and looked at her for understanding, his eyes riveted on her.

"You like this side better?" she asked. He shook his head and then pointed back to the flowered side.

"Do you prefer the flowered side?" He knotted up his face in frustration, and she began to cry.

"Allen, I'm so sorry, darling, I can't understand what you're trying to say." She turned to me, but I could provide no answers, except to say they both just needed to be patient.

"Maybe we should try again from the beginning?" I suggested.

Allen slowly pointed to the flowered cotton and Sandy repeated, "It's beautiful?" He smiled in acknowledgment and then pointed to the striped side.

"This side is beautiful, too?" she asked. He nodded vigorously, as if she was finally on to something. He repeated both steps, to which she answered each time with increasing confusion, "It's beautiful."

Suddenly June's eyes widened as she asked tentatively, "Allen, do you want me to know it's beautiful on *both* sides? That both sides of existence are beautiful—this side and the next?" He nodded, and tears of relief ran down his face. "Are you telling me you will be all right no matter which side you're on?" He openly wept as she wrapped him in her arms.

. . .

As death approaches, we often feel an overwhelming need to *do* something. But this is really a time to be still and simply be with the dying person. Even if the person can no longer speak, we can carefully watch his or her behavior. This mindful, sensitive approach will allow us not to miss the powerful final lessons a patient may be trying to teach. This is our invitation to share their journey.

THE BOTTOM LINE

The dying ask us to be still: "Be with me and watch my actions. They are my words when I can't speak."

PART VI

COMING TO THE END

WHAT'S NORMAL FOR DYING
ISN'T NORMAL

It is as normal to die as it is to be born. And yet somehow, when a terminal diagnosis is made, there is often a sense of being robbed, of a huge injustice, or of a punishment from God put upon us. But in truth, dying is our last developmental task. No one is spared. When and how we must confront it is the mystery. The fact that we must is not.

In our expectations of the natural order of things, deaths that seem to occur too young, or those that seem senseless or unjust shake us to our core. We subconsciously expect to die peacefully in our sleep at a ripe old age. So, of course, much of death seems unjust and wrong. Understandably, we feel that we must fight it, stop it, and change it.

When we care for the dying, the changes in their bodies—and sometimes in their minds—can make them look different and act strangely toward us. It all seems so tragic and *abnormal*. Our instinct, of course, is to stop it, fix it, make it normal again. And no matter what their age, saying a last goodbye to someone we love is always rife with pain and heartache. Because it's normal doesn't make it easy.

Just as one of the many normal symptoms of pregnancy is a swollen belly, there are also many normal signs of dying. I tell my patients and families, "I know this is breaking your hearts. You don't have to like these changes. They may not look or be acceptable, but they are normal for the process of dying. So let's not waste precious time and energy trying to change the unchangeable or fix the unfixable. There are many things we *can* change and fix, so that's where our energy and focus should be. We *can* make this better and easier for all of you."

FRANCES

Frances had been a beautiful, fashionable woman all her life—the kind of woman who never went out of the house without coordinated shoes and handbag and a fresh coat of lipstick. But when at seventy-eight she was diagnosed with liver failure, she surprised her family by abandoning any sense of vanity or self-consciousness.

"I don't care what I look like. It's too time-consuming!" she explained. "I just want to have my family here with me and appreciate every last minute we have together."

And they were there to do just that: her husband, their three children, their four grown grandchildren, and one great-grandchild all camped out in their three-bedroom condo for several weeks as Frances's health declined. The family shared stories, looked at photo albums, watched movies together, and read journal entries aloud. Two of the grandchildren played songs on their guitars at a respectful volume in honor of their grandmother, who had always loved music.

One day Frances's daughter, Lila, was going to massage her mother's feet as she lay in bed. Pulling up the sheet, she noticed that her mother's left little toe and the one adjacent to it had turned a bluish black. The hospice nurse went into the kitchen with Lila and explained that Frances's toes were becoming gangrenous. She no longer had adequate blood circulation to her extremities.

"It's possible that those toes might eventually fall off, but by that point she won't feel anything there," the nurse explained calmly. "As awful as it seems, it won't hurt her at all." But Lila was horrified.

When Lila returned to her mother's room, she tried not to show her distress, but she couldn't hold back the tears. Frances took her daughter's hand and said matter-of-factly, "You're worried about my feet, aren't you?"

Lila nodded.

"I've been a vain woman all my life, Lila. I was always caught up with how I looked. Believe me when I say it's almost a relief *not* to care anymore. Those toes, this body, is not who I am. It's merely a shell, Lila, nothing more." Frances went on, "It took me until the end of my life to realize that simple truth, but because of it, I am not afraid or even embarrassed."

At first Lila couldn't believe what she was hearing, but because of her mother's acceptance, she learned to relinquish her own fear and discomfort. She suddenly perceived in her mother a new strength she hadn't anticipated.

Symptoms at the End of Life

Each terminal illness has symptoms that are unique to that specific condition: the excessive bruising seen in blood diseases, the swollen abdomen (called ascites) and yellow cast to the skin (jaundice) characteristic of liver diseases, and fractures and anemia in some bone diseases, to name a few.

It's especially important to realize this in the case of cancer, which in fact includes a huge category of illnesses. Every cancer has a unique personality, and its symptoms also differ. Many people are frightened or misled when a friend tells them, "Oh, yes, my uncle died of prostate cancer and he had a terrible time with ..." when a person with a malignant brain tumor may have entirely different issues. This is another reason to rely on your medical team for information and always to check with them about anything you hear, no matter how well informed your friends or acquaintances may sound.

There also are universal symptoms that appear as death

approaches. Most people dying naturally show these signs and symptoms regardless of their disease and no matter what additional symptoms they have from their specific illness. These symptoms are the signs of the dying process itself, and as such they are normal.

Please note, however, that this is generally not true for people who are being maintained by artificial measures such as a respirator or tube feeding. Their dying may be delayed, but their deaths are often more sudden, less peaceful, less comfortable, and less intimate. They often die in intensive care units, surrounded by lights, noise, machinery, and medical staff. Family members are typically sent out of the room when a crisis happens, so they may not even be present at the time of death.

The universal changes I describe here happen to a body dying naturally, regardless of the illness. They are typically more upsetting to friends and family members than to the person who is actually experiencing them. Knowing what to expect can ease the distress of this transition.

Weight Loss

Imagine a weary mountain climber with a full backpack. As the mountain gets steeper, the exhausted, depleted climber discards more and more of the load. This helps the climber go on a little longer, until it is impossible to continue. Just so, the dying body, with its rapidly diminishing energy, instinctively rejects food that will simply take energy to digest. Appetite loss is a normal sign of dying. At this point, I recommend to caregivers that they put the scale away. Weighing the patient can only depress both of you. Why do it?

Appetite Loss

Red meat is often the first food to be rejected by the dying. The foods that they may show an interest in are typically bland and almost tasteless, such as very small amounts of cream of wheat, even if they hated it when they were well. Puddings or a sip or two of juice are also enjoyed. But most dying people have no appetite at all as death approaches, and if they do accept any nutrition, it is usually to please or placate the worried caregiver.

Difficulty Swallowing

Difficulty swallowing can occur earlier in throat diseases and when there are brain and neurological compromises from tumors, strokes, or degenerative diseases. But dying people nearly always become too weak to swallow in the last week or so of life. They start to sputter and cough even when taking just liquids, and the difficulty continues until they are unable to swallow at all.

It is critically important that the caregiver and family recognize this change and *completely stop feeding or offering fluid to the dying person.* As difficult as this is, feeding or giving fluids puts him or her at great risk for choking or aspirating—breathing what is fed into the lungs. This could precipitate a death of more drama and discomfort than is necessary. Keeping the mouth clean and moist with small ice chips or wet mouth swabs is usually enough to allay thirst and keep the dying person comfortable.

Weakness

A number of factors contribute to weakness: disease progression, organ failure, unavoidable changes in nutrition and hydration, and failure of the brain cells that send the limbs messages to move. The little energy the body has left is being used to fight the losing battle with the disease. There is no remedy for weakness. Exercises that may have been recommended earlier in the disease are now inappropriate. They do not rebuild wasted muscles; they only serve to increase the dying person's exhaustion. If pushed to exercise, he or she will feel a sense of failure and the caregiver will feel frustrated. As I've indicated in Chapter 11, forcing nutrition or hydration to try to build up someone's strength can instead have dire consequences.

All of the counterproductive interventions I've described are focused on what is *gone* rather than what is *still there* to work with. As the dying person gets weaker, his or her need for help and support with physical tasks, such as bathing, dressing, and getting around, increases. It's common for a patient to want to lie down and rest frequently. This will increase until he or she is in bed full time. The dying often want caregivers and friends to sit quietly with them. Healthy people don't understand that it actually takes energy just to follow a conversation. The patient may be too weak to talk much—or even to listen. This is normal for dying.

Swelling

As death nears, the heart is getting weak and the kidneys aren't filtering as they once did, so the body fluids accumulate and become a burden. In what is called "third spacing," these fluids are dumped into spaces that are far away from the heart and less important to maintaining survival. They move out of arteries and veins and into the surrounding tissues. This causes puffy, swollen feet, ankles, legs, and sometimes hands and face.

I'm sometimes asked why diuretics aren't used to reduce this kind of swelling. Diuretics are medications that stimulate the kidneys to increase the output of urine, and they are beneficial in some circumstances. But in the dying, the spaces where the extra fluid is deposited are often beyond the reach of diuretics, so by using them we achieve the opposite: we dehydrate the patient, who continues to be swollen.

It is futile and unrealistic to try to fix this problem. Also, giving diuretics means that the very sick and weak person must get up to go to the bathroom much more frequently, and this is exhausting. If they cannot make it in time, constant contact with urine, whether on bedding or clothes, can cause the skin to break down, forming bedsores that may become infected. A catheter may be inserted into the bladder to prevent this. However, it's important to weigh the benefits and burdens of this decision, because a catheter is embarrassing, invasive, and annoying to the patient. It's usually better and far simpler to decrease fluid intake and use ice chips or Popsicles to keep the mouth moist. Incontinence briefs may be needed, and frequent skin cleansing and care is essential.

If the skin is stretched and dry because of the swelling, keep it well moisturized with lotions. Moist skin is much more elastic and less likely to crack and break down than dry skin is.

"But won't he be thirsty? Doesn't dehydration hurt?" a worried caregiver might ask.

I ask in return, "Have you ever heard someone say, 'My arm is thirsty'?"

When the caregiver shakes his or her head, I continue, "Thirst is a mouth sensation and can easily be soothed with ice chips without adding more water to the edema, or body swelling."

Increased Sleeping

This often occurs very gradually and gently. A caregiver might tell me, "This week he's taking three naps a day. Last week it was two!" Or "He's resting longer each time, and it's a little harder to wake him up." I'll then suggest that the caregiver mark the calendar each day with the actual number of hours the patient slept. This shows the family that the dying person's need to sleep is increasing and his wakeful hours are decreasing. This is normal for dying.

Try to remember that the ill person's body is at war with the illness. This is a war that we can't see, and one that the patient ultimately can't win. Fighting this war takes energy and strength the patient no longer has—and in a compassionate attempt to replenish it, the body will require the person to rest more and more.

Confusion/Delirium

As hard as it is to watch someone you love lose weight and become gaunt or jaundiced, it is often more upsetting to deal with mental status changes such as confusion or delirium. The mind is the essence of who we are, so to deal with disorientation and dementia in someone we love is to deal with a stranger who has suddenly moved into a body that is still dear and familiar to us.

It is estimated that approximately 70 percent of people dying of illness experience some degree of confusion before they die. Confusion may come and go, or it may be more prolonged. There are many reasons why this happens: the confusion may be disease-related (as in kidney or liver failure, or with brain diseases); the patient may be too weak and overwhelmed to think clearly; or it may be a side effect of the medications being used. As I've discussed in Chapter 30, it may also be related to important experiences that the dying person is attempting to tell us about.

In caring for the dying, I think in terms of "good" confusion or delirium versus "bad" confusion or delirium. If the dying person is enjoying or benefiting from the confusion—if, for example, he or she is enjoying happy dreams and memories—but this upsets the family, leave it alone and reassure the family. However, if the confusion is causing the patient turmoil, agitation, or fear, talk to your medical team for possible solutions. Sometimes adding, subtracting, or rearranging medications can help.

But most important, and regardless of other treatments, listen to the words the dying person is saying and write them down, even if you don't know what they mean at the time. In time you may find hidden meanings that are not immediately apparent. Always reassure the dying person that he or she is in a safe place and surrounded by caring people, and that you are trying hard to understand what the person is trying to tell you. Try not to get frustrated or judgmental, for as hard as it is for the caregiver, the person who is experiencing the confusion or delirium may feel an increasing bewilderment or loss of control. *Listening* and *patience* are the operative words here. Be as loving and understanding as you possibly can. And be prepared for the possibility that you'll learn something new.

Restlessness and Agitation

I have often thought that this behavior may indicate the last psychic battle before a person resigns him- or herself to dying. But it may also be a sign that something isn't done, that something is bothering the patient. Because the dying person can no longer verbalize what is needed, he or she becomes agitated. This is the time for caregivers, family, and friends to think hard about what might be missing. Words of forgiveness? Permission "to go" from a loved one? Assurance that the family will be okay? Do you need to call an important person and ask him or her to come? Or send away a person whom the dying individual may wish to spare?

It's very common to see a dying person plucking at the bedcovers as though they were in the way or holding him or her down. I've often suggested removing most of the covers (always guarding the patient's modesty) to see if that helps.

Once again, family teamwork is important at this time. If the agitation is mild and not distressing to the patient, leave it alone. If, however, it escalates and the patient seems in distress or fearful, medications are available to help. Try every other intervention first, because medication can make it even more difficult for a compromised patient to communicate his or her needs.

Changes in Vital Signs

As death approaches, the blood pressure usually decreases. The pulse usually increases, and if it remains consistently above 120 beats a minute, this can indicate that death is only a few days to a week or so away. It is not uncommon for a dying person to have a fever in the final days. This is not caused by an infection and therefore does not need to be treated by—nor would it respond to—antibiotics. It is probably caused by the dehydration and by changes in the hypothalamus, which is the body's thermostat. Cool cloths on the face, neck, armpits, and groin, together with over-the-counter anti-fever suppositories, are usually all that is needed, but check with your doctor or hospice nurse first.

Decreased Urine Output

This is the natural result of decreased fluid intake and diminishing kidney function. The urine becomes concentrated and strong-smelling, and it may be as dark-colored as tea. It sometimes contains sediment from cells and mucus shed from the walls of the bladder. Nothing need be done about this. The body is simply winding down, and the patient is completely unaware.

Blood pressure must be above 70/0 to make the kidneys produce urine. (Normal blood pressure is 120/80, give or take a few points in either direction.) If it's below 70/0, there will be minimal urine made, if any. When the kidneys no longer make any urine at all, they shut down and fail. Kidney failure causes toxins to accumulate in the blood, which gently leads to increased sleeping, coma, and typically a peaceful death.

Changes in Level of Consciousness

It is actually rare for someone to be fully conscious and able to communicate until the very last moment of life. The dying will seem to become more and more "fuzzy" in their thinking and seem "spacy" or detached from the people and events around them. This generally happens gradually, and I suspect it is the body's natural mechanism of self-protection, so that dying is softened rather than being faced with fear.

Medications being given to the patient, typically for pain, can also cause this fuzziness. Some patients prefer this to having any discomfort. But others request smaller doses, choosing to have some discomfort rather than being mentally spacy. This is another reason it's so important to work with the patient: to find the amount of medication that best suits the dying person's wishes and needs.

Sleeping gradually increases, but the patient becomes harder and harder to rouse and may drift immediately back to sleep once awakened. This state of semiconsciousness is usually a very comfortable place for the dying to be—as if they were on a big fluffy cloud just gently drifting farther and farther away from us. We can pull them back by stimulating them to wake up, but as time goes by, more and more stimulation accomplishes less and less, until we cannot bring them back to us at all. And is it the compassionate thing to do to keep pulling them back from such a peaceful place?

Patients who drift in and out are in *semi-coma;* when they can no longer be pulled back, they are in *coma.* Semi-coma progresses to coma that is generally short-lived—a few hours to a day or so. The important thing to understand about coma is that although patients cannot respond to us, they do hear us and are aware of what is happening around them. We know that hearing is the last sense to die. (If anything, it seems that hearing becomes *more* acute as people approach dying.) So talk to the dying, even when they are in coma. They need to hear your reassurances and love. It's also important to remember to say *only* the things you want the dying to hear, even if you are in the next room.

Some people I talk to about dying tell me, "I wish I could just die in my sleep!" The vast majority of people dying naturally of illness (I would guess close to 95 percent) go into a brief coma—comparable to a profound sleep state—before they die, so the good news is that most of us *do* die in our sleep.

Changes in Breathing

In the final hours, or sometimes a day or so before death, a new pattern of respiration occurs. Called Cheyne-Stokes respiration, it is caused by messages sent from the breathing centers in the brain as it slowly dies. These changes are painless, and if the person is still conscious, he or she is usually unaware of them. The pattern starts with a loud, deep, sighing breath that sometimes sounds like a snore. This is followed by a breath with less volume and noise, then by a series of more shallow respirations, until no breath is seen or heard. This is followed by a long pause with no breathing at all that can last thirty to sixty seconds or more. Then respiration starts again with a loud, deep sighing breath, and the pattern repeats, over and over. The periods of no respiration gradually grow longer, and the shallow breaths become even fainter and more irregular, until breathing stops entirely. The final breath is usually so shallow, quiet, and soft that it is often missed. If the family is sitting around the bed talking softly or praying, someone may suddenly notice that the patient hasn't taken a breath for a few minutes. This is a normal, natural death—peaceful, quiet, and easy.

The "Death Rattle"

This disturbing sound causes much anxiety and concern in those around a dying person. Even its name is ominous and frightening. In actuality, however, it is simply the sound caused by a small amount of moisture or mucus in the back of the throat. A healthy person with this mild congestion, similar to a postnasal drip, would simply clear the throat or cough to relieve it. The dying person is too weak to do either. As he breathes in, the fluid or mucus moves down the windpipe. As he breathes out, it moves back up the windpipe. This occurs over and over with each breath. That is what causes the rattling sound— nothing more than a little mucus or fluid.

There are very good medications that can be given via a patch behind the ear or put under the tongue of a conscious or unconscious person to dry up these secretions and stop the rattling. While this sound is rarely a problem for the dying person, the medications make it easier on anyone witnessing the death. The "death rattle" seems to stay negatively in people's minds forever, so stopping it with medications is good, compassionate symptom control for the *observers,* while not being harmful to the patient.

Mottling

As the heartbeat becomes weaker and threadier, the blood is not pushed through the veins and arteries efficiently, so it pools or pockets in the low places on the body: along the back of the person lying in bed, and along other parts of the body that are against the mattress. Some areas become bluish or purplish, while others are very blotchy and blanched out. Mottling usually starts in the feet and moves up the body. It seems that our bodies die from the toes up.

At the same time, the body attempts to counteract the failing circulation by pooling the blood around the vital organs of the body. The hands and arms, as well as the feet and legs, appear bluish in color and feel much cooler or even cold to the touch compared to the trunk, which may still feel warm from the blood that has pooled around the heart and lungs.

Again, these changes are not problematic to the patient, but they can cause alarm in observers. Nothing needs to be done about them, but they are an important sign that death may be hours to a day or so away. This is normal for dying.

THE BOTTOM LINE

Understanding what is normal for dying can help prevent fear and alarm in the onlookers and help them focus on what they can do to help the patient.

33

"IT-ALL-GOES-TO-HELL-
IN-A-HANDBASKET DAY"

The plan has been working so well. The patient is comfortable, the family is functioning confidently, and
there is peace in the home. But suddenly, for no good reason,
everything falls apart. A frantic phone call comes from someone in the family: "It's all unraveling! We're miserable! We can't
do this anymore! He needs to be in the hospital! Please come
quickly!" This phenomenon is so common that I have named it
"It-All-Goes-to-Hell-in-a-Handbasket Day."

I've come to suspect that this day has more to do with the
patient's final *psychic* battle between life and death than it does
with anything physical. It is, I believe, the catalyst for the final
letting go: not only on the part of the patient ("I can't bear to
go on anymore. I'm finally ready to say goodbye. Let me go
now") but also on the part of the family ("I can't stand to see
him struggle any longer. This is not what any of us wanted
for him. It's selfish to hold him here. Because I love him, I must
let him go").

The darkest time of night is just before dawn, and the most
painful time of labor is at the very end, just before birth. Death
is usually in close proximity to this "It-All-Goes-to-Hell-in-a-
Handbasket Day"—often only a few days away. The good news is
that this awful day usually leads to a sense of resignation and
acceptance for both patient and family. When death comes, it is
usually comfortable and peaceful.

MARTY

Marty was only fifty when he was first diagnosed with leukemia. This crisis did not fit into his successful and orderly life. He had moved up the corporate ladder quickly to become his firm's vice president of information technology. He and Barbara, his wife of twenty-nine years, had two grown sons who were established in their own businesses. Together they had built a lovely home, which Marty had maintained meticulously until his illness worsened.

"This is definitely the palace and he is definitely the king," Barbara told me with a laugh. "It's always been that way!" She had recently retired from her career in banking because it was clear that Marty needed her at home full time.

In the seven years since his diagnosis, Marty had achieved two remissions with chemotherapy, but this time the chemo caused so many dangerous side effects that he could no longer continue. His doctor recommended that he call hospice, get his affairs in order, and enjoy the time he had left with his family. During the first two months after he was admitted to hospice home care, he remained fairly stable. The monthly transfusions he received kept up his blood counts and maintained his ability to function.

But soon the transfusions were helping for a shorter and shorter period, until he needed to be transfused weekly. He was experiencing frequent nosebleeds and a generalized feeling of profound fatigue. It became harder for him to keep up with the basic daily activities of life—bathing, dressing, having meals. Even daily transfusions could not have stemmed the tide of his loss of blood and energy.

He spent increasing amounts of the day reading, napping, or spending quiet time with family and friends who came for short visits. He still struggled to run the house as always, writing orders down on his clipboard: "Pay bills—electric due third of the month," "Turn heater down at night and install a pro-grammable thermostat," "Change filters every month." But as his energy decreased, the notes dwindled, too: "Pay bills," "Heat down," "Change filters." Despite his deterioration, he was com-fortable, the atmosphere was calm, and he felt loved and cared for by his wife and family, who also seemed to be focusing in a positive way on the time they had left to share.

Then came "It-All-Goes-to-Hell-in-a-Handbasket Day." For no apparent reason, Marty complained of unusual pain. His hospice nurse, Dulcie, was able to control it by increasing his pain medication, but his nose quietly dripped blood and he was having frequent bouts of bloody diarrhea. Despite being up and dressed, he was restless and anxious. Sitting up wasn't comfortable, but lying down wasn't, either. So he was up and down, up and down, as Barbara tried to find something to soothe him.

This sudden change in her husband made Barbara unset-tled and anxious, but she was doing a good job of staying fo-cused on the tasks at hand. By the next morning, however, Marty's symptoms had worsened, his behavior had become in-creasingly erratic, he occasionally said something that didn't make sense, and she worried that he should be in the hospital. She called for Dulcie to come back and evaluate him.

Marty stirred slightly as Dulcie said, "Hi, sleepyhead," then checked his vital signs and listened to his lungs. "I'm glad to see you are finally able to rest," she told him. He murmured some-thing in reply, smiled, and drifted back into sleep.

"He's very pale and bleeding more now. His pulse is rapid and his blood pressure is very low," Dulcie reported to Barbara. "As fast as we're giving him blood, it's coming out, so the trans-fusions aren't helping him anymore. But he does seem a lot more peaceful and comfortable now than he did when you called. You're doing a great job of helping him, Barbara." She gave her a hug.

"I don't want him to struggle anymore. It's just too hard," Barbara said tearfully.

"I understand," Dulcie said. "Sit here with me. We need to talk about what's going on." Barbara sat down slowly, her eyes wide with fear. Dulcie continued, "I think there's only a little time left, so you just stay near him and let him know how much you love him, how much he has mattered to you and your family. Assure him that you will be all right."

"Isn't there anything else we can do to help him?" Barbara asked plaintively.

"Unfortunately, there's nothing that can be done. What you are already doing is what means the most to him—just being here with him."

A while later Marty woke up briefly, glassy-eyed and seemingly puzzled. "Who's going to make the final decision?" he anxiously asked Barbara.

Barbara had read *Final Gifts,* and Dulcie had also coached her in ways to understand such "confused language." So now Barbara calmly said to Marty, "You will, sweetheart, whenever you're ready. It'll be okay." She stroked his face. "I love you, and I promise you I'll take care of everything here. So don't worry about a thing."

He visibly relaxed. "Oh, good! That's fine, then," he said, settling back into his lounge chair. He slept there comfortably through the night and at some unnoticed moment slipped into a coma. He died peacefully and quietly the next morning with Barbara at his side.

It would have been so easy to panic and insist that Marty be hospitalized. If he had been, his final hours would have been spent in the turmoil of being jostled into an ambulance, moved into strange surroundings, and being poked and prodded for IVs by people he'd never seen before. Because of Dulcie's reassurances and Barbara's courage, Marty was able to die peacefully at home, knowing that he could decide to go whenever he was ready, that his family would be okay, and that those who loved him would care for his "palace."

Time to Do What We Do So Well

Hospice is remarkable in what it can do to help patients and their families cope with an illness that cannot be cured. What it can do is very impressive, *but only if the hospice staff are given enough time to do it*. I've been assigned to patients who died during my visit to admit them. Of course the hospice team and I did the very best we could, but I couldn't help but think that all we really did was add to the confusion as the family tried valiantly to understand and adapt to yet another group of new people during a time of severe stress, turmoil, and crisis. If anything, such timing seems more detrimental than helpful.

As I've said, some patients and families hold off until the last bitter minute, as if by not calling for help, they are also holding off death itself. Some are afraid that "it's like giving up to call hospice." Others say, "We waited until she was unconscious, because she'd figure out that she's dying if she heard the word *hospice*." Unfortunately, in situations of denial such as these, little time is left to do what we do so very well—really help the dying and their family deal with this ultimate life crisis.

In most cases, a prognosis of six to twelve months is the best entry point into a hospice program. However, I've cared for a patient for as long as two and a half years. This patient had Lou Gehrig's disease—also called ALS, amyotrophic lateral sclerosis—a terminal, progressive neurological illness that ultimately took her life but did so very, very slowly.

When the dying patient has children, additional time is needed to help the young ones understand at an age-appropriate level what is happening. A plan for emotional support should be put in place for children as young as two. Bereavement support is essential for little kids and young adults to learn how to understand their feelings and cope in grieving.

Having hospice in place early allows for enough time to find a level of comfort and emotional support for all involved, and will also help the family manage crises in order to honor the dying person's wish to die at home, or if necessary in a hospice bed in an inpatient facility.

THE BOTTOM LINE

When it all seems to be falling apart, it may really be coming together.

34

BEING *WITH,* NOT *AT,*

THE DYING PERSON

I was blessed to be the birthing coach for my daughter as she brought her baby girls into this world. I was equally blessed to be the "birthing" coach for my parents and uncle as they left this world. They had taught me how to live, and in their dying they taught me how to die. It was the beautiful full circle of truly living this life.

ANNETTE AND SIMON

When I first met Simon, a retired army general, I was struck by the fact that everything about him, his family, and his life was so in order, so "spit-and-polished," that there seemed no room for anything less than perfection. Knowing that the experience of dying is full of moments that cannot be controlled or planned for, I wondered if he could be flexible enough to handle his wife's illness. Still, he clearly adored his wife, Annette, and had the financial ability to provide her with anything and everything she might want and need.

His military success was clearly exhibited by the ribbons and medals framed on the walls of their home. The old photos of him alongside Eisenhower, MacArthur, and other senior military officers—most in battle fatigues—spoke of someone who had looked at the enemy dead on, expected to win, and always had. But Simon could not control or defeat the fact that the love of his life was dying.

In dealing with caregivers, my basic approach is that knowledge is power. What is ahead is less frightening if it is discussed, anticipated, planned for, and understood. However, I *never* push information on anyone who is unsure or prefers not to know. As I have said before, I have great respect for denial, which is a wonderful crutch. Unless I have something better to put in its place, I leave it alone unless the denial is causing harm or putting anyone in danger.

I also keep in mind that while many terminal illnesses follow a predictable path, there are factors that vary from patient to patient, including age, previous state of health, mental and emotional determination, and previous treatments and care received or rejected. Each course is somewhat predictable, but it is always unique to the person.

Since Simon told me he wanted to know everything, we collaborated from the beginning on a plan to deal with the deterioration that was ahead for Annette as her disease progressed. He was receptive to this information, and he prepared as though he was going into the battle of his life—which in many ways he was.

Annette, on the other hand, was clear that she didn't want to know *anything*. "I never worry at all when Simon's in charge, and as you can see, he always is, " she told me.

After a week or so of visiting Annette, I could see that Simon was becoming burdened with the various medicines to keep track of, meals to prepare, doctors' appointments to keep, and chores to do. I suggested tacking a handwritten chart on the kitchen wall to help schedule and plan for some of the weekly responsibilities. Simon liked the idea. He quickly developed a strict routine. But as the plan of care changed with the course of Annette's illness, so did the chart, and such changes in medications or other treatments require adaptability and flexibility. An untrained caregiver, particularly one who is an organized, in-control person like Simon, can soon feel over-whelmed as the "perfect plan" is modified. While I never in-tended the chart to be a list of rigid marching orders, it seemed to evolve into that as Simon's need for control increased.

Annette remained comfortable as her condition gradually deteriorated, but I noticed that Simon was becoming more and more obsessed with the house and yard. He spent so much time pruning his bushes, they looked artificial. He now insisted that the bedsheets be lightly starched and ironed by the caregivers he had hired, who understandably balked at such a waste of time when Annette's physical need's were increasing daily. One after another, the private-hire home health aides resigned, and the constant turnover upset Annette and added to her mild confusion. She called for Simon incessantly, and he was becom-ing frustrated by being regularly pulled away from his "work." "Tell her I'll be there when I'm done," he would briskly direct the hired caregiver.

A new chart outlining Simon's version of the schedule had now appeared on the bedroom door, and the expectation was that it be followed exactly:

10:00 A.M.: Head of the bed up 45 degrees

10:30 A.M.: Head of the bed down flat

10:45 A.M.: Lotion on feet

11:00 A.M.: Lotion on hands

And this was hardly the beginning or the end of it! Poor Annette did not have a moment's peace the whole day, as her in-creasingly limited time was flying by in the company of strangers doing insignificant "stuff" to her.

One sunny afternoon I found Simon in the backyard, wear-ing earplugs with a hedge trimmer screeching in his hands. "We need to regroup, Simon," I shouted, gesturing for him to come inside. He fixed me a cup of tea and became visibly nervous, anticipating bad news, as we talked at the kitchen table.

I said, "Simon, you've done such a spectacular job of taking care of Annette all along. But these last days and hours are few and precious, and she has only a little time left. Do you want to spend it doing yard work while a different face every week tries to follow this intense schedule? They are always turning her, changing her, moving her, rubbing her with lotions, setting her hair, doing her nails. Some of those activities are good and comfort-producing, but rest and peaceful quiet time are also essential for her now. The schedule is just too much. What she wants and needs is you to just be with her, not strangers fussing at her all the time. Having everything look perfect does not make it perfect."

"Want some more coffee?" he asked absentmindedly, forgetting he'd made me tea only moments before. He jumped up from the table, straightened the papers scattered in front of his place mat, and grabbed my half-empty teacup. Then suddenly he rinsed it out and put it in the dishwasher. *Poor guy*, I thought. *This is so hard for him. He's rushing around in a frenzy so he doesn't have to stop and really look at what's happening.*

He finally sat down at the table again and at last met my eyes. "Is this the end?" he asked hoarsely.

"No, I think she has a few days left, but I can't guarantee that, so I'd hate to have you miss this last opportunity to be with her. I just need to be sure you understand where she is in her journey. She loves you and trusts that you will know what's best for her and how you want to spend this precious time." He slowly got up and disappeared into the dining room. I quietly waited as I heard him blow his nose many times over the next few minutes.

He returned red-eyed and sat down with purpose. "You know, Maggie, the make-it-or-break-it point in a battle is realizing when your battle plan isn't working anymore and having the courage to regroup and change it," he said. "I just didn't realize we had gotten to that point. Or maybe I didn't want to re-alize. So, how do I do this now?"

I had known from the start just how much Simon loved his wife, but in that moment it was clear that he was even willing to shift his whole attitude when he realized it would serve her better. I was so moved. I said softly, "Let the home health aides do what they have been trained to do. Such detailed direction is demeaning. It doesn't recognize their judgment and skills. Meanwhile, you do as much of the comfort-providing as you like. For example, I'll bet Annette would love to have you give her gentle back rubs, hand rubs, and foot rubs. But it's also very important just to be with her quietly.

"As she gets closer to leaving us, the thing she'll want most of all is your presence. You really don't have to do anything at all. Simply put a cozy chair in her room and bring in your news-papers and books. She's sleeping most of the time now, so imagine how soothing it will be for her to open her eyes and just see you there. This will also help her not to worry about where you are and how you're doing. She's comfortable enough so that it'd be okay if you want to lie down beside her and just snuggle for a while. Spend as much time with her as you can. If she's quiet, you be quiet. If she's awake and talkative, talk with her. If she's sleeping, take a nap yourself. *That* is how best to share her journey. You know her so well—just follow your in-stincts about what she needs, and keep doing the wonderful job you've been doing."

A week passed with Simon spending time with his wife in just that quiet, loving way. And then one morning, while he was napping beside her on their bed, Annette died so peacefully and quietly that he didn't realize it until he awoke.

"I gradually became aware that it was just too quiet. She wasn't breathing anymore," he told me. "I don't know how long it took, but I just wanted to keep every bit of her warmth close to me. I held her until it was gone. Then I called hospice to tell you she'd died." He sadly smiled as silent tears slid down his face.

I spoke with Simon at the gathering after Annette's funeral. "You did a wonderful job, Simon, and I know it was heartbreaking for you. But every wife should be so blessed to be cared for as lovingly as you cared for Annette."

He openly wept. "Of course I wish she were still here, but I'm at peace that I did everything I could for her. I want you to know that we shared some of the most beautiful moments during those final days!"

LISA

One devoted and fastidious daughter named Lisa worried out loud to me about making her mother's dying just right. "I just want this to be perfect for her!" I had already noticed the fresh floral arrangements by the bed, the sheets and covers that were changed at least daily to match her mother's nightgown, and the soft classical music always playing in the background as Lisa's mother drifted in and out of coma. The "Hallelujah Chorus" of Handel's *Messiah* was all ready to be turned on for the last minutes before death—which was probably still some weeks away.

"I just keep feeling like there's something that I've overlooked to make this right, but I don't know what it is I've missed!" she told me.

"You know, Lisa," I replied, "doing *nothing* is often the right thing to do, even though I know that doesn't help with that panicky feeling. Right now, as your mother slips in and out of coma, she's very busy transitioning from this life into whatever comes next. Even though it may not look like it, she has a high level of awareness of what's going on around her. She may also be having experiences that we can't see and hear.

"Do you remember what it was like being in labor?" I went on.

"Yes, I do," she said with a laugh.

I continued, "Without the monitors, nobody can see what's going on, and yet the mother is very focused and busy. A lot is going on, isn't it? That baby is transitioning from the mother's womb into this world. A laboring mother even gets a certain look on her face as she focuses inward and tries to work with what's happening in her body.

"Now imagine if Miss Nellie Nurse had a need to be busy and tidy and kept fussing at you while you were in labor. 'Do you want ice chips? Let me fluff your pillow. Are you hot? Let me fan you. Let's sit up. Let's lie down. Your hair's a mess, I'll comb it. You're sweating—I'll bathe you.' Can you imagine how that mother would react? I suspect if there was a chair within reach, she'd throw it at her and shout, 'Leave me alone! I'm busy!' "

Lisa smiled.

"That's what I mean when I say that sometimes the best thing to do is nothing," I finished. "The best way to make this perfect for your mother is to quietly be there with her and share the journey as far as you can." Tears of relief came into her eyes, and she nodded silently again and again.

As I work with families and friends facing the death of someone they love, it often strikes me that their anticipation of how that time will be is usually much worse than it actually turns out to be. Their busy behavior is a way of not looking at the inevitable as it approaches. But when they are given the opportunity to be completely present, most caregivers are grateful to have shared those last days, hours, and minutes. A large percentage of them miss the actual moment, as Simon did, because it is so quiet and peaceful. I often hear, "I couldn't believe it was so easy!"

Many others have said, "I will never again be as afraid of dying as I was before," or "It was the hardest job I ever loved." To witness and help facilitate such realizations is an honor and blessing in *my* life.

THE BOTTOM LINE

The best way to share the journey of dying is simply to be with the dying person, sharing quiet times and gentle moments.

35

"I NEED YOUR
PERMISSION TO GO"

As hard as it is for the dying to leave the people they love, it's an added distress to think that their loved ones will be caught off guard, unprepared, and overwhelmed at the time of their death. "Does my family know that I am leaving soon, and will they be too devastated by this?" "Are they ready?" "Will they ever recover?" "Will they be all right without me?"

It appears that even unconscious patients have these concerns. It is not uncommon for a dying person who seems to be lingering to be finally able to go when the family gives verbal permission and assurances that they understand what is happening and that they will be okay.

GARY

The CEO of a prominent international company, Gary was living in Brussels with his young family when he was diagnosed with end-stage lung cancer. Immediately they moved back to the States, to a suburb of the city where much of his extended family still remained. "This is where it all began," he said. "So this is where it should end." He was only in his fifties, a tall, imposing ex-athlete and a real no-nonsense kind of person, used to being in control and accustomed to succeeding.

His thirty-eight-year-old wife, Belinda, was a strong achiever in her own right, the attentive mother of two school-age children, now doing occasional work for the corporate law firm where she had been an attorney before going to Brussels. They lived very comfortably in an impressive contemporary house tucked away in a manicured neighborhood. But no amount of power or success could change the fact that Gary was dying too soon.

On my admission visit, I was struck by how advanced Gary's illness was and wondered why they had waited so long to call hospice. My nursing partner, Judy, and I needed to move quickly and aggressively to relieve his symptoms of pain and shortness of breath, and we didn't have a lot of time to make things better for him and his wife and children. I cannot reiterate strongly enough that, particularly when there are children involved, the more months we can work with a family, the better.

Gary was always polite and cordial to me and my other team members, but our relationship remained very businesslike. Belinda, on the other hand, treated us like long-lost friends. Having lived overseas for many years, she had few social supports here, and our visits always ended with tea and cookies in the kitchen nook as Gary dozed in his room down the hall.

Our kitchen table meetings covered many topics: their life together overseas, how her roles were changing here, marital problems they'd overcome, how the kids were doing in school, how Belinda was managing to juggle all the aspects of her life, and how her own grief was affecting them. "I'm way too young to be a widow!" she'd say sadly.

We managed, for the most part, to maintain good symptom control, but it was much harder than usual, as his disease was so far advanced, challenging, and unusually tenacious. I recall reviewing with Belinda the concept that people usually die as they live, and her response surprised me.

"Well, then, get ready, because Gary came into this world fighting, and he's been fighting ever since. If what you say is true, this may not be an easy death for him or any of us." Her words concerned me, and I secretly prayed that she was wrong. I asked her to tell me more about Gary.

"He was a twelve-pound baby, and his delivery was incredibly long and difficult. The doctors couldn't promise he'd be all right. His mother ended up having an emergency hysterectomy because she hemorrhaged so heavily after the delivery.

"His family was hardworking, with little education," she continued. "His parents both worked two jobs, so he raised himself on the city streets. We later realized that he had an undiagnosed learning disability, but from the time he was a little boy, he was told, 'You'll never amount to anything!'

"Struggling as hard as he did in school, he believed them. He dropped out of high school and ran with a bad, dangerous crowd. He had regular brushes with the law and spent time in juvenile detention. He experimented with drugs and alcohol and was clearly going nowhere good fast, until on his own he decided to join the navy. He always seemed to know how to survive by the skin of his teeth!"

She heated up a kettle of water for tea and put out a plate of biscuits. Then she went on, "He loved the structure and discipline of the military. He really flourished—he finished his GED and eventually struggled through college classes, one at a time, until he got his engineering degree. His commanding officer saw his tenacity and potential and recommended that he apply to officer candidate school. It was a long shot, but he was accepted, became an officer, and eventually got a master's degree in engineering. With the exception of his commanding officer, he had absolutely no support or encouragement, even from his family. It was all a battle for him, a real fight every step of the way. But he persisted, left the navy, and moved into business technology.

"We met at a party. I was in total awe of him. He seemed larger than life, and I was certain there was nothing he couldn't conquer. Sure enough, he fought his way up from the bottom and soon was at the top of his field as the CEO of a huge international company," she said with pride. "But then the cancer . . . he became so ill so fast.

"When he was diagnosed, he swore he would conquer this just as he'd conquered all the other hurdles in his life." Her eyes filled with tears. "He pursued the toughest treatments and refused to accept 'no' from any oncologist. He'd simply move on to a new doctor who would push the envelope and give him what he wanted. I can't begin to tell you how sick he's been, but he'd just keep pushing. Eventually, though, it all failed him, and here we are. He conquered every other hurdle in his life, but we're told he will lose this battle. It's impossible to even think about it!" she sobbed as Judy and I tried to soothe her.

On what turned out to be my last visit with Gary, he was clearly near death, but unfortunately he wasn't at peace. He was agitated and wild-eyed as he struggled and fought to breathe. I immediately medicated him and assured him I would not leave him and Belinda until he was comfortable and Belinda no longer needed me. Gasping too much to be able to speak, he grabbed my hand and held it firmly on his chest. I administered more morphine to ease his breathing, and the struggling started to abate. Once he was calmer and more comfortable, I called the doctor to report the problem. He supported my actions and gave me ongoing orders for whatever Gary needed. He also offered to put Gary in the hospice inpatient unit if it was too difficult at home.

As I returned to Gary's room, Belinda stepped out into the hall, where he couldn't hear us talk. "Do you think he's dying?" she asked anxiously.

"Yes, I think he is, and very soon—possibly within a few hours," I replied.

She thought for a long moment, then suddenly stood very straight and declared, "I am *not* going to give him over to strangers in the hospital now! I will keep him here to die with me and our children. I should wake them up soon. I want to make sure they say goodbye to their daddy."

I was moved by this young woman's courage. "Would it help if I stayed with you for a while?" I asked.

She put her arms around me and wept on my shoulder. "Please, please do. I'm so afraid!"

The pain medication had fully taken effect now, and he was sleeping comfortably. I sat with Belinda over a cup of tea and said, "Boy, were you right about him being a fighter. I gave him a *lot* of morphine, but he just kept fighting it. He is a *very* strong and determined man. He's definitely dying as he lived."

About ten o'clock that evening we heard him stir, and rushed into his room. He was awake, energized, and bright-eyed, seemingly in awe of something we couldn't see. Urgently he cried out, "Hurry, Bindy! Quickly, quickly, get the kids! We have no time to waste!"

"What *is* it, darling?" Belinda held his flailing arms and leaned close to his face. "What's wrong? I'm right here with you, sweetheart. What do you need?"

"There's no time left!" he said frantically. "The *Gull* [the name of his corporate jet] is gassed up and ready to go! We have to go *now*!" He pulled her body close to him. "Now, darling, now!" I was stunned at this burst of strength and urgency from a man so close to death.

Belinda took his face in her hands and, leaning very close to him, said, "Gary, sweetheart, the children and I can't go with you right now. But we'll be in the plane right behind you. We need you to go ahead and make sure everything is set up and ready for us, as you always do. *Please,* darling, we're depending on you. You go now. We love you, but we'll be fine and we'll be along very soon, I promise! So go now, go. It's okay."

The children had been wakened by the commotion down the hall, and they were standing wide-eyed in the doorway, listening. Now they climbed right onto Gary's bed and, following their mother's lead, said, "It's okay, Dad. We'll take care of Mom. We promise! And we'll see you soon, deal?" they said, surprising me with their maturity and strength. Gary slowly relaxed his grip on Belinda. His breathing slowed down and became easy as he slipped into the coma that would hold him peacefully for the last few moments of his life while Belinda and the boys curled up around him like kittens, holding him and kissing him goodbye.

After settling the kids back in bed, Belinda and I sat in the dark on the front porch, waiting for the people from the funeral home to arrive. She sadly chuckled, "I *told* you—he fought his way into this world, he fought his way through it, and now he's fought his way out of it and into whatever comes next!"

I hugged her and said, "I have learned so much from all of you. I will never forget this night!"

It's difficult for the loving, devastated heart to say, "It's okay with me that you die!" We are never completely ready to say that final goodbye to someone we love, and yet the dying person still needs to hear that loving permission. The words can be simple:

"I understand what's happening, and even though I'm very sad, I'll be all right."

"Please don't worry about me. I can see you're getting so tired, so it's okay if you need to let go. I love you, and I'm all right."

Such support helps our loved ones complete their journey more peacefully, relieved of the fear, and knowing that their family understands and is prepared for their leaving.

THE BOTTOM LINE

The dying ask of us: "Let me know you'll be okay—then please let me go."

36

THE FINAL HOURS

You've digested difficult information that you never wanted to know. You've confronted fears and anxieties that seemed insurmountable. And you've done a huge amount of very hard work. Now you've been told that the person you love is dying very soon, possibly in a few hours. As ready as you thought you'd be, you're *not*, and you can't shake the panicky feeling of *"Do something, do something!"* So, how do you survive these final hours? What do you do?

Typically by this last stage, the dying person has already detached from the physical journey, and possibly from all those around him or her as well. The patient may be in a semi-coma or coma, which usually lasts a few hours to a day or so and is followed by death. He or she may be running a fever, which you are relieving with cool cloths and anti-fever suppositories. The person stopped being able to swallow a day or so ago.

Friends and family may be converging on your home. Out-of-town relatives arrive and face the gravity of the situation and the losses all at once, and their grief may be extreme. As exhausted and stressed as you are, you may find yourself comforting *them*! Now you realize that as hard as this journey of caring has been, you've done little bits of grieving all along, as each loss was faced and every deterioration recognized.

Some family members may feel guilty about not having helped out more, so now they go into a hyper "do" mode. They may ask you to come up with significant tasks they can tackle

to make up for their past lack of involvement. So now you become responsible for finding ways to ease someone else's guilt.
Feelings—both good and bad—run high, and hypersensitivity
abounds.

You probably feel muddled and overwhelmed. Your concentration is terrible, and you feel like you're walking into walls.
This is early grieving, and it is normal. The arrival of other family members and friends initially felt like caring support, but it
may ultimately seem like a distraction that is keeping you from
being with the dying person in these final hours. How do you
protect your time for what is really important?

Now you have new jobs: make up the beds, put out clean
towels (if you can find any), make sure everyone's needs are being met. Is there enough food for lunch? Who's going to sleep
where? Is somebody picking Uncle Charlie up at the airport? Is
there enough gas in the car? Has the minister (or priest or
rabbi) been called?

Just as an obstetrician who has been involved throughout a
pregnancy wishes to be there for the delivery, you want to share
the final hours of the journey you have been making with the
dying person for so long. And yet these tasks of caring for your
family and friends are pulling you away.

Eventually, though, jobs have been assigned, the house and
kitchen are accommodating the company, and everyone seems
to be settling in. Now what do you do? Fight all the normal in-
stincts to *do* something. Just sit quietly near the dying person.
Watch and try to imagine where the person is and what he or
she is experiencing. A gentle, loving touch is wonderful, but try
not to distract the person or attempt to pull him or her back.
Remember that the patient is busy transitioning from this life to
whatever may come next. This is a busy time for the dying. Even
though we can't see exactly what's happening, a lot is going on.
This should be a quiet time simply to be with the dying person.

Some caregivers and families find peace in having beautiful, soft music playing in the background—perhaps some of the

patient's favorite selections. Others lie quietly next to the patient, gently touching or stroking a face or arm. Some choose to "keep the death watch," while others look through family albums, quietly reminiscing together about the life of the dying person. Imagine how wonderful it would be to spend your final hours comfortably, surrounded by those you love as they review your life and how meaningful it has been to them, how much it has mattered that you were here on this earth. Laughter and tears should not be suppressed. They are normal expressions of love and grief, and you're not fooling the dying person by not being emotional. In fact, if emotions are restrained, the dying person may be concerned that you're "not getting it" and will often struggle to linger until you do. So be present, but also take care of yourself.

The terminally ill cannot avoid dying, but they have shown us that they have an amazing ability to choose the actual moment of death. If the dying person wants you there as he or she takes that last breath, you will be. The person will wait for you.

There are countless stories of the dying grandmother who lingered waiting for her grandson to arrive before she died, or the mother who hung on until her daughter's wedding was over, or the many who avoided dying on special days such as holidays to spare their family from changing joyful times into days of mourning.

And we know that the opposite is also true: if a dying person doesn't want the people he or she cares about to be there at the moment of death, the person will pick a time when you are *not* present. Your loved one is giving you the gift of sparing you, or perhaps he or she has always been a very private and introspective person. Remember, it is the dying person (even in coma) who will choose—and often for the most loving of reasons. It is not your failure, nor any reason to feel guilty. The decision was out of your hands to begin with, so be at peace with this.

. . .

I hope you feel good about what you've done, not only in helping the person you love to die peacefully at home, surrounded by love, but also because of what you've taught those around you, especially children. You have shown them that this journey called dying does not have to be about fear, pain, or anguish. Instead, you have shown them that it is a difficult yet loving opportunity to learn how to live every day until you die, rather than die every day until your life ends.

You have learned powerful and uplifting lessons from this dying person you love, you have shared them with others, and you will carry this knowledge forward into any future dying experiences you may have. Now you can see ahead to your own dying—not in fear, but as a most brilliant opportunity to write the last chapter of your life in a way that truly reflects the unique, caring, and generous person that you are. Appreciate what you've done, and who you are.

THE BOTTOM LINE

Surviving the final hours in a positive way can provide comfort to you on your new journey—grieving.

PART VII

ONE JOURNEY ENDS, ANOTHER BEGINS

37

ON THE TOLL ROAD

The Healing Power of Crying

I've never thought crying was a bad thing. There are times I'll even seek out a sad movie because I feel the need for a good cry. The ability and willingness to cry has been a tremendous asset to me professionally. It's a great catharsis, and it's one of the best remedies for grief. Because it is so effectively healing, I have managed to continue my work as a hospice nurse since 1981, much longer than most.

I have taken care of more than two thousand dying people and still love the challenge of my work. It is true that it's painful to witness the physical and emotional hurdles of a terminal illness, but wrapped up in each dying person is such profound beauty and meaning that I cannot imagine working in any other profession. My work is like being a birthing coach at the other end of life.

There is no question that there is also a lot of sadness in the work I do. My patients are dealing with a series of losses as death approaches. I have sat, talked, and listened for hours at their kitchen tables or next to their recliners, or knelt beside their beds and leaned in to hear their weak whispers. I have cared for and about them for weeks, months, and sometimes years, and for their families as well. And I will not forget them.

The families are dealing not only with the patient's losses—of independence, of health, of a former identity—but also with the anticipated loss in their own lives. They must start a whole new journey of grieving when my work is done. I, too, quietly grieve. But in keeping with hospice policy, my relationship with the patient's family must end when the funeral does. Their grief journey deserves the assistance from the best professionals—the hospice bereavement team—and that is not my area of expertise. So losing the patient is an issue of grief for me, but even more so is losing the family. I often worry about them and wonder how they're doing. Every time I drive by their street I think of them. My map is full of unique monuments: *That's around the corner from where Tony used to live,* or *That's Mary's development,* or *Donna's children attend that school—I wonder how they're getting along.*

Often I'm asked, "How do you keep from crying?" Well, I don't. I cry. I cry a lot, actually. I sometimes cry with my patients, I sometimes cry with my families, I most often cry alone. When I say cry alone, I don't mean just genteel sniffling and tears dabbed with a tissue. I mean head-back, mouth-open wailing, the louder the better—aerobic crying. It's like an investment: the more you put into it, the bigger the payoff, and the less you have to do it in the long run. But I do try hard not to cry in front of my own family, although it's very difficult. Hospice work is the kind of work that should not be taken home every night.

I have a favorite place to cry—the toll road that spans the last miles home. A few times a month, with no particular warning, I feel the tears come as I approach the entrance. So I grip the steering wheel and get into it. I'm often racked with sobs by the time I get to the tollbooth. Early on, I was concerned about the tollbooth attendants. They stood looking at my face streaked with tears as I fumbled for the dollar that I placed in their outstretched hands, and they heard my sobs as I waited for my change. After a few times of trying to suppress my tears, I stopped worrying about how they saw me. *What the heck,* I figured, *I'll probably never know these people, and this spares my family.* The toll road was where I felt free to grieve.

A few years ago, the first visit to a new patient took me to a nearby town. I rang the doorbell that I would ring many times in the following weeks as I cared for the wonderful matriarch of this large, loving family. When the adult son opened the door, I was taken aback by his reaction to me. His mouth dropped open in surprise and his eyes grew large as he stared at me and my name tag. He looked familiar somehow, and yet I just couldn't place him. A few awkward moments later he said softly, "Oh! *Now* I understand. Please...please come in." At that moment I recognized him as one of the tollbooth attendants.

"Better to cry in my car than at dinner with my kids," I offered sheepishly.

"You must really care if you face such losses again and again," he said, smiling. "I'm happy that you'll be taking care of my mom," he added. Instead of questioning my stability, he respected my vulnerability and caring.

As the weeks passed and I came to know him better, he told me how he and the other attendants used to talk during breaks about "the crying woman in the silver car." They wondered what was such a constant problem in my life. He told me that one of the younger guys was tempted to shout out to me as I went by, "Dump the bum!" The next day I had to laugh remembering that suggestion as I went through the toll lane.

As I drive past them now, I sometimes get a "Hey, nurse!" or a knowing smile, a nod, or little wave. Together, these unknown attendants and I recognize a grief thread that weaves through the mundane daily activities of our workaday lives and binds even strangers together in the sad journeys we share. Unspoken, my show of sadness validates their own tragedies, and perhaps they too have since found their times and places to cry.

THE BOTTOM LINE

Providing good care for others depends on your providing good care for yourself.

38

DOING THE GRIEF WORK,
DAY BY DAY

Colonel Hobart was not my regular patient, but I was on call for the weekend when the answering service paged me with the report that he had just died. I immediately phoned his wife to express my condolences and to tell her how long it would take me to drive from my house to theirs. As it was three in the morning and I was unfamiliar with their neighborhood, I asked her to put on as many lights as possible so I could easily pick out the house in the dark. "Oh, believe me, you'll know!" she replied.

As I turned the corner of one of the quiet, tree-lined streets, I could not miss it: a house ablaze with lights in every window and with a spotlight illuminating the house numbers by the front door. Although both sides of the street were filled with parked cars, the wide driveway was empty. The three-car garage was also empty—and brightly lit.

Then I saw her and immediately knew what she had meant. Mrs. Hobart was in her bathrobe, kneeling in the middle of the garage, surrounded by heavy bags of soil, and planting large red geraniums in great big pots.

As I walked down the driveway toward her, she looked up, the tears silently streaming down her cheeks. "I know it's totally crazy," she said, "but I just *have* to do this *right now*!"

I leaned over, gave her a little hug, and said, "Yes, I completely understand. You're not crazy, and the name of this behavior is *normal*!"

"Thanks for that," she said, laughing a little through her tears. Then she got up to lead me into the house, where her lifeless husband lay.

The Work of Grieving

After my father died, I suddenly understood the old tradition of wearing black clothes and black armbands and hanging large black ribbons on the front door of the family home. The world around you has no way of knowing that your grief has made you feel like a robot, going through your required daily chores, while your heart and brain are saturated with the numbness of grieving. Twice in the grocery store I spotted something that dropped me unexpectedly and instantly into grief. Once it was the Dromedary dates my father loved, then it was his favorite semisweet chocolate. Both times I fled the store in tears, leaving my nearly full grocery cart still in the aisle. I was able to prepare and shield myself against the obvious entry points into raw grief—the holidays, his birthday—but it was these unexpected, innocuous moments that brought me to my knees.

My young son, trying to express his grief, told me, "When I think of Granddad I feel a big lonely in my throat." How well he captured that feeling of a lump in the throat, and how often our grief is felt physically! I never realized that a broken heart actually feels like a heart that has been broken into pieces, until mine was. I was amazed that I could actually point to the pain.

Grief is hard work, but if we are to go forth positively in our lives, it *must* be done. Unless we find healthy outlets for our grief, the pain will last much longer than necessary, and it may very possibly disrupt our relationships and even cause physical illness.

Grief can be acknowledged and expressed, both inwardly and outwardly, or it can be suppressed and denied, only to reveal its presence in insidious ways. Too many of us were taught as children to "not act like babies" and "pull ourselves together" when we cried, yet tears, sadness, and even depression are normal signs of grief.

Less obvious signs of grieving include poor concentration, agitation, changes in sleeping and eating patterns, weight gain or weight loss, guilt, panic, anger, resentment, and dwelling on regrets. Some people are frightened by the intensity of these symptoms and feel like they're going crazy. But in fact these are normal ways of getting the grief work done and are common, even healthy signs of grieving.

I personally would rather not prolong the process of grieving any longer than I have to, so I go right into the vortex of the storm. If I didn't, I wouldn't be able to continue experiencing so many losses through my work and still live with as much joy and fulfillment as I do. I often tell my families, "The better you grieve, the worse it feels, at least for a time. Just get down into it and *do it*!" Cry often and do it with gusto. Get help with it if you need to. Grief will control you less as you express it more. It *will* get better, as will you, day by day.

But if crying isn't your style, seek out other ways to open the valve and let the pain out. There are many ways to process a loss: through artistic expression, physical activity, prayer, meditation, talking with friends, professional counseling, spending time in nature—even whacking the heck out of a golf ball! The important thing is to find as many healthy outlets as possible for *your* experience. Of course, if your instinct is to quell your pain with alcohol or drugs, or if you feel the pain has grown unbearable, seek professional help to get your life back on track without causing yourself or anyone else harm.

Another way to heal is by reaching out to others who have experienced similar pain. Many of the volunteers at hospice are widows and family members of former hospice patients. They know firsthand how to help when others may not. They are remarkable volunteers because they've turned grief into something positive. They have learned that grief is a part of the path. But it is not the destination, and the path can get gentler as one goes on. They have also learned that their path is private and that their work as volunteers is to focus on the grieving person's path. After all, no two grief experiences are the same.

If you do it right, it will get better. The grief never completely goes away, but it does start to fit into your life in a more manageable and less painful way. The hole caused by that loss in your life is never completely filled, but we *can* begin to shift from unbearable pain when we think of our deceased loved one to sweet reminders of the wonderful ways that person impacted our life. And however we grieve, our acceptance of it also helps others when they confront unbearable sorrow.

Styles of Grieving

Friends and family may be joined in their loss, yet the *way* they react is always personal and individual. The very person who has been the rock of Gibraltar through the last months of a loved one's life—nurturing others, actively involved in the daily care of the dying person—may need the greatest dose of support after the person is gone. Another person might feel overwhelmed and unable to cope during the entire time their loved one is dying, yet after the death they seem to be able to offer their strength to the entire family. Still others may need active support through all phases of the journey.

While I embrace the *idea* of a family experiencing the loss of a loved one together, it is important to bear in mind that we will each have our own *way* to grieve and *time* to grieve. One person might become more introverted, choosing to spend time quietly and alone. Such a person might read or write or paint, or might want to walk alone in the woods every morning. Another person might find solace in humor, or in cleaning frantically. And the very person who controlled all aspects of her father's care in his last days may become incapacitated after his death, suddenly not wanting to help in any way. *It is essential during such a difficult time to be as sensitive as possible to others experiencing the loss, whatever their style of grieving.*

Support During the Journey

The world seems to give you an unspoken month or two to grieve. Then you're supposed to put a smile on your face, perhaps get a new relationship, and "move on." The casseroles stop and friends' calls start to taper off. The length of your grieving might begin to make other people uncomfortable, so to deal with their sense of frustration and failure to make you feel better, they pull back—ironically and without meaning to, creating more loss for you to deal with.

Seeking the support of a grief group is highly recommended, and wonderful groups can be found through counseling centers, hospitals, and places of worship. Grief support is also part of the services provided by hospice programs, and typically it's free. To share your journey with similar travelers is very helpful. And sometimes wonderful new friendships are formed from the common bond of shared loss and sorrow.

A special note to friends: be prepared for your grieving friend to repeat the story of loss over and over as if you had never heard it before. Understand that each time the story is told, your friend loses a bit of grief pain. It's as if a small puff of air is released from a balloon that is so overinflated it threatens to pop. Puff after puff, the balloon becomes more relaxed. When you patiently listen to the story time and time again, you are providing the most caring and helpful support.

And for the bereaved: above all, do not isolate yourself, but allow others to help nurture you through your grief. This is particularly difficult for so many of us who have grown accustomed to being independent, self-reliant, and stoic. Peel yourself out of bed or off the couch, shower and get dressed each day, and make sure you eat well. Then answer the door to receive your friends' and co-workers' gifts of soup or flowers, welcome their hugs, pick up the phone when they call, go out for walks or for lunch with them, let them coax you to the gym or to get your nails done, and *try to be as honest as you can about how you feel*. Remember, there's no right amount of time or right way to process your grief. The important thing is to be where you are, and feel the support of those who love you.

We all need to invite some kind of healing work in when we are wounded. We can reach for any or all of the various ladders that are dropped down to us when we are in that dark emotional hole, but the important thing is to start climbing, rung by rung, step by step. There are people and things that will help. Seek them.

THE BOTTOM LINE

Grief will control you less as you express it more.

39

"WHEN I THINK OF GRANDDAD, I FEEL LONELY IN MY THROAT"

How Children Grieve

To this day, a soft-boiled egg brings me right back into my nana's kitchen. I was only four when she died, and yet all these years later that taste rekindles the pleasant memories and feelings I had sitting with her at the breakfast table. It's a good memory, one that I cherish.

But not all memories are good. I can still feel my young child's fear at being whisked out of the room when Nana had one of her dramatically spurting nosebleeds. Perhaps if I'd been given a simple explanation about "Nana's messy nose," I would not have felt the same panic. Instead I was forced to sit upstairs in my room with my imagination running wild.

Children perceive sickness and death differently at different developmental levels. But they *always* perceive them, and even very young children grieve just as significantly as adults, though not in the same way. As a parent, you may benefit from reviewing your own history with death and dying. Are you struggling with any lingering inhibitions or fears? What experiences have you had—positive and negative? You have the power to actively shape your child's experience to be a positive and healthy one.

The best policy is timely honesty. Use correct language, provide simple explanations and definitions, and ask the child if he understands. If not, try again with a different approach or explanation. Using indirect or symbolic language will confuse young children. (If you say, "We took your grandfather to the hospital and lost him," be prepared for questions about when the search will begin!) With older children and young adults, indirect language conveys the message that death and dying—and the grief that follows—are things to euphemize and avoid discussing. When you delay sharing information with a child, you demonstrate to him that you are not available and trustworthy. A child's security is shaken and his imagination is encouraged to build mountains out of molehills.

You may be thinking that it's too hard to talk honestly and openly with your child and that it will be too upsetting for him to listen. It's natural to want to shield children from unpleasantness and pain. But it's important to realize that you *cannot* hide the truth from children. Even if you manage to do so for a time, the emotional consequences can be far worse than the initial pain you tried to avoid. Involving children early in the process of dying allows them the chance to prepare for this loss, to say goodbye, and to start healthy anticipatory grieving. If you do not involve them, they will imagine far worse than the reality. You and they also suffer another loss: the opportunity for bonding through a shared ordeal.

On September 11, 2001, my granddaughters Ellie and Tallie were two and a half years and eighteen months old, respectively. My daughter and son-in-law have one television set, and they have blocked all channels except PBS for the kids. They did everything they could to shelter the girls from the news and from the unstable feeling in the world during those terrible days. However, driving into Boston a number of months later, they passed a factory with smoke coming out of the chimneys. Tallie pointed and said, "Fire!" to which Ellie responded very matter-of-factly, "No. An airplane hit it." You can't shelter children 100 percent.

When someone is dying, the entire environment changes.

Even the smallest infant can sense tensions and show signs of distress. Nonverbal clues abound: worried looks, unusual visitors, hushed conversations, and unusual absences. And don't assume all the clues are nonverbal. Neighborhood gossip can provoke all sorts of wild rumors on the playground. Without a truthful explanation to thwart the gossip, children are quick to draw their own conclusions: "Did Grammy go away because she didn't love me?" "If I touch my sick brother, will I get sick, too?" Given the power of magical thinking and creative imagination, these fantasy explanations can be far more hurtful or anxiety-producing than the reality. You can help prevent anxiety by assuring children that they will not be kept in the dark when something important is happening.

It's important to confirm the death for a child. It's not until the ages of eight to ten that most children start to understand the finality and universality of death. Younger children often believe (or want to believe) that death is a temporary sleep-like state.

On the other hand, children do understand life, so they may be able to grasp that death is the absence of life. Life means you can run, jump, breathe, eat, sleep, feel sad, get hurt. When you can't run, jump, breathe, eat, sleep, feel, or get hurt, that's what death is like. Watch for signs of guilt or regret that they somehow caused the sickness or death by something they did or failed to do.

Ceremonies help confirm the finality of death and stimulate active grieving. It is important to include children in rituals whenever possible, but only if they want to be there. Older children can feel honored to be involved in the planning and implementation of a memorial. Children model their behaviors on what they see around them, and ceremonies give them the opportunity to observe natural expressions of grief. However, brief stays at events such as a viewing may be advisable. Children can easily become overwhelmed by the touches and words of strangers. For a newly fatherless boy to be told that he is "the man of the family now" or a grieving little girl to be informed that "you need to take care of Daddy" is extremely damaging. You can help protect children from such insensitivity by assuring them that the remaining parent will continue to be a parent and is capable of taking care of both him- or herself *and* the child.

If a child declines to attend a ceremony, it is often because he is afraid of the unfamiliar or unknown. Respect his decision but be prepared to support him later if he grieves the choice he made. It is helpful to explain that a wake, funeral, or memorial service is a chance to say a final goodbye and to be with other people who also loved the deceased. Describe where the ceremony will take place and what will happen step by step, including what a casket is, how the body will look (if the casket is to be open), and that the child can touch the casket or the body if she wants to. Discuss feelings and give the child permission to express emotions as they come and however they come: by crying, being quiet, doing a reading, going outside to be alone for a few minutes, or even letting out a giggle.

Plan some time for you and your child to be alone with the deceased before a service or cremation. I usually suggest that families start a public viewing with fifteen to thirty minutes of private time for immediate family only. This is an ideal time to let the child touch and ask questions. Ask the child if there is anything she would like to have buried with the loved one.

Well into early adulthood young people are the center of their own universe. This is normal. As such, they are very powerful beings in their own worlds. Understand that they are concerned, whether openly or inwardly, about how the experience relates directly to them. At every age, children need reassurances that life will return to normal and they will always be cared for.

An infant may need to be held and rocked more frequently; a toddler may need to see familiar food on the table at the usual time and may want to have favorite storybooks read over and over. Older children may wonder if it's okay to play and have fun; teens need permission to be with their friends. Teens are also likely to worry that financial hardship might require a move or a change in college plans. If possible, reassure them on this score—or be prepared to discuss your new situation openly and realistically.

All children grieve sporadically in short intense stretches, followed by "What's for lunch?" Their apparent self-centeredness and periods of normalcy shouldn't be interpreted as a lack of grief, insensitivity, or uncaring behavior.

Children of all ages need help to find ways of articulating their feelings and expressing their grief. Sharing helps, whether it is time spent with family or sessions in a support group with other kids of the same age who have suffered a loss. Like adults, children will go through phases of denial, searching for the deceased, depression, anger, and confusion, and these difficult emotions may be expressed as disruptive behavior. It's important not to alter your discipline. Children need boundaries to feel safe and secure. Be patient but firm. Find outlets for the energy these highly charged emotions create.

One of the leading books on this topic, *The Grieving Child: A Parent's Guide,* by Helen Fitzgerald, provides invaluable guidance on the types of behaviors and emotions to anticipate, signs to be concerned about, and numerous activities that help a child release feelings, including role-playing with puppets, clay modeling, drawing, journaling, and keeping a "memory box" for treasures. Fitzgerald also offers detailed suggestions for a "children's funeral," a short service designed by, and held for, the children that might precede the main funeral or memorial service.

Children even younger than two are known to keep memories of such early experiences. After the funeral, you can reinforce your child's recollections by keeping pictures of the deceased visible and by frequently retelling favorite family stories. You will give your child the priceless gift of strong memories and a lasting connection to the one they loved and lost.

Grieving Through the Ages

The First Year

Young infants most likely perceive death only as an absence or separation, and if the deceased is not a primary caregiver, the child may not be aware of the death at all. Babies are, however, very sensitive to disruptions in their schedules and routines and can sense a change in their environment caused by unusual absences and the emotional state of caregivers. As for any stress or discomfort, they may react with irritability and with changes in normal activity levels and in feeding and sleeping patterns. The intensity of their reaction is linked to the level of change and distress around them.

Babies find reassurance in normal routines and familiar faces. They will respond well to playtime, smiling faces, and increased cuddling. Try to minimize unusual sights, sounds, and smells in the child's environment. If the primary caregiver is dying, gradually introduce a surrogate—such as an aunt, grandmother, or friend—to care for the infant's needs.

Verbal Infants and Toddlers (to About Age Three)

Children in this age group will feel the terrible loss of someone very close to them, although they don't really understand death and may easily confuse it with sleeping or going away. Toddlers may not be much affected by the loss of someone who is not in their inner circle—a grandparent who lives far away, for example. But they readily react to turmoil in their surroundings, and they may express their concern through simple sentences such as "Daddy gone" or "Mommy sad." Mirroring back these kinds of statements is often enough response for very young children.

Children this age may also respond with distress to new experiences such as having many strangers in the house or making long hospital visits. Keep routines as close to normal as possible, including playtime, story time, and lots of cuddle time. Expect outbursts of bad temper, anger, or frustration. Unlike older siblings, toddlers' language skills are still not adequate to deal with these new and strange emotions. They may try to bring back a loved one by displaying behaviors, positive or negative, that were responded to in the past. (If Mommy always came to comfort him when he cried in his crib, you may see more tears at bedtime.) They need to be repeatedly reassured, in words and actions, that they are still loved and cared for, especially if they have just lost a primary caregiver. Everyone can get involved in showing extra love and support. The comfort you provide to the child will in turn be comforting to you.

Young Children (Ages Three to Five)

Preschoolers are magical thinkers with immensely active imaginations. At this age, you can speak to them directly about the diseased, but they will interpret your explanation in their own way, and often very literally. If you tell a child, "Your father was sick. He went to the hospital and died," a preschooler may become mortally fearful of any sniffle or sneeze and terrified of what happens in hospitals. So it is important to use simple language, explain words they may not understand, and emphasize key points. For example, a preschooler might need to hear that her father was so *very, very, very* sick that he couldn't get better.

Because of their magical thinking, children at this age are particularly prone to believing the death could have been prevented by, or was caused by, something the child did or said. Since children display grief through play, watch as they act out scenes for clues that they are suffering from guilt or regrets.

Children this age ask many questions—often repetitively, sometimes inappropriately. They often perceive death as temporary or confuse it with sleeping. Answers to questions like "Where will Mommy go to the bathroom if we bury her?" help them grasp the reality of the situation. Sometimes a question like this will pop up long after you think your child has accepted the loss. It is common for children to test reality by confirming that the answers are the same every time they ask.

As with children of every age, it is important to prepare your child by describing in detail what the child might see in each new situation, such as a hospital visit. How scary is it to see an IV line and oxygen mask on your grandfather if you don't know what they are or that they are helping him? Encourage your child to ask questions before and during new experiences, and allow her to approach them at her own pace whenever possible.

School-Age Children (Ages Six to Nine)

School-age children can differentiate between fantasy and reality. They toy with the finality of death, athough they often think of it in frightening cartoon images: a ghost, a skeleton, a hand reaching up from a grave. Yet magical thinking lingers: they can imagine that death is something that can be outsmarted or prevented, or even that it happens only to other people, other *old* people. (Don't be surprised if they keep asking you how old you are!)

Children caught in the overwhelming wave of unfamiliar emotions and feelings of abandonment often alternate between asking many specific questions and active denial. Denial can emerge in bursts of increased happiness or playfulness. Speak with the child honestly and openly, and explain details factually. Encourage him to speak freely and listen without interruptions. When children in this age group do express their grief, it is often very dark, which helps to release the inner chaos. They may become more cautious and create new "rules" to protect themselves from their fears. Like three-to-five-year-olds, they are prone to guilt and regrets, but experience them more intensely. As with other age groups, inappropriate or aggressive behavior needs to be corrected firmly but gently, separating the actions from the child.

"Tweens" (Preadolescents Ages Ten to Twelve)

By age ten, most children understand the permanence and universality of death and realize the significance of rituals. Because they are also learning their roles in society, a death may trigger many complex questions about religion, faith, and cultural beliefs.

Friends become paramount in these years, when your social ties can make or break you. Although most kids this age will try to act unaffected—and may even believe that they are—a death in the family, especially of a parent or sibling, makes you different from other kids and may also cause many changes in your daily life. This is an enormous added stressor for this age group, as they fear rejection by their peers. They want to act "cool," so they will repress feelings or emotional reactions, which in turn can cause uncharacteristic moodiness and unusual behaviors. Their fears often manifest physically with stomachaches, irritability, sleep disruptions, and changes in appetite. Tweens may also take on caretaking roles while losing interest in school and activities they previously enjoyed. Emotions can percolate into impulsiveness, rebellion, aggression, and/or bullying.

Since the social network is so important to self-esteem and

emotional health, encourage interaction with friends. Let your child know it is okay to have fun, joke around, and laugh out loud. Reassure your child about the future, and show that you are there for her by setting aside quality one-on-one time. Be aware that your child may also need increased time alone with her thoughts, photos, or memorabilia. As with other ages, don't tolerate bad behavior or lower your standards.

Teens and Young Adults (Ages Thirteen and Over)

These young people are preparing to enter the "real world," emotionally and intellectually. A death can devastate their plans and dreams. Although they have an adult concept of death, it is hard for them to face their own mortality and to deal with the emotional turbulence caused by the loss. Remember what you were like as a turbulent teen...and now add grief on top of it.

Guilt is amplified as well. Clashes between teens and parents are a natural part of the separation process by which they establish their own identities. Conflicts can come back as painful regrets or guilty memories. Teens are not beyond drawing the conclusion that they caused, or failed to prevent, the death. They may retreat temporarily into depression, spending increased time alone or asleep, trying to shut out reality. Encourage them to seek out someone to talk with about their feelings. (Parents, don't be offended if it's not you!)

Teens get satisfaction from being trusted with important tasks. They benefit from being included in planning and decision making for commemoration rituals, and they may be quite willing to take on a more important role in managing the family through this period of upheaval. Encourage a return to a "normal" routine as soon as possible at home, in school, participating in activities, and socializing with friends.

As mature as they may seem, teens and young adults still need a sense of security in the family and the future. Answer their questions with frank, open, and honest answers. Even when met with resistance, maintain limits and boundaries to keep them from acting out, performing poorly in school, developing unhealthy relationships, or abusing substances. And, like their younger counterparts, they may need explicit permission to cry, as well as suggestions for ways to release their feelings.

Teach Your Children Well

As you grieve, so grieve your children. Little eyes are watching and learning. Laugh, cry, and show your frustration, joy, and exhaustion. The natural process of grieving is a journey that cannot be avoided, but it can be drawn out and made more difficult if it is ignored or delayed. As your children adjust to the new life ahead of them, be aware that grief will ebb and flow. Be sensitive to events, dates, and circumstances that may trigger an episode of increased grieving for you and your family. Involve your children in the disposal of possessions, allowing them to choose personal reminders of this person who played such a significant role in their life.

There are many excellent references and resources that can help you support your child through this difficult time. I encourage you to check the Recommended Reading section for suggested books, and to consider seeking professional counseling and/or a support group for grieving children. A school guidance counselor (who should be informed as soon as you know your child will be facing a death in the family) may be able to provide some local resources as well as helping your child ease back into normal life at school. Hospices provide grief support for children of all ages, and some have grief camps where your child can laugh and play with other children experiencing the same journey.

THE BOTTOM LINE

As you grieve, so will the children. Teach them well, as grief is a normal part of life.

40

"FOR A MOMENT I COULD
SMELL MOM'S PERFUME"

I was recently shopping in a local department store and was pleasantly surprised to bump into Ruth, the widow of a former patient of mine. Her husband, Larry, had died three months before. I soon became concerned, however—she looked so exhausted and depressed. I wondered if she was receiving help from our bereavement team. Hospices provide this invaluable service to family and friends for thirteen months after the death, long enough to help the grieving person through the "first" of everything—the first birthday, the first Thanksgiving, and so on. This enormously beneficial support is typically free of charge.

But when I asked Ruth if she had requested help, she said quickly, "No. I'm too much of a mess right now. They'll think I'm crazy!"

"What's the matter?" I asked.

She took my elbow and pulled me into a quiet corner of the dress department. Her eyes filled with tears. "I knew it would be hard to grieve Larry's death, but now I think I'm losing my mind, Maggie!" She looked around to be sure we couldn't be heard. "Even my kids are worried about me and want me to see a psychiatrist!"

"Tell me what makes you feel there's something wrong," I asked.

"I've woken up out of a sound sleep a couple of times because I hear Larry calling me. It's so clear and *loud*! I've even gone into the den where he died, and of course the hospital bed's not there anymore. Then I really feel terrible, burst into tears, and can't get back to sleep. Now I'm having trouble getting to sleep at all. I'm afraid I'll hear him again! I don't understand what's happening to me!"

"Oh, Ruth," I said, "you'd be surprised how common this is. You're not losing your mind. This kind of experience happens often to people in grief. I'm sorry you haven't started with the bereavement team yet, but I think you should right now. They can help you understand that this is normal." A flood of relief washed over her face.

I also recommended that she read the book *Hello from Heaven* by Bill and Judy Guggenheim, which is based on more than three thousand firsthand accounts of what the Guggenheims have named "after-death communication," or ADC. Before I read this book, I had also recognized just how many of my patients' loved ones recounted similar experiences. I used to call such moments "angel kisses."

People often feel isolated in their grief and therefore fearful of these rather normal occurrences. One feeling can easily compound the other, causing a person to question his or her sanity. This is what had so upset Ruth. Our bereavement team could have told her it's fairly common for the grieving survivor to have some kind of very vivid experience of the person who has died.

"Perhaps it really was your husband trying to contact you," I suggested.

"I hadn't considered that at all," she said. "I come from a family who only believes what is provable and rational. I must admit, it's a relief to know that so many other people have this experience, that I'm not going crazy! Why doesn't anyone talk about this stuff? I'm going to pick up that book right now." And Ruth hugged me goodbye.

In *Hello from Heaven*, the Guggenheims offer the following definition of ADCs:

An after-death communication or ADC is a spiritual experience that occurs when someone is contacted directly and spontaneously by a deceased family member or friend. It is a direct experience because no intermediary or third party such as a psychic, a medium or hypnotist is involved. The deceased relative or friend contacts the living person directly on a one-to-one basis. It is a spontaneous event because the deceased loved one always initiates the contact by choosing when, where and how he or she will communicate with the living person.

The experiences can happen in many ways, all of which are beyond the realm of what we would consider "normal." Someone might inexplicably feel the presence of someone who is deceased. The daughter of one patient told me, "I can't explain it, but I felt my mother here with me in this room. It gave me such a sense of peace."

Many loved ones recount seeing a vision: "I saw my cousin at the bus stop as I drove by, and felt instant joy. I turned quickly to call to him, but there was no one there."

Others may hear something inexplicable. One mother told me the following story: "As I sat crying in the surgical waiting room while my son was having emergency surgery, I heard my father's voice telling me everything would be all right. Then I felt a great sense of peace and relief. And he was right: my son recovered beautifully."

Patients' loved ones have also felt the touch of someone they've lost: "I was sleeping soundly when I felt the brush of a kiss on my cheek and awoke to a feeling of love and warmth. An hour later the phone rang to tell me my sister had died in a car accident an hour before."

It is not uncommon for people to smell things that remind them of the deceased. One man confided, "I've lived alone the last two years since my wife died. Holidays especially have been difficult. Last week when I was driving home, I couldn't help noticing all the homes lit up with Christmas decorations and lights, families carrying trees down the street. I felt so depressed and alone. Yet something miraculous happened as I got home and unlocked the door. The smell of my wife's turkey and stuffing, her specialty, filled the house, and I knew she was with me."

Some family and friends recount receiving important messages from the deceased. One family member of a patient said, "We were house hunting when my grandmother's voice told me not to put a deposit on the house I wanted. Her voice was so insistent. We ended up buying another house. A month later the house I had wanted burned to the ground from faulty wiring in the middle of the night. If we'd bought that house, we could have all died in our sleep!"

Finally, individuals often have vivid dreams in which those they lost reveal to them that not only are they happy, but their former physical strength and vitality are restored. It is as if our loved ones want us to know that no matter how worn down anyone is by life, when we get to the other side, we are perfect and whole again. One man told me just such a story.

"My nephew Ross's leg was amputated when he was twelve, but tragically, that didn't save him from dying of bone cancer a few years later. While Ross was going through his treatments, he made friends with a young girl named Lisa who was getting chemo for leukemia. Her hair had fallen out and it embarrassed her, but Ross always told her how beautiful and brave she was. Sadly, Lisa also died a year later.

"Maggie, I have to tell you, I believe they are both at peace now. I had a very vivid dream one night that they were running in a beautiful, sun-filled field together. They both seemed so happy. He turned, smiled, and waved to me. He had both legs, and Lisa's beautiful hair was back. That dream seemed more real than any other I've ever had. I woke up feeling calm, as if they really had contacted me to let me know how they're doing. I visited Lisa's mother to tell her. She cried so much, but she was grateful to know her daughter was whole and happy. It gave her peace as well."

These experiences may seem irrational to some, yet they often happen in a wakeful state and are quite vivid. Many people brush them off as a coincidence, a daydream, or the result of too much wine with dinner; some, like Ruth, feel they are losing their minds. However, all the evidence makes it easy to conclude that powerful and important communication can happen at, around, and after the time of death. Whether we "get it" or not, it happens. If we don't "get it," we lose this wonderfully validating and uplifting information. If we accept it, this knowledge can decrease our fear of dying and grieving and give us the precious awareness that someday we will be reunited with those we love. These experiences teach us that love is eternal. It never dies.

THE BOTTOM LINE

Love never dies. Be receptive to the "angel kisses" or "after-death communications" that may comfort you and guide your journey.

APPENDICES

Your Strongest Tools Are Made of Paper: Advance Directives

Although none of us get out of this world alive, only 10 percent of us die suddenly, without any warning. What that means is that 90 percent of us have the opportunity to think ahead, plan ahead, and make our wishes known for our unique last chapter.

PUT YOUR PLANS IN WRITING

- Give copies of your written plan to:
    Each family member involved
    Your designated decision maker
    Your doctor(s)
    Your attorney
- Keep a few copies in a secure place in your home—*not* your safe deposit box, as they must be readily accessible.
- Take a copy with you anytime you are hospitalized. The hospital will keep it with your chart, so you will need other copies available.

Remember, you can always change your mind. As long as you are mentally competent, your verbal wishes always override your written wishes.

IMPORTANT DOCUMENTS YOU SHOULD HAVE

Health Care Power of Attorney

A health care power of attorney, or HCPOA (also known as a durable medical power of attorney, a durable power of attorney for health care, or a health care proxy) is the document that identifies the person you choose who understands your wishes and will make health care decisions according to your wishes if you are unable to do so yourself. This need not be a relative. By law, in most states, one or two physicians must certify that you are unable to make these decisions before your HCPOA authority is recognized legally. It is wise to have a backup HCPOA in the event your designated HCPOA is unable to carry out these duties. Your HCPOA has no legal rights to make financial decisions for you or access your money. It is helpful, but not required, to seek legal assistance with your HCPOA, but you will need to have your HCPOA document witnessed (by a non-family member or someone who will not benefit from your estate) and notarized. In some medical facilities verbally appointing a health care proxy is not enough and a written HCPOA is required.

Important points to consider before choosing your HCPOA:

- Is this a trustworthy person who understands your wishes and values?
- Is this someone who is not an emotional person, and can stand firm against family and medical personnel during times of controversy and stress?
- Can this person gather the information needed to make necessary decisions in keeping with your wishes?
- Is the person available and able to take on this responsibility?

- Can the person recognize that family stress reactions at this time should be handled gently and treated as possible grief reactions?

Power of Attorney for Finances

This is the legal document necessary to allow someone who does not already have the right to access your bank accounts and other financial accounts to pay your bills and act on your behalf financially only if you are unable to do so or choose not to do so yourself. This person can only make financial decisions for you, not health care decisions.

Important characteristics to consider before choosing someone to hold your power of attorney for finances:

- Is this person honest and trustworthy enough to understand your wishes and values?
- Will this person stand firm against your family and billing organizations that may not have your best interests at heart?
- Will this person take time and gather the information necessary to make decisions in keeping with your wishes?
- Is this person available and able to keep up with your bills and financial needs?
- Can this person recognize that family stress and grief reactions (such as overspending for the funeral) often affect financial issues?
- Can this person be alert to the potential for greed?

Living Will

In this document you state your wishes about life-prolonging or -sustaining treatments in the event you become terminally ill or could not benefit from these treatments. You may list as many treatments as you wish and be as specific as needed. You may qualify your choices; for example, "I only want antibiotics

in pill form—no needles or IVs—if need be," or "I want any artificial feedings discontinued if I don't gain weight or show improvement in my condition in two weeks." As laws about advance
directives vary from state to state, it is helpful, but not required,
to seek legal assistance in drawing up your living will. It should
be witnessed (by a non–family member or anyone else who would
not benefit by your dying or your estate) and notarized.

Do-Not-Resuscitate (DNR) Form

In many states your living will and/or your health care power of
attorney is *not* recognized by the paramedics who will come if
you dial 911. What most people don't understand is that by dialing 911, you have taken step one of a legal process that can
only be stopped by the order of a physician. The 911 system is a
state-mandated system established to save lives at whatever
cost. Once 911 is called, you cannot, by law, stop or interrupt
what they do—even in your own home. In some states the only
legal document that will give you control over the 911 system is
the state-generated do-not-resuscitate form, signed by your
physician. It is important to check the requirements of your
state. Your local hospice or fire department with ambulance
service can clarify this. Once you have this form, it must be kept
in a readily visible place and should be with the dying person
anytime he or she leaves the home—perhaps in a pocket or wallet. The safest way to avoid unwanted treatments, such as cardiopulmonary resuscitation or respirators, is not to call 911 to
begin with. If you are a hospice patient, call hospice. They will
send help and direct you what to do.

Last Will and Testament

Your will is a legal document that states your desires for the dis-
bursement or disposal of your tangible goods and property. At
death your wishes will be enforced by your executor, a person
you appoint or hired to do this after you die.

A point to consider: if you have an estate large enough to pay a lawyer to prepare a will and appoint an executor, hire someone rather than asking a family member to do this. The burden of grief is difficult enough; often families are ripped apart by conflicts over what is and is not inherited and by whom. This puts an executor who is a family member in a very difficult position. Grieving is a time for families to pull together and support each other, not be torn apart in conflict.

The Ethical Will

Common in Judaism, the ethical will has been used since the eleventh century. It is typically a letter written by the dying person as a way to share last thoughts, hopes, and principles of moral behavior with those who will be left behind. It often contains an overview of the person's life story, including the wisdom gained and lessons learned during that life. Basically, the message to the family is something like: "This is who I am, where I came from, what I've learned along the way, and what wisdom I wish to leave to each of you." It affords a unique opportunity of a life review that is shared with loved ones.

Five Wishes

Five Wishes is a new form of advance directive that looks to all of a person's needs: medical, personal, emotional, and spiritual. It also encourages you to discuss your wishes with your family and physician.

Five Wishes lets your family and doctors know:

1. Which person you want to make health care decisions for you when you can't make them
2. The kind of medical treatment you want or don't want
3. How comfortable you want to be
4. How you want people to treat you
5. What you want your loved ones to know

Five Wishes was written with the help of the American Bar Association's Commission on Law and Aging and is valid under the laws of forty states and the District of Columbia. It is easy to use. All you have to do is check a box, circle a direction, or write a few sentences. For more details, and to preview the document, go to www.agingwithdignity.org/5wishes.html.

You may order a copy online or by phone or mail:

Aging with Dignity
P.O. Box 1661
Tallahassee, FL 32302-1661
Phone: 850-681-2010
Toll free: 888-5WISHES (888-594-7437)

ORGANIZE YOUR INFORMATION

Last, but by no means least, is what you do with all the information and documents you have gathered and completed. It is of great help to you, your family, and other important people if you put all this information in one, readily available place, such as in a special notebook. What's important is that everyone who needs to know this information knows where it is kept and what your notebook contains. The originals of your legal documents should be kept with your attorney and/or in your safe-deposit box. Be sure someone else is on the signature card of your safe-deposit box and can have access to it if you are unable. Be sure to put a copy of the card in your special notebook. It is also wise to put a card in your wallet with or next to your identification indicating that you have completed advance directives and where they can be located in case of emergency if you are unable to speak for yourself.

It is often difficult to know when it's time to talk to the important people in your life about your concerns and desires. Involving them in this process, or just asking them to look through your notebook when it's completed, can be a very helpful way to open a dialogue about your wishes, needs, and plans. It is so much easier and less emotional to have these discussions when you are not in the middle of a crisis and dying is a remote concept of the future. Ideally, we would have all these discussion with each other *before* we are even ill.

CONGRATULATE YOURSELF

Only 25 percent of the population have taken advantage of these wonderful legal tools. By taking advantage of them, you have given yourself peace of mind and given your family and friends a most loving gift.

The Dying Person's Bill of Rights

- I have the right to be treated as a living human being until I die.
- I have the right to maintain a sense of hopefulness however changing its focus may be.
- I have the right to be cared for by those who can maintain a sense of hopefulness, however changing this might be.
- I have the right to express my feelings and emotions about my approaching death in my own way.
- I have the right to participate in decisions concerning my care.
- I have the right to expect continuing medical and nursing attention even though "cure" goals must be changed to "comfort" goals.
- I have the right not to die alone.
- I have the right to be free from pain.
- I have the right to have my questions answered honestly.
- I have the right not to be deceived.
- I have the right to have help from and for my family in accepting my death.
- I have the right to die in peace and dignity.
- I have the right to retain my individuality and not be judged for decisions that may be contrary to beliefs of others.
- I have the right to discuss and enlarge my religious

and/or spiritual experiences, whatever these may mean to others.

- I have the right to expect that the sanctity of the human body will be respected after death.
- I have the right to be cared for by caring, sensitive, knowledgeable people who will attempt to understand my needs and will be able to gain some satisfaction in helping me face death.

This Bill of Rights was created at a workshop, "The Terminally Ill Patient and the Helping Person," in Lansing, Michigan, sponsored by the Southwestern Michigan Inservice Education Council and conducted by Amelia J. Barbus (1975).

The Hospice Medicare Benefit

Hospice care is available as a benefit under Medicare Hospital Insurance (Part A). To be eligible, Medicare beneficiaries must be certified by a physician to be terminally ill with a life expectancy of six months or less. While they no longer receive treatment toward a cure, they require close medical and supportive care, which a hospice can provide. Hospice care under Medicare includes both home care and inpatient care, when needed, and a variety of services not otherwise covered by Medicare. The focus is on care, not cure. Emphasis is on helping the person to make the most of each hour and each day of remaining life by providing comfort and relief from pain.

Medicare covers:

- physicians' services,
- nursing care (intermittent with 24-hour on call),
- medical appliances and supplies related to the terminal illness,
- outpatient drugs for symptom management and pain relief,
- short-term acute inpatient care, including respite care,
- home health aide and homemaker services,

- physical therapy, occupational therapy, and speech/ language pathology services,
- medical social services, and
- counseling, including dietary and spiritual counseling.

How long can hospice care continue?

Special benefit periods apply to hospice care. A Medicare beneficiary may elect to receive hospice care for two 90-day periods, followed by an unlimited number of 60-day periods. The benefits periods may be used consecutively or at intervals. Regardless of whether they are used one right after the other or at different times, the patient must be certified as terminally ill at the beginning of each period. A patient also has the right to cancel hospice care at any time and return to standard Medicare coverage, then later reelect the hospice benefit in the next benefit period.

Are other Medicare benefits available?

When Medicare beneficiaries choose hospice care, they give up the right to standard Medicare benefits only for treatment of the terminal illness. If the patient, who must have Part A in order to use the Medicare hospice benefit, also has Medicare Part B, he or she can use all appropriate Medicare Part A and Part B benefits for the treatment of health problems unrelated to the terminal illness. When standard benefits are used, the patient is responsible for Medicare's deductible and co-insurance amounts.

To determine whether a Medicare-approved hospice program is available in your area, contact the nearest Social Security Administration office, your state or local health department, your state hospice organization, or call the National Hospice Organization Hospice HelpLine (800) 658-8898.

Source: www.hospicenet.org

For the complete U.S. Medicare publication on hospice care, go to www.medicare.gov/publications/pubs/pdf/02154.pdf

Recommended Reading and Resources

ON DEATH AND DYING

Byock, Ira. *Dying Well: Peace and Possibilities at the End of Life.* New York: Riverhead Books, 1998

Byock, Ira. *The Four Things That Matter Most: A Book About Living.* New York: Free Press, 2004.

Callanan, Maggie, and Patricia Kelley. *Final Gifts: Understanding the Special Awareness, Needs, and Communications of the Dying.* New York: Bantam, 1993.

Kiernan, Stephen P. *Last Rights: Rescuing the End of Life from the Medical System.* New York: St. Martin's Press, 2006.

Kushner, Harold. *When Bad Things Happen to Good People.* New York: Schocken Books, 1981.

Lattanzi-Licht, Marcia, et al. *The Hospice Choice: In Pursuit of a Peaceful Death.* New York: Fireside, 1998.

Lynn, Joanne, and Joan Harrold. *Handbook for Mortals: Guidance for People Facing Serious Illness.* Oxford: Oxford University Press, 1999.

ON CARING FOR THE TERMINALLY ILL

Capossela, Cappy, and Sheila Warnock. *Share the Care: How to Organize a Group to Care for Someone Who Is Seriously Ill.* New York: Fireside, 2004.

Kessler, David. *The Needs of the Dying: A Guide for Bringing Hope, Comfort, and Love to Life's Final Chapter.* New York: Harper-Collins, 2007.

Ray, Catherine. *I'm Here to Help.* New York: Bantam, 1997.

ON ADVANCE DIRECTIVES

Doukas, David John, and William Reichel. *Planning for Uncertainty: Living Wills and Other Advance Directives for You and Your Family.* Baltimore: The Johns Hopkins University Press, 2007.

McManus, Roger. *From Here to Hereafter: Everything My Family Needs to Know.* Greensboro, NC: Planner Press. To order: http://www.yourfamilyneedstoknow.com. This is a well-done filing system that assists patients and families in collecting and organizing all necessary documents for end-of-life issues.

Whitman, Wynne A., and Shawn D. Glisson. *Wants, Wishes, and Wills: A Medical and Legal Guide to Protecting Yourself and Your Family in Sickness and in Health.* New Jersey: FT Press, 2007.

ON GRIEF AND GRIEVING

Grollman, Earl A. *Living When a Loved One Has Died*. Boston: Beacon Press, 1977.

Kessler, David, and Elisabeth Kübler-Ross. *On Grief and Grieving: Finding the Meaning of Grief Through the Five Stages of Loss*. New York: Scribner, 2005.

Lewis, C. S. *A Grief Observed*. New York: HarperCollins, 2001.

Rosof, Barbara D. *The Worst Loss: How Families Heal from the Death of a Child*. New York: Henry Holt, 1994.

ON THE DEATH OF A SPOUSE

Colgrove, Melba, et al. *How to Survive the Loss of a Love*. New York: Prelude Press, 1993.

Davis Ginsburg, Genevieve. *Widow to Widow: Thoughtful, Practical Ideas for Rebuilding Your Life*. Cambridge, Mass.: Da Capo Press, 2004.

Didion, Joan. *The Year of Magical Thinking*. New York: Vintage, 2007.

ON NEAR-DEATH AND AFTER-DEATH EXPERIENCES

Atwater, P.M.H. *The Big Book of Near-Death Experiences: The Ultimate Guide to What Happens When We Die.* Charlottesville, Va.: Hampton Roads Publishers, 2007.

Atwater, P.M.H. *Coming Back to Life: Examining the After-Effects of the Near-Death Experience.* Kill Devil Hills, N.C.: Transpersonal Publishing, 2008 (forthcoming).

Cox-Chapman, Mally. *The Case for Heaven.* New York: Putnam, 2001.

Guggenheim, Bill, and Judy Guggenheim. *Hello from Heaven: A New Field of Research—After-Death Communication Confirms That Life and Love Are Eternal.* New York: Bantam, 1997.

Moody, Raymond, Jr. *Life After Life.* New York: Bantam, 1975.

Moody, Raymond, Jr. *The Light Beyond.* New York: Bantam, 1988.

Morse, Melvin. *Closer to the Light: Learning From Near-Death Experiences of Children.* New York: Villard, 1990.

Osis, Karlis, and Erlendur Haraldsson. *At the Hour of Death: A New Look at Evidence for Life After Death.* Norwalk, Conn.: Hastings House, 1997.

FOR CHILDREN

Clifton, Lucille. *Everett Anderson's Goodbye*. New York: Henry Holt, 1988.

DePaola, Tomie. *Nana Upstairs & Nana Downstairs*. New York: Putnam, 1987.

Heegaard, Marge. *When Someone Very Special Dies: Children Can Learn to Cope with Grief*. Minneapolis, Minn.: Woodland Press, 1988.

Johnson, Joy & Marvin. *Tell Me, Papa*. Omaha, Neb.: Centering Corp, 1978.

Mills, Joyce C. *Gentle Willow*. New York: Magnation Press, 1993.

Schwiebert, Pat, and Chuck DeKlyen. *Tear Soup*. Grief Watch, 2005.

Simon, Norma. *The Saddest Time*. Morton Grove, Ill.: Albert Whitman & Company, 1986.

Thomas, Pat. *I Miss You*. Barron's, 2001.

Viorst, Judith. *The Tenth Good Thing About Barney*. New York: Aladdin, 1971.

Zolotow, Charlotte. *My Grandson Lew*. New York: HarperCollins Children's Books, 2007.

FOR ADOLESCENTS

Agee, James. *A Death in the Family*. New York: Vintage, 1998.

Blume, Judy. *Tiger Eyes*. New York: Laurel Leaf, 1982.

Deaver, Julie Reece. *Say Goodnight Gracie*. New York: Harper Trophy, 1989.

Fry, Virginia. *Part of Me Died, Too: Stories of Creative Survival Among Bereaved Children and Teenagers*. New York: Dutton Children's Books, 1995.

Grollman, Earl A. *Straight Talk About Death for Teenagers: How to Cope with Losing Someone You Love*. Boston: Beacon Press, 1993.

Krementz, Jill. *How It Feels When a Parent Dies*. New York: Alfred A. Knopf, 1981.

FOR CAREGIVERS OF GRIEVING CHILDREN

Doka, Kenneth, J., ed. *Living with Grief: Children, Adolescents and Loss*. Hospice Foundation of America, 2000. Call 1-800-845-3402 to order.

Emswiler, Mary Ann, and James P. Emswiler. *Guiding Your Child Through Grief*. New York: Bantam, 2000.

Fitzgerald, Helen. *The Grieving Child: A Parent's Guide*. New York: Fireside, 1992.

Wolfelt, Alan. *Helping Children Cope With Grief*. Indiana: Accelerated Development, Inc., 1983.

ABOUT HOSPICE

For information about hospice programs within the United States, contact:

The National Hospice and Palliative Care Organization
1700 Diagonal Road, Suite 625
Alexandria, Virginia 22314
(703) 837-1500

The organization's extensive website offers many services, including a searchable guide to hospice care providers, information on advance directives, and dozens of other helpful links to end-of-life care resources.

http://www.nhpco.org

WEB-BASED SUPPORT FOR PATIENTS AND FAMILIES

CaringBridge is a nonprofit web service that connects family and friends during a critical illness. It offers free, personalized websites that enable you to easily keep loved ones informed through a patient-care journal and photo gallery, and enables them in turn to send guestbook messages of support that you can access at any time. Setting up a website is easy, and the site is accessible *only* to those to whom you choose to give your web address. (Individual sites are not available through search engines, and you may also add additional layers of privacy and security.) For more information, please see:

http://www.caringbridge.org

ACKNOWLEDGMENTS

The writing of this book has been difficult and painful: too long a journey, too many roadblocks, too many unexpected potholes—from misplaced trust and computer crashes to losing my home and possessions in a terrible fire—and too many serious illnesses and deaths of dear ones.

Throughout it all, however, it never escaped me that the final journeys of the brave patients and courageous families in this book were far worse in every way imaginable. So perhaps it is only fair that it was such a struggle for me to get this book completed as my tribute to them. Always and in every way, my patients and families keep me grounded. This labor of love embodies the lessons learned from them, and my gratitude to them forever.

Throughout this entire journey my most stalwart, supportive, helpful, reasonable, dependable, and multitalented companion, who suffered all the potholes and problems right along with me (while raising three of my wonderful grandchildren), has been my precious, beautiful, and amazing daughter, Erin Nikitchyuk. My love, pride and gratitude to you always.

In order to bring you the best and most current information, I have relied upon and been generously assisted by those I consider the true experts in the field of dying and death. I have been honored to know and work with the best and the brightest and am grateful for their support and the contributions of their special and important talents:

To my research assistant, Katie O'Neil, who now represents the new generation of nurses;

To Ron Culberson, whose great talent "injects humor into healthcare";

To Mary Narayan, who deftly opens our eyes to respect and recognize the needs of other cultures;

To Sherry Showalter, for blending the richness of Native American traditions with the importance of good grieving;

To Bill Guggenheim, for opening our hearts and minds to the comfort of "after-death communications";

To Stephen Kiernan, for his informed and passionate support of patients' rights.

To the other best and brightest clinicians, who have graciously reviewed and contributed to *Final Journeys* and were always available for encouragement and support:

Cindy Defer, RN, Director, and Jan Walterscheid, RN, Education Coordinator, Lakeside Christian Hospice, Carlsbad, New Mexico;

Silvia and Helen Peralta, wonderful cheerleaders, Houston, Texas;

Cinni Cummings, RN, CHPN, my best supervisor ever, and Natalie Kerr, RN, BSN, former hospice colleague, Delaware;

Dulcie Kaplow-Cohen, a skilled and appreciated colleague, Virginia;

Chaplain Rev. Barbara Cullum, Maryland, whose expertise in ethics guided me.

My acknowledgments would be incomplete without being grateful for the support of the teams of Hospice Care, Inc., of Madison, Wisconsin, under the sterling leadership of "Doc Rock" and Kelly Fischer, RN, Clinical Director for Long Care Teams, and of Sister Georgeann Roudebush, who assisted me with information on spiritual influences.

All of these very talented people have been wonderful to me in this journey.

To the finest physician experts in the fields of hospice, palliative care and oncology my great thanks go to:

Alex Peralta, MD, Houston, Texas;

Ira Byock, MD, the Dartmouth Hitchcock Medical System of the Dartmouth Medical School, Lebanon, New Hampshire;

Mary Jo Lechowicz, MD, Emory University Medical School, Atlanta, Georgia.

Their contributions added greatly to the medical accuracy, and therefore to my comfort level and confidence, in this book.

To my agent, Gail Ross, and editor, Toni Burbank: In showing me the many sides of the publishing world, you have affected my life in ways innumerable.

I suspect most of my readers will be approaching a frightening and difficult journey themselves, or will be caring for a special person who is dying. I applaud the courage it took for you to open this book. It is my fervent prayer and hope that it may be a guide through the problems and concerns you may be facing. If *Final Journeys* lightens the burdens or eases the fear and suffering for even one person, I will have accomplished my goal.

I honor you who choose to travel this difficult but tender journey. It will change your life forever, as it has mine.

ABOUT THE AUTHOR

Originally trained in high-technology emergency and intensive-care nursing, Maggie Callanan, RN, has specialized in the care of the dying since 1981, working in both metropolitan and rural settings as a hospice home-care and in-patient nurse and nursing coordinator.

Based on her hospice experiences, she co-authored *Final Gifts: Understanding the Special Awareness, Needs, and Communications of the Dying*. Now a classic published in nine languages, it received the *American Journal of Nursing*'s Book of the Year Award when it was released in 1993. Maggie was also the 1996 recipient of the Hospice and Palliative Care Organization's prized Heart of Hospice Award for clinician of the year, given for outstanding achievements in and beyond hospice.

Since publication of the research on which *Final Gifts* is based, she has spoken nationally and internationally before medical and lay audiences and also provides training on topics related to death and dying, grief, bereavement, and hospice care. She also created and directs the National Hospice, Palliative and Home Care Speakers Bureau (www.nhphc.org), a collaborative group of dedicated expert speakers in the field.

Maggie's first love and primary interest continues to be providing hands-on care to dying people.

To contact the author, please visit her website: www.Maggie Callanan.com.